by **MARIA REIDELBACH**

COMPLETELY

A
History
of the
Comic
Book
and
Magazine

Designed by
**ALEXANDER
ISLEY
DESIGN**

LITTLE, BROWN AND COMPANY

BOSTON TORONTO LONDON

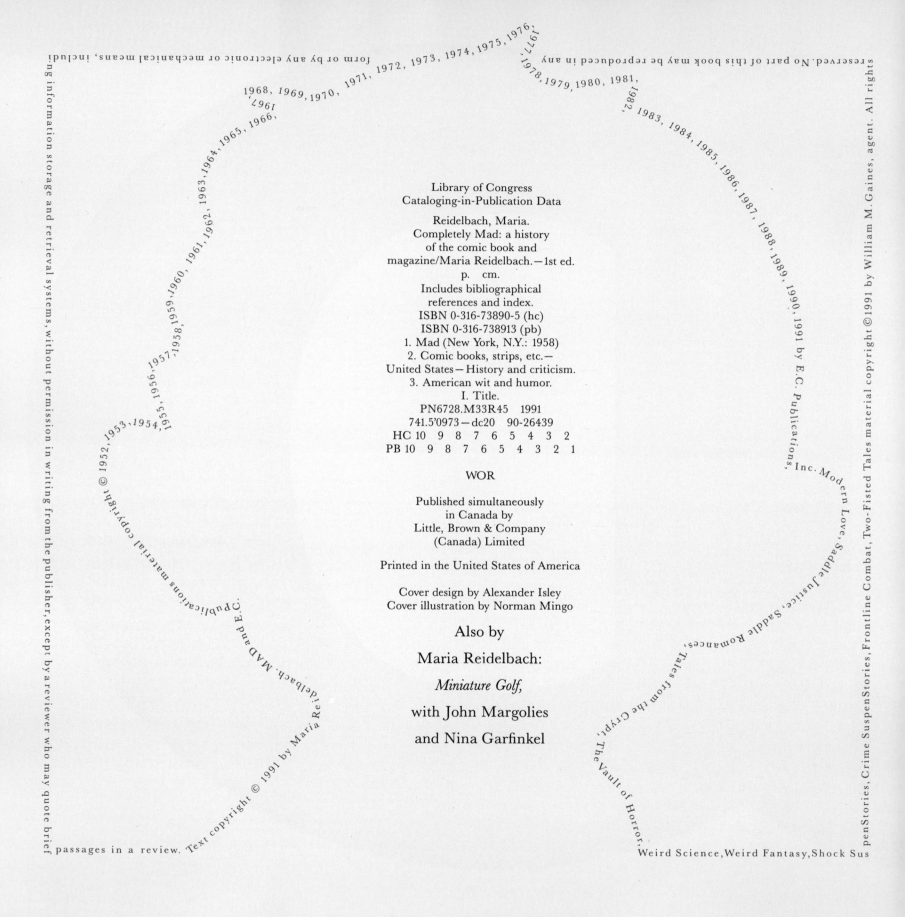

Library of Congress
Cataloging-in-Publication Data

Reidelbach, Maria.
Completely Mad: a history
of the comic book and
magazine/Maria Reidelbach.—1st ed.
p.   cm.
Includes bibliographical
references and index.
ISBN 0-316-73890-5 (hc)
ISBN 0-316-738913 (pb)
1. Mad (New York, N.Y.: 1958)
2. Comic books, strips, etc.—
United States—History and criticism.
3. American wit and humor.
I. Title.
PN6728.M33R45   1991
741.5'0973—dc20   90-26439
HC 10 9 8 7 6 5 4 3 2
PB 10 9 8 7 6 5 4 3 2 1

WOR

Published simultaneously
in Canada by
Little, Brown & Company
(Canada) Limited

Printed in the United States of America

Cover design by Alexander Isley
Cover illustration by Norman Mingo

Also by

Maria Reidelbach:

Miniature Golf,

with John Margolies

and Nina Garfinkel

FIRST THANKS must go to Walter Lehrman for a careful reading of the manuscript and help in many ways, to Nina Garfinkel, who provided the spark that became this book, and to Anne Doran for early feedback on the text. Many thanks also to my agent, Clyde Taylor, my editor, Pat Mulcahy, Alex Isley for his inventive book design, and Dorothy Crouch. My gratitude to the "moral support squad" for encouragement and wise counsel; the roster includes David Comins, John Coplans, Dorothy Reidelbach, June Kostar, Dieter Kearse, Diane Bertolo, Jeanne Houck, Lorna Koski, and Sarah Auld, who are only the tip of the iceberg. For help with research, technical matters, or for advice, I'm indebted to Frank Jacobs, whose biography of Bill Gaines laid much groundwork, Bhob Stewart, Susan Kendzulak, Kelly Donovan, Michael Mattil, Tom Damraur, Jim Salicrup, Monte Beauchamp of *Blab!*, Greg Baisden of *The Comics Journal*, Allon Schoener, Art Spiegelman, Howard Schneider, Lyle Stuart, DesignerType, and the father-son team of Bob Muehlhof and Tom Lewis, whose computerized *Mad* index is a wonder. Thanks also to Eric Baker, Lottie Brandel, Peter Coates, Steven Heller, Don Preziosi, Irving Schild, Charles Schulz, Brad Silversmith, Bill Spicer, Ben Z. Swanson, Jr., Eric Wolfe, Don Wright, and Craig Yoe for their contributions. Otherwise unattributed quotations are culled from interviews with Jack Albert, Dave Berg, Lenny Brenner, Bob Clarke, Paul Coker, Jr., Dorothy Crouch, Jack Davis, Dick DeBartolo, Jerry De Fuccio, George Dougherty, Mort Drucker, Don Edwing, Will Elder, Al Feldstein, John Ficarra, Sara Friedman, Anne Gaines, Bill Gaines, Chris Gaines, Kelly Freas, Stan Hart, Frank Jacobs, Al Jaffee, Charlie Kadau, Tom Koch, Arnie Kogen, Harvey Kurtzman, Sheldon Mayer, Nick Meglin, Harry North, Tom Nozkowski, Gloria Orlando, Joe Orlando, Joe Raiola, Seymour Reit, William Sarnoff, Larry Siegel, Lou Silverstone, Angelo Torres, George Woodbridge, and Don Wright. Many thanks for precious time and thought generously given.

FINALLY, my deep appreciation to Bill Gaines, Nick Meglin, John Ficarra, the staff of *Mad*, Al Feldstein, and Harvey Kurtzman for everything they've done to help this book along.

LEMME OUTTA THIS FURSHLUG-GINER PLACE!

"But I don't want to go among mad

people," Alice remarked.

"Oh, you can't help that,"

said the Cat: "we're all mad here.

I'm mad. You're mad."

"How do you know I'm mad?"

said Alice.

"You must be," said the Cat,

"or you wouldn't have come here."

LEWIS CARROLL

*To the memory of my mother, who, upon hearing I was
to write this book, hesitated only a moment
before she exclaimed, "Why, Maria, what an honor!"
And to Rip, Dot, Pat, Tom, Sonia, and Erika.*

CONTENTS

MAD

AMERICANA
FOR A DIME

The day was not unlike many others at *Mad* magazine. The morning's *New York Times* brought a humorous anecdote about a woman who had just moved to pastoral Bucks County in Pennsylvania. Lost in a bucolic haze while perusing the local library's magazine selection of *Country Journal* and *Quilter's Newsletter*, she was startled to see a small sign notifying patrons that due to problems of theft, *Mad* magazine would no longer be stocked on the lending shelf. From *Mad*'s fax machine came another story, this one from the Canadian *Calgary Herald*, about a junior high school teacher who was in trouble for embellishing his students' exam papers with small cartoons from *Mad*. A

The first real comic book sold—*Famous Funnies*—64 color pages for a dime. Max Gaines reprinted favorite Sunday comic strips like "Toonerville Folks," "Mutt and Jeff," and "Hairbreadth Harry." Newsstands quickly sold it out and Gaines knew he had a hit. —*Famous Funnies, #1*

mother in Indiana who had been in the habit of buying *Mad* as a treat for her grandson. The boy had taken a copy of the magazine to school, where a classmate had tipped off the teacher that it had a nude woman on the back cover: a topless mermaid. When the boy's parents found out, he received a beating and suspension of his allowance, and he was grounded. The grandmother was distraught. "Why can't you be like you used to be?" she charged. "I used to buy this magazine for my daughter when she was her son's age. It certainly wasn't like it is now." In fact, in this case, *Mad* was exactly as it had been: the very cartoon in question had first been printed in the magazine nearly twenty years before.

For almost forty years, Americans have loved to hate *Mad*, or hated to love it. How has *Mad* managed to carve out such a precarious, yet durable, niche in the American psyche? The history of *Mad* is really many stories, with many characters. It is the story of an eccentric publisher, an awkward rich kid who thought he'd grow up to be a high school chemistry teacher. It is the story of an enraged psychiatrist and the most gruesome horror comic books ever created. It is the reports of Senate subcommittee hearings and Supreme Court cases, and the tale of a mysterious orphan boy with an unforgettable gap-toothed grin. It is also the personal histories of talented editors, writers, and artists, many of whom were outsiders of one sort or another, immigrants, or children of immigrants. It is the evolution of an obscure ten-cent comic book into a cult magazine with an audience of millions in countries all over the world. But first of all, it is a story that begins with the invention of the comic book itself in a small apartment in the Bronx.

parent had charged that the drawings "carried sexual and Satanic overtones" and "encouraged disrespect for authority." While William M. Gaines, *Mad*'s publisher, called the school to see what could be done to save the teacher's job, *Mad*'s editors pondered a letter just received from an irate grand-

It was 1933, the year that Hitler was appointed German chancellor, then granted dictatorial powers, and it was also the year that Franklin Delano Roosevelt was inaugurated and created the Public Works Administration, a ray of hope for a country caught in a deepening depression. Television was patented, while a court ruling was necessary to allow James Joyce's *Ulysses* into the United States. Book burnings raged in Germany, and sixty thousand artists fled the country. An international exposition opened in Chicago; it was optimistically named "A Century of Progress." Prohibition was repealed and Mae West reigned in Hollywood, at least until the newly appointed movie censors saw her latest movie. The *Graf Zeppelin* ruled the air and the first German concentration camps were erected. Bread lines grew, and the hit song was the Disney ditty "Who's Afraid of the Big Bad Wolf?"

Max Gaines and his wife, Jessie, had more local concerns as they struggled to feed their two children, Elaine and William. They had been scraping by since the onset of the depression; Max had tried everything, from work in a munitions factory to producing a "We Want Beer"–emblazoned necktie for Prohibition-weary bar-goers. Eventually, they found themselves living with Max's mother in New York City and wondering what to do next.

One day, while rummaging through the attic, Max became absorbed in reading a yellowing stack of Sunday funnies. He was struck by inspiration: if he enjoyed rereading the colorful stories, there might be others out there like himself. He approached a friend at a company called Eastern Color Printing and found that they had been experimenting with just that idea for several years, producing tabloid-sized reprints of Sunday comics as promotional giveaways for newspapers and product manufacturers. Gaines became an enthusiastic salesman, reducing the size of the books to that of a tabloid folded in half, and selling hundreds of thousands of copies to companies like Wheatena, Canada Dry, and Milk-O-Malt.

It had never occurred to the men at Eastern that the public might pay for these booklets, and this was Gaines's stroke of genius. He tested the market by stamping the giveaways with a ten-cent price and dropping off stacks to a couple of cooperative newsstands. The books were a hit. Under Max's supervision, Eastern Color Printing printed *Famous Funnies* No. 1, the first issue of the first monthly comic book ever, and in May 1934 it hit the stands. Finally, all of the features of modern comic books were in place: the "half-tab" size, the ten-cent price, monthly issues, and newsstand distribution. Although it took several months to build a readership, *Famous Funnies* was an obvious success. Max, Jessie, Elaine, and Bill moved to their own house in Brooklyn.

One day, not long after *Famous Funnies* became a monthly, Max was suddenly fired from his job at Eastern. If he knew why, he didn't tell; the family story has it that he arrived for work one day to find a locked office. Once again he managed to land on his feet. He learned that the McClure Syndicate had a pair of two-color printing presses idle. Being the magnate of giveaway comics, he struck a deal whereby McClure would let him use their presses for the comic books in return for 50 percent of the proceeds. Gaines capitalized his end of the operation in a deal

"Relativity theory in 1905 announced the dissolution of uniform Newtonian space as an illusion or fiction, however useful. Einstein pronounced the doom of continuous or 'rational' space, and the way was made clear for Picasso and the Marx brothers and Mad.*"*

MARSHALL McLUHAN
Understanding Media

with George Delacorte of Dell Publishing Company. Soon he was in direct competition with his earlier creations, publishing *Popular Comics,* which contained reprints of "Dick Tracy," "Little Orphan Annie," "Gasoline Alley," and "Terry and the Pirates."

Sheldon Mayer, hired as a teenager by Gaines to be an editor and production man, remembers the early comic books as being crude and experimental. Both of McClure's presses had been previously used to print black ink, which left unsightly blotches in the margins when other colors were run. Gaines and Mayer had to clean each of fifty sample comic books by hand with gum erasers. The Sunday strips they reprinted had to be rearranged to fit the proportions of the comic book. Photocopies were very expensive at the time, and so Mayer's job was to peel original drawings by master cartoonists from the cardboard on which they were drawn and cut them up. "Oh, how it disturbed me—it was pathetic," he says. "Yet, we had first-class names. Even though the books were basically thrown together, those first comics had a certain style and quality."

Gaines and Mayer embarked on a program to upgrade their product, soon running continuity strips in chronological order and including "Scribbly," an original character created by Mayer, who was a talented cartoonist in his own right. Several other companies sensed the market and had begun printing their own books, but *Popular Comics* had become the best.

Gaines became known as "Charlie" in the trade, a joke on his nonexistent middle name, and his business style evolved. "If you said he wasn't difficult, there would be lots of people who would say you were talking about the wrong guy," Mayer says. "He did everything at the top of his lungs, and he found that being in a nasty temper got him a lot more than any other technique, so he used it. But when things really got bad, if you were in a real jam, he would take his coat off and roll up his sleeves and help you fix it. He was basically a very sweet guy, but you never knew which one you were going to meet."

By 1936 the business was stable and ready for growth. Gaines became friendly with publisher Harry Donenfeld, who was a partner in a small company called Detective Comics. Donenfeld was ambitious—he was the first to use original, previously unpublished material in a comic book, he owned some presses and had a stake in Independent News Company, which distributed comic books. He intended to build a comic book empire. Gaines and Mayer knew that Donenfeld was hungry for more original material, and one day in 1937 a proposal for an unusual newspaper comic strip hero caught Mayer's eye. Created by Jerry Siegel and Joe Shuster four years before, the potential strip had passed over the desks of every newspaper and newspaper syndicate, who had all thought that the hero was too unbelievable. But there was something in the concept that captured Mayer's imagination, and he pointed out the drawings to Gaines.

Gaines had Mayer paste the strips into comic book form and send them over to Donenfeld. Warily, Donenfeld decided to give the comic a try. Dubbed *Action Comics,* the first cover featured the premier of the red-caped, blue-suited Superman holding an automobile aloft with one hand.

With the groundbreaking success of Superman, Max and Donenfeld's business

Shortly after Bill Gaines took over his father's company in 1947, Educational Comics was publishing comic books like these. In 1948, Gaines hired Al Feldstein, and the two began to tinker with the staid, conservative titles, even writing the advice columns for the romance comics. —*Modern Love, #2; Saddle Justice, #4; Saddle Romances, #11*

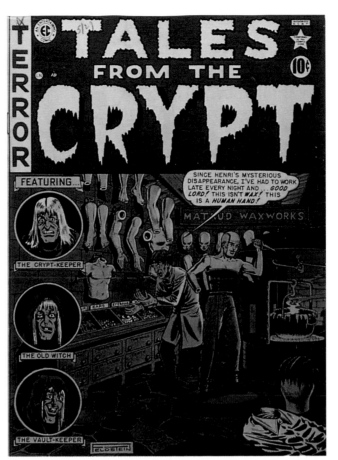

Gaines and Feldstein discovered a shared love of suspense stories and old radio programs like "Lights Out" and "The Witch's Tale." Together they created a new concept in comic books: horror. The stories were told by a trio of fiendish ghouls whose personae Gaines and Feldstein gleefully adopted when responding to readers on the letters pages. Here we see two typical covers. *Tales from the Crypt*'s cover, by Feldstein, shows a mannequin-maker's surprise as he discovers the whereabouts of his missing assistant. Johnny Craig's *Vault of Horror* cover depicts a fear that caught the tenor of the time: a late-model car menaced by the living dead. —*Tales from the Crypt*, #25; *The Vault of Horror*, #26

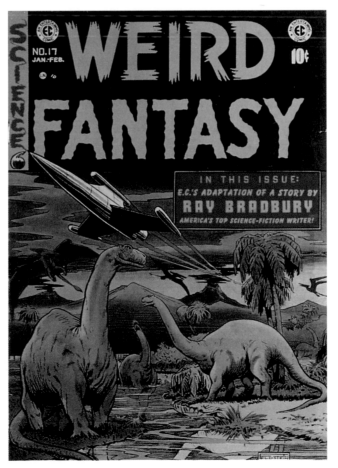

EC's two science-fiction comic books were Gaines's and Feldstein's favorites. Intricate plots of space travel and nuclear annihilation abounded, while passionate fans responded in large numbers about correctly and incorrectly depicted technical details. These covers, by Feldstein and Wally Wood, are showcases for drawings of dinosaurs, rocket ships, and gravity-defying guys and dogs. —*Weird Science*, #12; *Weird Fantasy*, #17

Although comic books in general were disdained by parents and educators, crime comics had the worst reputation of all. *Shock SuspenStories* and *Crime SuspenStories* spelled trouble for EC. Even though they were not technically a part of the "true crime" genre, and contained less explicit violence than some comics by other publishers, they were singled out as being offenders. One look at these covers by Johnny Craig and Feldstein shows why—EC artists were just too good. *—Shock SuspenStories, #7; Crime SuspenStories, #16*

 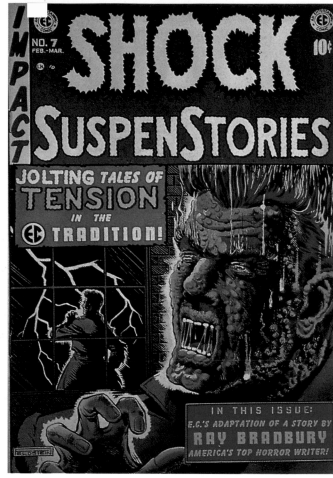

relationship grew; they formed a publishing business together, inaugurating the All-American line of comic books. Donenfeld was uptown in ritzy carpeted offices with a full staff, while Max was on Lafayette Street in the Lower East Side, running a shirtsleeve operation. Donenfeld supplied the money and Max the know-how. The AA Group, as it was known, produced *The Flash*, *Hawkman*, *The Mighty Atom*, *Hop Harrigan*, *Movie Comics* (using movie stills), and others, totaling twenty comics in all.

Gaines's concoction had become one of the few success stories of the Great Depression. By 1941 there were over thirty comic book publishers producing 150 different comic books each month, with combined sales of fifteen million copies a month, and a projected readership of sixty million. Comic books were produced at great speed using Ford's newly developed assembly-line methods. Writers produced formula plots that were drawn, inked, and lettered by a succession of artists. Publishers treated it all as hackwork; artists and writers often weren't credited for their work—sometimes because they were ashamed, other times because publishers wanted the creative talent to be easily interchangeable. Sensing an appetite for the more lurid themes of good against evil, in 1942 Charles Biro created *Crime Does Not Pay*, spawning a new genre for the burgeoning publishers to plunder. "True" crime comics were slapped together and became increasingly violent, with stories such as "Murder, Morphine and Me," and "Boston's Bloody Gang War."

The growing popularity of comic books among youth put the public eye on the publishers. A debate by alarmed parents on the worth of comic books developed, and editorials appeared in papers across the country, with writers tossing off terms like *id* and *super-ego*, in their attempts to explain the danger or harmlessness of the craze.

Reproducing newspaper strips had been safe, but as AA began creating more comic books containing original material, Gaines became conscious of the content of his stories. He invited a number of educators, psychologists, and other concerned public figures to join a board of advisers to AA. One of them was William Moulton Marston, a psychologist who had been advising movie producers on how to make interesting movies that wouldn't be censored by the Hays Office, and who had also written several articles on the bad influence of comic books. Gaines asked Marston to help him create a superhero with certifiably positive traits for children to emulate. Marston's solution surprised everyone: the character was female. Wonder Woman was, in Marston's words, "a feminine character with all the strength of a Superman plus all the allure of a good and beautiful woman." The comic was signed with the name "Charles Moulton," a combination of Marston's middle name and Gaines's nickname.

By 1943 comic book sales had almost doubled again, to a new high of twenty-five million copies a month. Gaines and Donenfeld's AA Group and Donenfeld's DC group accounted for one-third of them.

Gaines and Mayer made continuing improvements, drafting these guidelines for artists and writers:

Never show anybody stabbed or shot,
Show no torture scenes,
Never show a hypodermic needle,
Never show a coffin, especially with anybody in it.

At the same time, Gaines published under the imprint of Educational Comics a series of his own: *Picture Stories from the Bible*, *Picture Stories from Science*, *Picture Stories from American History*, and *Picture Stories from World History*. In 1944 his distributer reported: "He is a staunch believer of wholesomeness in the comic publishing business, and the board of advisors he helped to round up to keep his publications immune from criticism is just what the doctor ordered." Gaines's consultations with clergymen helping with the *Picture Stories* were memorable. "I don't give a damn how long it took Moses," he would scream, "I want it in two panels!"

In 1945, Donenfeld split his share in AA with his accountant, Jack Liebowitz, and through no doing of his own, Gaines had a new partner. Gaines was passionate about comic books, and Liebowitz was a businessman with his eye firmly on the bottom line. When Liebowitz pressed for more advertising in the books than Gaines felt was fair, Gaines decided the time had come to cash in on his success. World War II was going on, and AA's paper allotments were worth almost as much as the comic titles themselves. Gaines sold out to Donenfeld and Liebowitz for half a million dollars, tax-free, said goodbye to Mayer, who went along with the deal, and announced his retirement.

A change of heart came quickly; two weeks later, Max was back in business, on his own this time. He evaluated the few titles of which he retained ownership: *Tiny Tot Comics*, *Animal Fables*, and his own favorites, the *Picture Stories* line. With groups like the General Federation of Women's Clubs on the comic book warpath, the timing seemed right for a line of educational and strictly juvenile comic books. With evangelistic fervor, he started the presses rolling. For two years EC produced these comics to mixed response. They may have been what the parents thought wholesome, but kids would have none of it — on the street it took ten *Picture Stories from the Bible* to trade for only one *Batman*.

THE MADMEN: *William M. Gaines*

William M. Gaines is a man of many enthusiasms and just as many contradictions. He has plotted some of the most gruesome horror stories ever to see print, and at the same time is a sap for the schmaltzy music of Al Jolson. He cultivates a reputation as a skinflint and a miser, going so far as to spend days hunting down the staff person responsible for a brief long-distance telephone call, yet gives lavish bonuses to both staff and free-lance artists and writers, and takes them on expense-paid international trips with luxurious accommodations. Although Gaines is a gourmand who has traveled the world for love of food and wine, frankfurters from Nathan's Famous on Coney Island are still one of his favorite meals. He despises smoking, but neither is he a health enthusiast, just as strongly disliking exercise, or even walking. He is an atheist who purchased a doctor of divinity degree and a minister's title from the Church of the Universal Brotherhood so that he could perform marriages.

A collector of airship models and toys, Gaines has been a member of the Lighter-than-Air Society for the last twenty-five years. He is a great fan of Frédéric-Auguste Bartholdi's "Liberty Enlightening the World," and his collection of Statue of Liberty objects ranges from plastic snow bubbles to major bronze studies by Bartholdi himself. In fact, Gaines—a large man—seems to like all things mammoth, and also has special fondness for King Kong and the flamboyant Elephant Hotel in Margate, New Jersey (once going so far as to investigate buying it).

How did Gaines become one of the great eccentrics? "I was a behavior problem, nonconformist, a difficult child," he confesses. His father, Max C. Gaines, would have been the first to agree with that assertion, although it may have described him, as well. The elder Gaines spent his first working years at several occupations. While an elementary school principal, Gaines, who was Jewish, fell in love and married Jessie Postlethwaite, a teacher of Pennsylvania Dutch extraction. Although Max was known in the community as generous and kind, he was a hard taskmaster of the younger Gaines, and also was said to have a hair-trigger temper with his family. Bill was an especially awkward child, and the problem was made worse by his father's demands and tirades. Max adopted the opinion that Bill would never be a success, and as Bill grew up he lived down to Max's expectations. By all reports, he *was* a rather obnoxious child, his playfulness tending toward the worst

Suddenly, tragedy struck. While boating on Lake Placid, Max Gaines, his friend Sam Irwin, and Irwin's son were struck by another boat. Max had time only to throw Irwin's son to the back, probably saving the boy's life, while his own was instantly lost.

The Gaines family was in a state of shock and disarray. Bill, twenty-five years old and entering his last year as an education student at New York University, had been left just weeks before by his wife, Hazel. Thinking quickly, the newly widowed Jessie convinced Bill to move in with her and take over the family business.

Bill had little hope for what he describes as "the smallest, crummiest outfit in the field" with the "weakest distributor"—Leader News. EC was $100,000 in the red, but Bill reluctantly complied with his mother's request, stopping by the EC offices between classes to sign checks while Frank Lee, Max's business manager, and Sol Cohen, his circulation manager and editor, attended to the day-to-day business.

At this point daily business meant playing catch-up with the larger publishers. There was big money in comics, and most compa-

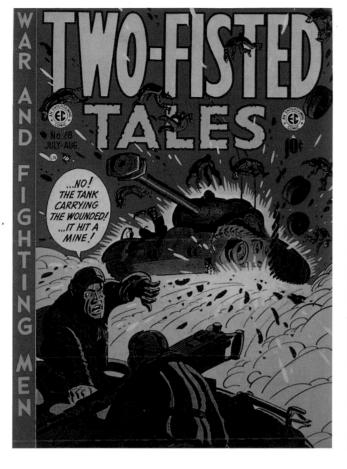

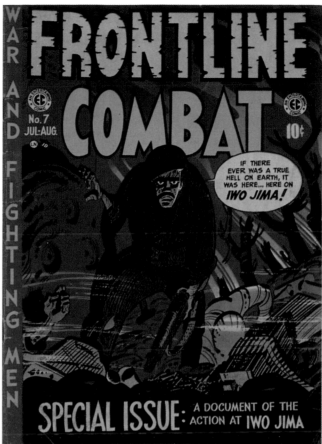

nies tried to keep up with the popular themes of the moment. The first big fad had been superheroes, then "true crime" comics. As one publisher found success with a genre, all the others would jump on the bandwagon, and within weeks hundreds of similar comic books, or titles, as they're called by the trade, would flood the market. Just as suddenly as it had begun, a fad would usually topple under its own weight.

In early 1948, the trend of the moment was teenage comics, and Sol Cohen put out the word that EC was looking for an artist who could draw *Archie*-style adolescents for a new comic. Al Feldstein applied for and got the job, but *Going Steady with Peggy* never saw ink; before even one story had been finished the

bottom fell out of the craze. Bill Gaines, however, had one look at Feldstein's curvaceous cuties and concluded, in his first major decision for the company, that he wanted to keep Feldstein around. Feldstein graciously allowed EC to cancel their contract with him for *Peggy* in a handshake agreement to develop the newest trend, western and romance comics.

Bill had an immediate liking for Feldstein, and he needed someone his age around the offices. Feldstein was twenty-three years old and interested in breaking into writing, as well as drawing for the comics. Together, they began editing several comics: *Modern Love*, *Saddle Justice*, and *Moon Girl*. Under the names Adrian, Amy, and Chuck, the two even wrote

practical jokes of the sort involving sneezing powder and fake ink blots.

As a student, Gaines's grades were unremarkable, yet he received a perfect score in chemistry on the New York State Regents Examination, so he enrolled in the Polytechnic Institute of Brooklyn with a major in the subject. Polytechnic is a college known for its large entering classes and small graduating classes and Gaines became one of the casualties. He dropped out in 1942 as a junior and disguised his failure by convincing his father that he had been drafted into the army.

During his three years in the service, Gaines, who had never been a lady's man, was matched by Jessie to his second cousin Hazel Grieb. They married in 1944 and lived offpost for his last year in the service. On his return to New York he enrolled in New York University and began work toward a degree in education.

After his divorce and the death of his father in 1947, Gaines's life turned around. He moved back in with Jessie and finished his studies, while slowly taking over a role as head of the family and of the failing Educational Comics. During this time he developed a penchant for neatness and orderliness that became an obsession; he counted handkerchiefs and towels at home and stayed late at the office to empty ashtrays and tidy desks. He measured his own desk for optimum placement of blotter, pen, and other tools and adhered strictly to the planned locations. He smoked then, and had a cigarette lighter for each day of the week.

By 1952 he finally seemed to be out of Max Gaines's shadow. EC had not only come out of debt, but was making good profits. This, of course, was due to the horror and suspense comic books, a genre that would have been anathema to Max. As the staff turned over he hired Al Feldstein and Harvey Kurtzman as editors, keeping on Johnny Craig from the earlier days. Gaines seemed to be a natural leader, and his growing enthusiasm for comics and regard for artists encouraged them to bring him their best work. He began dieting at that time: The diet pills prescribed by his doctor kept him up most of each night, so he spent the time plotting fiendish stories for EC's horror, suspense, and science fiction comics. **(To be continued.)**

advice-to-the-lovelorn columns. As the comic romances grew more popular, the pair responded with *A Moon, A Girl . . . Romance*, and *Saddle Romances*. These slightly bizarre (not to say kinky) titles are the result of what Bill describes as "a flagrant trick to fool the post office." Since new titles required a new second-class permit, Bill tried to save time and money by altering titles rather than coming up with completely novel ones.

After finishing college, Bill began spending more time at the offices and with Al. They became friends, having lunches and dinners, and going to the roller derby together. At the same time, Gaines drew the young artist Johnny Craig, who had worked for the AA group as a teenager, further into the fold.

By the following year, Gaines, Feldstein, and Craig were editing six western, crime, and romance comics. Together, they began building a stable of artists; Gaines began to take particular care with the books. At EC artists were chosen for their suitability for their subjects, and were encouraged to develop their own styles.

Al and Bill discovered a shared love of the old suspense radio programs like "Lights Out" and "The Witch's Tale." In a fit of enthusiasm one day they wrote two horror stories, "Crypt of Terror" and "Vault of Horror," and ran them in EC's *Crime Patrol* and *War Against Crime*. Like the radio programs they emulated, these stories each had a ghoulish host who welcomed the reader into worlds of the macabre. The Crypt-Keeper stood guard for "The Crypt of Terror" and the Vault-Keeper for "The Vault of Horror." The two had such fun that they didn't bother waiting for reader response to their stories, feedback which would take months. They began work immediately on more stories. Sol Cohen, convinced that the new direction was a mistake and that EC was finally going to go under, left for a job at Avon Comics.

Bill Gaines was beginning to enjoy the comic book business. Rather than hire a new editor in chief, he and Feldstein took over

From a comfortable position near the top of the heap, Feldstein and Gaines wrote this satire for the last issue of *Modern Love*. The story pokes fun at the comic book industry itself, telling of the boom and bust of the romance comic market. Tiny Tot was the name of one of Max's companies, and the two yes-men are Gaines and Feldstein.
— Gaines and Feldstein/Feldstein, "The Love Story to End All Love Stories," *Modern Love*, #8

Cohen's duties and plotted a new course for EC. In early 1950, they dropped the crime comics and premiered *The Crypt of Terror* and *The Vault of Horror*, two of the first horror comic books the world had seen. With writing a cut above the usual and truly frightening drawings, the editors invited reader participation with regular letters columns, where inquiries would be answered by the Crypt-Keeper and Vault-Keeper themselves.

Gaines changed the company name from Educational Comics to Entertaining Comics, adopting the motto: "A New Trend in Comic Books." The first New Trend titles were followed closely by comics based on another of Gaines's and Feldstein's shared interests, science fiction, and *Weird Science* and *Weird Fantasy* were born. The group was then rounded out with *Shock SuspenStories*, and *Crime SuspenStories*, two guaranteed money-makers, and yet another horror title, *The Haunt of Fear*, hosted by the Old Witch. As each new title appeared, one from the old days was dropped.

In order to keep up with the demand for stories for the comics, Gaines and Feldstein developed what Gaines called the "springboard" technique, with which they generated one tale a day. Gaines would stay up most of the night reading horror and science fiction for inspiration. He would keep a stack of cards at his side, and each time he came up with a potential story idea he would jot it down. The next day, he and Feldstein would sit in his office: in Gaines's words, "It was my job to 'sell' him a springboard. As it would get to eleven or twelve o'clock, I'd be getting desperate, 'cause I knew he had to finish a story—it used to give me stomachaches. Finally we'd hit something he liked." Feldstein would race into his office and lay out a draw-

ing board, dashing out the panels, text, and dialogue on the boards, composing while he worked. At the end of the day Gaines would read the story aloud. "This was the fun part," he remembers. "We always thought of our work as being theatrical, and it had to read right. We suggested to our readers that they also do this, and a lot of them did."

The stories got wilder. Gaines and Feldstein egged one another on with ridiculous plots, each one more farfetched than the last, embellished with titles like "Ants in Her Trance," "'Tain't the Meat, It's the Humanity," "Ooze in the Cellar," and "Coffin Spell." *SuspenStories* entered some of the murkier areas of marital relations and family life with stories of love triangles, crimes of twisted passion, and of murderous offspring. Also included were what Gaines called the "preachy stories," a running series of morality tales that appeared in the suspense comics, each one dealing with a different aspect of social inequality. Plots revolved around misguided patriotism, prejudice against African Americans, Mexican Americans, and Jews. The science-fiction comics, their favorites, featured the strangest aliens. In most of their stories, EC specialized in the "O. Henry" ending, a shocking plot twist intended to leave their readers gasping.

Meanwhile, EC premiered two more New Trend comics: *Two-Fisted Tales* and *Frontline Combat*, edited and written by a new free lance, Harvey Kurtzman. Misled by the name Educational Comics, Kurtzman had approached the company in 1949 to do nonfiction educational work. Among the drawings in his portfolio were some one-page funny comics that Gaines and Feldstein couldn't forget.

Nevertheless, Kurtzman had his mind on

A shell-shocked Korean War veteran is the subject of this story from Harvey Kurtzman's *Two-Fisted Tales*. While other war comics depicted victory and annihilation, Kurtzman's often explored other points of view, such as stories told by adversaries or civilians from occupied territories. — Kurtzman/Wood, "Bug-Out," *Two-Fisted Tales*, #24

A new family on the block is the basis of this morality tale from EC's crime comic *Shock SuspenStories*. Gaines and Feldstein's early 1950s series of tales about bigotry and race relations was strong stuff for comics and was often misunderstood by critics, who focused only on the occasional use of racial epithets and ignored the context. — Feldstein and Gaines/ Wood, "Blood Brothers," *Shock SuspenStories*, #13

Aliens from another planet review a copy of EC's *Weird Fantasy*, which depicts— aliens from another planet reading an EC comic. EC's science-fiction comics were full of clever plays with time travel, recursiveness, and paradoxes as well as some of the best art in the business. — Feldstein and Gaines/ Al Williamson, "The Aliens," *Weird Fantasy*, #17

EC's unredeemed line was its horror comics. Although Kurtzman hated them, Gaines and Feldstein relished coming up with ever-more-grotesque plots. Critics failed to notice that even the most ghoulish stories were lightened with tongue-in-cheek humor, like this nauseating tale of a man who accidentally happened upon a town populated by vampires. The stories were traditionally opened and closed by a ghostly host, in this case, the Old Witch.
—Feldstein and Gaines/Orlando, "Midnight Mess," *Tales from the Crypt*, #35

other things. "One thing I was working on," he says, "was trying to explain the ulcer graphically." He was dispatched to David Gaines, Bill's uncle, who *was* producing educational comics, and Kurtzman's first job for the family was *Lucky Fights It Through*, a western/syphilis tale, the highlight of which was a singalong entitled "That Ignorant, Ignorant Cowboy."

Kurtzman also began doing art for some of EC's horror and science-fiction titles. By late 1950, he was given his own two adventure titles, but again turned his attention to nonfiction work. "I became obsessed with the idea of communicating real events," Kurtzman says. His comic books became heavily researched. In his quest for realism, he sent his assistant, Jerry De Fuccio, down in a submarine to gather sound-effects, and he himself conned a ride in a Grumman rescue plane, only later to find that it was a test flight of an unproven craft.

The adventure comics had become war comics, and they were quite different from the others. "I was reading the news of the Korean War along with everybody else," he says. "It struck me that war is not a very nice business, and the comic book companies dealing in the subject matter of war tended to make war glamorous. That offended me— so I turned my stories to antiwar."

It was also clear that Kurtzman knew there was more than one side to any war story. "When I wrote about Iwo Jima," he explains, "I avoided the usual glamorous stuff of the big, good-looking G.I. beating up the ugly little yellow man." Some of his Korean War comics were even told from the point of view of a North Korean. "I felt that people should know the truth about war and everything else," Kurtzman says. "As a matter of fact, I finally came to the conclusion that it's the truth that one should be interested in, that if you aim your thinking toward telling the truth, then you'd be doing something worthwhile."

As Al Feldstein put it, "EC was a brain-storming operation." Artists continued to be encouraged to develop unique styles, and Gaines and Feldstein's stories grew even more outrageous. Kurtzman worked more on his own, producing the most realistic war comics ever seen, with his own art and that of his favorite fellow artists.

The new titles began to attract attention. Entertaining Comics were unlike any others. The horror comics, with their intricately, lovingly detailed rotting and diseased corpses; the science-fiction titles, with an endless supply of BEMs (bug-eyed monsters); the *SuspenStories*, with sensational tales of love and evil; and the war books, with a decidedly pacifist bias, were the most intense comics available on the stands. The plots had surprising twists, and "good" did not always triumph. The inside front covers were used to introduce a different artist each issue, and every comic had its own letters page, which developed loyal and involved readers. Among teenagers EC stock rose; each EC comic book was worth five or more by another publisher.

Triumphantly, Gaines published the last of the old comics, *Modern Love* (No. 8), in which he and Feldstein told the self-satirizing story of a comic book publisher, his two yes-men, and their never-ending efforts to cash in on the latest comic book rage. Now EC was the trend-setter, and other publishers were rushing to keep up with the newly discovered appetite for horror and ghost stories.

Unfortunately, not all of the attention was good. Concerned parents, realizing that a comics code initiated within the industry in 1946 was not being enforced, again became worried about the effect of the gore and carnage churned out in the hundreds of horror and crime comics. Concerned community leaders wrote increasing numbers of editorials denouncing them. In 1951 Canada passed a law calling for two years imprisonment for anyone making, publishing, printing, or selling crime comics. Crime comics were then smuggled across the border.

At EC, Gaines was in deep. He had concocted an unusual business philosophy in which it seemed perfectly sensible to him to fund EC's less profitable science-fiction and war comics with the profits from the horror and suspense comics, the cash cows of the operation. In what *A Smithsonian Book of Comic-Book Comics* calls "a rare and probably unique instance of a publisher's supporting comic books because he cared about them," Gaines had unknowingly laid his own booby trap.

HEH, HEH! AND THAT'S THE STORY, KIDDIES! THAT'S WHAT 'CIVILIZED' VAMPIRES DO THESE DAYS! THEY DINE IN *BLOODITARIAN RESTAURANTS*, OPEN *SUNDOWN* TO *SUNRISE*. WHERE IS THERE ONE IN *YOUR* TOWN, YOU ASK? WELL, SOME *NIGHT* IF YOU FEEL *UP* TO IT, *LOOK* FOR IT! YOU CAN TELL IT BY THE *SIGN* INSIDE! IT'S IN *RED*... AND IT SAYS, "POSITIVELY NO *NIPPING* THE *WAITERS*"! THE GUY WHO *STARTED* THIS CHAIN OF DRINKERIES IS A *VAMPIRE BARNUM!* HE *KNOWS* THERE'S A 'SUCKER' BORN EVERY MINUTE! NOW I'LL TURN YOU BACK TO THE *CRYPT-KEEPER!* 'BYE!

NOTES

"He is a staunch believer . . ." Wilkes, "Charley Gaines — Comics Pioneer," 7.

"ten Picture Stories from Bible to trade . . ." Wilson, "Don't Go Away, Mad," 37.

"When I wrote about Iwo Jima . . ." Jacobs, William M. Gaines, 61–62.

By 1951 Gaines had pulled EC out of the slump it had been in when he'd taken over the company four years before. It was a small, though profitable, publishing house, with an influence 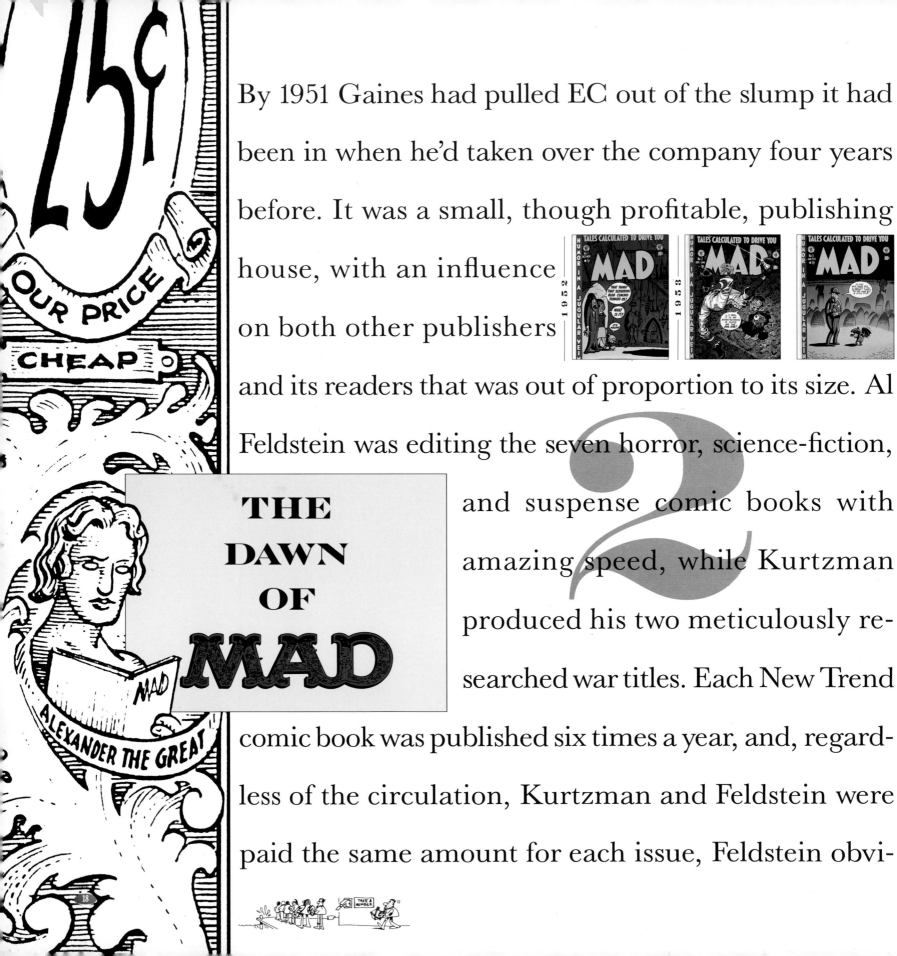 on both other publishers and its readers that was out of proportion to its size. Al Feldstein was editing the seven horror, science-fiction, and suspense comic books with amazing speed, while Kurtzman produced his two meticulously re-searched war titles. Each New Trend comic book was published six times a year, and, regard-less of the circulation, Kurtzman and Feldstein were paid the same amount for each issue, Feldstein obvi-

THE DAWN OF MAD

ously making quite a bit more money than Kurtzman, though both worked for EC full-time.

Finally, Kurtzman brought the discrepancy up to Gaines, who found himself in a difficult situation. Gaines felt that if he paid Kurtzman more, it wouldn't be fair to Feldstein. Gaines thought back to Kurtzman's first meeting with EC, the hilariously funny

THE MADMEN: *Harvey Kurtzman*

"I wanted to be a cartoonist from the word go," says Harvey Kurtzman. His childhood activities give credence to his claim. Mondays would find the young Kurtzman picking through his neighbors' trash searching for the Sunday papers his own family didn't get, so that he wouldn't miss even one comic strip. Small and unathletic, Kurtzman would join in on the local stickball games by drawing elaborate scoreboards on the sidewalk with chunks of plaster found in vacant lots.

Kurtzman had a childhood that was not unusual for a Russian Jewish kid born in Brooklyn in 1924; he was a "red diaper baby" whose progressive parents subscribed to the *Daily Worker* and sometimes sent Kurtzman and his brother to Camp Kinderland, a left-wing summer camp in upstate New York.

As Kurtzman grew older, he found that cartooning "was a way of getting attention in high school. I was the class cartoonist, and I was good at it. I could think up little funny things about any given student." This distinction was no small feat, since the school to which Kurtzman refers was the newly formed High School of Music and Art, a special New York City public school in Manhattan for the most artistically talented students in the city. The precocious Kurtzman was also a couple of years younger than most of the students, having been moved ahead in his classes. There he met many of his lifelong friends, Will Elder, Al Jaffee, Harry Chester, and John Severin among them.

After graduating high school in 1939, Kurtzman got work with Louis Ferstadt, a portrait painter who paid the rent by supplying drawings to DC Comics, Timely Comics (now Marvel Comics), Ace Magazines, and the *Daily Worker*. At the same time, Kurtzman attended the Cooper Union for the Advancement of Science and Art in Manhattan, where he honed his skills.

In 1942 Kurtzman was drafted into the army; two and a half years later, back in New York City, Kurtzman regrouped with Will Elder and Charles

material he'd presented to them, and conversations they'd had over dinners at the Kurtzmans'. He suggested that Kurtzman try a humorous comic book, one that could be put together in a week or so, thus increasing his income by 50 percent.

Kurtzman came back with a proposal for a satire magazine, one that would lampoon the comics themselves. "I picked up in the garbage, or somewhere, some college magazines. They impressed me as being a new kind of humor, a unique kind of humor. Of course what they were, were youth magazines, which didn't particularly exist for anybody but the students."

Accounts conflict regarding the origin of *Mad*'s title. Kurtzman himself believes that he came up with the title in a personal brainstorming session. Gaines remembers that it was he or Feldstein who suggested "EC's Mad

Mag," a phrase often used in the letters columns to refer to EC's horror comics, and that Kurtzman shortened it, "in a brilliant move," to simply "Mad."

Kurtzman brought his small crew of artists, with whom he had been working on his war titles for a year and a half, to the project. "We had a good bunch of funny-men, and it was great," Kurtzman recalls. "The people who worked out the best were on a wavelength. Not only did we work together, but we played together, we picnicked, we had dinners at our houses, we were socially active

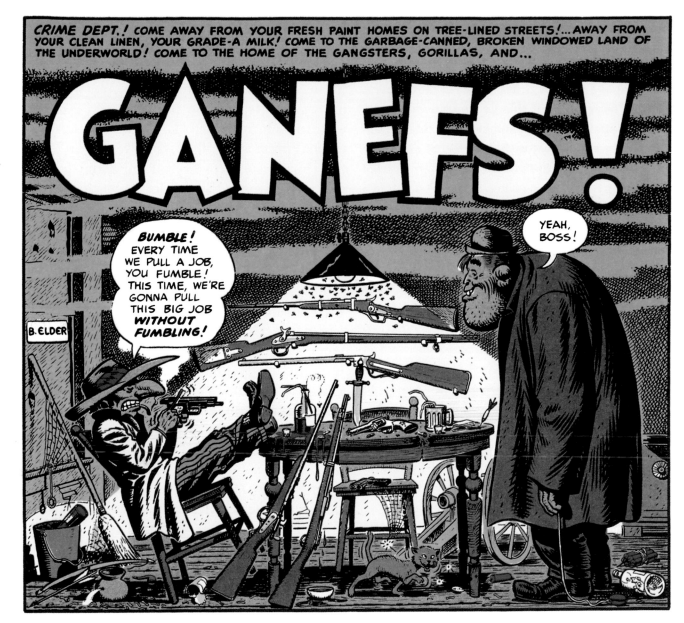

CRIME DEPT.! COME AWAY FROM YOUR FRESH PAINT HOMES ON TREE-LINED STREETS!...AWAY FROM YOUR CLEAN LINEN, YOUR GRADE-A MILK! COME TO THE GARBAGE-CANNED, BROKEN WINDOWED LAND OF THE UNDERWORLD! COME TO THE HOME OF THE GANGSTERS, GORILLAS, AND...

GANEFS!

B. ELDER

BUMBLE! EVERY TIME WE PULL A JOB, YOU FUMBLE! THIS TIME, WE'RE GONNA PULL THIS BIG JOB *WITHOUT* FUMBLING!

YEAH, BOSS!

Mad's original material was the comics themselves. In this splash panel from issue number one, Will Elder and Harvey Kurtzman lampoon crime comics. Kurtzman worked closely with his artists, often penciling in rough drawings for each panel. This one is filled with the kind of outrageous wit for which *Mad* became known: here, the comic detritus of the gangster lifestyle. Seldom is a new concept so well evolved as this. John Benson, an EC scholar from way back, has pointed out that "though *Mad* changed and developed over the years, there was an organic unity, a kind of perfection, from the start, which was undoubtedly due to the fact that editor/writer Harvey Kurtzman and his small crew of artists had already developed into a closely integrated team on the EC war titles over the previous year and a half....The final essential ingredient was a publisher who was willing to gamble on something as untried and irreverent as *Mad*...."
—Kurtzman/Elder, "Ganefs!," *Mad*, #1

with each other as well as being active with the work." The first 32-page issue of *Mad* contained four stories, all written by Kurtzman, and each spoofing a different EC comic. The look and writing were wild, a combination of the outrageousness and violence of Tex Avery's animated cartoons with the polyethnic dialogue and logic of George Herriman's Krazy Kat. "Hoohah!," a horror send-up, was drawn by Jack Davis and followed the adven-

tures of Daphne and her boyfriend Galusha, stranded on a dark and stormy night. "Blobs!" displayed new aspects of science-fiction cartoonist Wally Wood's style, while "Varmint!" took advantage of John Severin's skill with the western. Will Elder mopped up with "Ganefs!," a crime story of a gangster and his fumbling assistant, Bumble.

The first issue of *Mad* reached the stands in late summer 1952. Actually, Gaines didn't

Stern to form the Charles William Harvey Studio. The studio pursued commercial drawing and illustration work, and made extra money by renting out spare space to other artists. René Goscinny, Dave Berg, and John Severin were three of the many artists who passed through the studio in those years.

In the 1940s superhero comics were hot, but this genre was not Kurtzman's forte. He was best at funny, absurd comics. Bucking the tide, he approached the young Stan Lee at Timely/Marvel with a series of one-page comics called "Hey Look!" Lee found a place in Marvel's superhero comics for these, keeping a stack of them on hand for use when a comic book had a single page that needed to be filled. The ongoing work with Marvel changed Kurtzman's life. Through it he came to know many of the best cartoonists of the time, and at Timely/Marvel he met Adele Hasan, a proofreader whom he married in 1948.

It was the "Hey Look!" comics that Kurtzman carried with him to EC in 1949 when he approached Bill Gaines and Al Feldstein for work on educational comics, although the first work Kurtzman did for them was illustrating horror and science-fiction comics. When Kurtzman demonstrated in several science-fiction stories that he could write as well as draw, Gaines made him editor of EC's two new adventure comics, *Two-Fisted Tales* and *Frontline Combat*.

Kurtzman wrote, edited, and produced some art and covers for the two comic books. He was known as a tough taskmaster, and supplied the artist with tissue paper overlays of the panels; woe betide those who strayed from his rough sketches. Nevertheless, he was very well liked by the artists who worked with him. "Harvey is a great teacher," Jack Davis explains, "he would give dramatic readings of the scripts that were very inspirational."

With *Mad*, Kurtzman introduced a host of innovations to comics; he was the first to use mainstream humorists as writers; he parodied many aspects of life, including movies, television, magazines, and advertising. In the *Mad* comics he pushed the boundaries of what a comic was supposed to look like, incorporating photographs, fine art, and pop iconography. Finally, reaching the limits of the comic book medium, he supervised the transition of *Mad* from a comic book to a magazine, devising new and better printing and layouts.

After leaving EC in 1956, Kurtzman joined forces with Hugh Hefner, who offered him his own slick satire magazine. Kurtzman's *Trump* was a leap beyond *Mad* magazine, incorporating typesetting and a magazine style of layout, and produced in full color on slick paper. Although the first two issues of the magazine sold well, the high production costs caused an over-

have much hope that the humor magazine could make money, but he liked the idea and found Kurtzman's comics side-splittingly funny. He was willing to support *Mad* with the horror profits, hoping that it would eventually find an audience. Luckily, the abysmal sales figures on the first issue weren't in until the third issue was on sale and the fourth was in the works. By the fourth issue, something began to click, and Kurtzman's parody "Superduperman!" flew off the stands.

Mad was developing a following, and it wasn't entirely made up of the usual comic book fans. One member was Lyle Stuart, then publisher of the muckraking tabloid *Exposé*. Gaines, a fan of *Exposé*, was delighted when Stuart wrote for a subscription, and took the opportunity to meet him and cultivate a friendship. When EC's business manager, Frank Lee, retired a short time later, Gaines was happy to hire Stuart to do the job.

By mid-1953 business at EC was astonishing. *The Haunt of Fear*, *The Vault of Horror*, and the renamed *Tales from the Crypt* had a circulation of 400,000 copies each; *Crime SuspenStories* and *Shock SuspenStories* did almost as well, with a healthy 300,000 copies per title; *Weird Science*, *Weird Fantasy*, *Two-Fisted Tales*, and *Frontline Combat* lagged behind, at about 225,000 copies each. The company's horror books had spawned a host of imitators—by one count, 150 different horror comic books by other publishers now glutted the stands.

In November *Ladies' Home Journal* ran an excerpt of a forthcoming book that would set comic book publishing on fire. The author, Frederic Wertham, was an influential liberal psychiatrist, director of a "mental hygiene" clinic at Bellevue, and founder of several other mental hygiene clinics (one in Harlem).

Luckily, the numbers weren't in on the first three issues of *Mad* when this *Superman* parody hit the stands. For the first time Kurtzman was satirizing something other than an EC comic. Slapstick humor, busty women, and ridiculous detail by Wally Wood combined to make "Superduperman!" a big hit, finally turning the corner to profitability for *Mad*.

Almost immediately National Periodicals, the owners of *Superman*, threatened *Mad* with a lawsuit for infringement. Coincidentally, EC and National shared the same lawyer, who simply told Gaines to lay off. Gaines considered submitting, but Kurtzman knew that the future of *Mad* lay in doing satires and parodies, and he was not about to let the success of his new comic be threatened.

Ever the researcher, Kurtzman found a legal precedent that seemed to imply that *Mad*'s parody was legal and protected, also. Gaines hired the lawyer who wrote it to write up an opinion specifically to substantiate EC's right. When the opinion had been written, Gaines and Kurtzman were dismayed to see that this time the lawyer sided with National, not EC. Finally, Gaines consulted Marty Scheiman, his adviser Lyle Stuart's lawyer, about the situation. Scheiman suggested that they simply ignore the threat and continue with their parodies, which they did, without further problems. —Kurtzman/Wood, "Superduperman!," *Mad*, #4

The doctor was ready to publish the result of seven years of his observations of the ravages of comic books on youth, the fearsomely titled *Seduction of the Innocent*.

Wertham's book was a scathing indictment of almost all dramatic comic books, but his main targets were horror and crime comics. He saw them as having a bad effect on literacy and pointed to the dangers of such words

as "yeow, arghh, thunk, blam, glurg, and kurrack." He cited case after case of children committing crimes, murders, injuries, and suicides, all after reading comics. He attacked superhero comics as well. Batman, he claimed, was having a homosexual relationship with his boy sidekick, Robin. Wonder Woman, the superheroine created by a fellow psychologist, was a perfect lesbian role

eption when you're tense...." JAY LYNCH *A History of Underground Comics*

extended Hefner unexpectedly to withdraw his backing.

After *Trump*, Kurtzman founded and edited several short-lived but influential humorous periodicals. *Humbug* was a small, two-color publication funded by Kurtzman and his crew of diehard artists. From 1960 to 1965 Kurtzman and his assistants Terry Gilliam and Gloria Steinem produced *Help!*, which pioneered the photo-funny, and also included the first published work of the now well-known underground cartoonists Jay Lynch, R. Crumb, and Gilbert Shelton.

Since then Kurtzman has remained active, contributing his work to the *New York Herald Tribune, Esquire,* and other publications. His best-known work today is "Little Annie Fanny," considered to be the most lavish comic strip ever produced in America, which he and Will Elder have contributed to *Playboy* magazine since the 1960s. His latest comic is *Harvey Kurtzman's Strange Adventures*, published in 1990 by Marvel and including illustrations by R. Crumb, Sergio Aragonés, Sarah Downs, and others. He teaches a class in cartooning at the School of Visual Arts in Manhattan while enjoying the international rounds of comic book conventions, where he is a revered guest.

Al Feldstein's *Panic* was EC's own imitation of *Mad*. Its premiere issue in December 1953 included a spoof of "A Visit from Saint Nicholas" that caused the issue to be banned in Massachusetts, as well as a Mickey Spillane parody that aroused the ire of the New York City police.
—Cover: Feldstein/Feldstein, *Panic,* #1

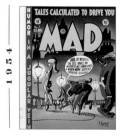

model.

In strange counterpoint to this diatribe, November also saw the first issue of an EC newsletter called *The Fan-Addict Club Bulletin*. Sent to nine thousand charter members of the club, the bulletin was friendly, newsy, and innocuous. Births and marriages among EC's staff and free lances were announced, and a trading post for old EC comics was set up.

The bulletin also touted the immediately forthcoming premier of *Panic*. By this time *Mad* had proven so popular that it had begun to have its own imitators with names like *Whack, Unsane, Bughouse, Crazy, Eh!,* and *Nuts.* Gaines figured EC should take advantage as well, and had Feldstein develop the new comic book.

Panic's December issue, its first, quickly lived up to its name. Feldstein had decided to celebrate the holiday by having Will Elder illustrate Clement Clarke Moore's "A Visit

from Saint Nicholas." Not a word of the original poem was changed, but the drawings illustrating it were an outrageously surreal trip through the pair's psyches. While the children dreamed of Marilyn Monroe, Jane Russell, and lifetime subscriptions to EC comics, Dad drank himself to sleep.

In Massachusetts, the attorney general reacted with outrage, describing the story as "pagan" and "desecrating Christmas." An American institution had been insulted, and the Governor's Council requested that the comic be banned throughout the state. The story received national coverage in the press. "I was the most shocked person in the world," Feldstein recalls. "What we didn't realize back then," Gaines clarified, "is that Santa Claus is a saint."

Gaines and his lawyer, Martin Scheiman, realized that EC had to defend itself, and

On a two-month time schedule, Kurtzman sometimes had difficulty coming up with enough material for the two war comics he edited plus *Mad*. Here, he lifts the artwork directly from an EC suspense comic and supplies new dialogue, much of it also clipped from other sources and dropped into the word balloons. The effect is strangely surreal and at the same time absurdly funny. — Kurtzman/Davis, "Murder the Husband!," *Mad*, #11

quickly. Scheiman released a statement to the *New York Times* charging "wanton damage" to his client in the defense of "a wholly imaginary, mythological creature."

Meanwhile, the hoopla kicked up by Massachusetts moralists drew the attention of the New York establishment to the comic. Soon, EC was visited by the New York City police, who purchased a copy of *Panic* from EC's mail room from Lyle Stuart (who had advised Gaines to stay out of sight) and promptly arrested him for selling "disgusting" literature. This time it was "My Gun Is the Jury," a sledgehammer Mickey Spillane parody, that provoked. The charge was serious: Stuart faced a potential year in prison.

The American Civil Liberties Union became interested and recommended that Scheiman wait until the case reached a higher court before settling it. A nervous Gaines wanted the situation resolved, however, and Scheiman argued the case so successfully that it was thrown out in lower court. EC had won two battles, but the worst part of the war was yet to come.

By early 1954, at the peak of McCarthyism, the hue and cry against comic books was being raised everywhere. The *Hartford Courant* waged an ongoing editorial battle against "the filthy stream that flows from the gold-plated sewers of New York." The ever-vigilant *Reader's Digest* began attacking comics in earnest. In April, Wertham's *Seduction of the Innocent* went on sale in bookstores and through the Book-of-the-Month Club, and added fuel to the fires. The book detailed many of the charges made earlier and included illustrations from the worst offenders, several from the EC line. Communities and church groups began to sponsor comic book burnings, and the call for a Senate Judiciary Hearing on the subject grew.

On April 21 the Hearings Before the Subcommittee to Investigate Juvenile Delinquency of the Committee on the Judiciary opened at the Foley Square Federal Court House in Manhattan. Witnesses called included Wertham, Walt Kelly, creator of *Pogo*, and Milton Caniff, creator of *Steve Canyon*. Gaines, noticing that the roster contained no witnesses for the defense of his kind of comics, and encouraged by Stuart, had volunteered to speak. His offer to appear was snapped up. He was scheduled to follow Wertham himself.

Gaines and Stuart stayed up the entire night before writing his opening statement. It said in part:

It would be just as difficult to explain the harmless thrill of a horror story to a Dr. Wertham as it would be to explain the sublimity of love to a frigid old maid. . . . My father was proud of the comics he published, and I am proud of the comics I publish. We use the best writers, the finest artists; we spare nothing to make each magazine, each story, each page, a work of art. . . . Our American children are for the most part normal children. They are bright children, but those who want to prohibit comic magazines seem to see dirty, sneaky, perverted monsters who use the comics as a blueprint for action.

The truth is that delinquency is the product of the real environment in which the child lives and not of the fiction he reads. . . . The problems are economic and social and they are complex. Our people need understanding; they need to have affection, decent homes, decent food.

After reading his statement, Gaines was questioned in detail about particular stories from his comics that had been submitted as evidence. The queries from the subcom-

mittee grew increasingly absurd, as in this exchange about an EC story of a girl abused in a haunted foster home:

GAINES: Most foster children, I am sure, are not in homes such as were described in those stories. Those were pretty miserable homes.

HERBERT HANNOCH: You mean homes that had vampires in them, those were not nice homes?

GAINES: Yes.

HANNOCH: Do you know anyplace where there is any such thing?

GAINES: As vampires?

HANNOCH: Yes.

GAINES: No, sir; this is fantasy.

Gaines sat patiently through Wertham's accusations that EC comic books promoted "racial intolerance," explaining that the particular story in question (one of EC's moral-

ity tales) was one of a series "designed to show the evils of race prejudice and mob violence."

In the most infamous passage of the closely watched hearings, Gaines was confronted with an issue of *Crime SuspenStories* with a particularly gruesome cover by Johnny Craig.

ESTES KEFAUVER: This seems to be a man with a bloody ax holding a woman's head up which has been severed from her body. Do you think that is in good taste?

"Gasoline Alley" was perhaps the only comic strip where the characters grew and aged. Kurtzman and Elder had great fun with this convention as evident in this strangely Freudian passage from "Gasoline Valley." — Kurtzman/Elder, "Gasoline Valley!," *Mad*, #15

GAINES: Yes sir; I do, for the cover of a horror comic. A cover in bad taste, for example, might be defined as holding the head a little higher so that the neck could be seen dripping blood from it and moving the body over a little further so that the neck of the body could be seen to be bloody. . . .

CHAIRMAN (SENATOR ROBERT C. HENDRICKSON): Here is another one I want to show him.

KEFAUVER: This is the July one. It seems to be a man with a woman in a boat and he is choking her to death here with a crowbar. Is that in good taste?

GAINES: I think so.

HANNOCH: (*despairingly*) How could it be worse?

In fact, the covers *could* have been worse. When Craig first submitted the "severed head" cover to Gaines and Feldstein, it showed both bloody neck stumps as he had described to the committee. Gaines had asked Craig to make changes, feeling that it was too gory for even a horror comic.

With that exchange Gaines became the star of the inquiry, but the result was infamy rather than support. Public sentiment turned decisively against the young publisher, as television and print news reports widely quoted the severed head exchange.

Gaines attempted to marshal a two-pronged attack and issued a call to arms. In May, a proposal was sent out to almost all the major comic book publishers. "If fools rush in where angels fear to tread," the letter began, "then I suppose EC is being pretty foolish. We may get our fingers burned and our toes stepped on." Gaines went on to suggest several strategies by which the publishers could fight the would-be censors, including a publishers organization to mount a public relations campaign, a research fund to sponsor independent scientific research on the effects of the comic books on children, and an effort to involve the American Civil Liberties Union in the fight against censorship.

Second, June's issue of the *EC Fan-Addict Club Bulletin* listed the address of the subcommittee and exhorted its now seventeen thousand subscribers to begin a letter-writing campaign. Kids were encouraged to have their parents make their voices heard, whether they were for or against comics.

You can almost hear Kurtzman chortling in this biting parody of Mickey Mouse. He points up every outlandish premise of Disney's comics while Elder supplies mousetraps, pet humans, a five o'clock shadow, and an amazing imitation of Disney's style. "Will understood parody," Kurtzman elaborates. "Of course what it is, is mimicry. Willy was just so good at it. He understood that you had to have an exact duplicate of what you're parodying." The satire becomes self-reflexive as the drawing style devolves to Elder's own and Darnold gets suspicious. —Kurtzman/Elder, "Mickey Rodent!," *Mad,* #19

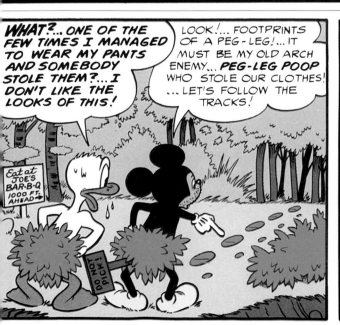

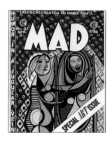

Summer, usually the high season for comic books, arrived, but sales throughout the industry flagged. The call to eliminate comic books became international as an exhibit of horror and crime comics, prominently labeled "Made in the U.S.A.," toured Great Britain. Even though Winston Churchill, on seeing

"There were two things banned from the Griffith household (Levittown, New York, mid-'50s): Mad *magazine and Elvis Presley. My parental unit's wrath was specifically directed at the Kurtzman* Mad*'s, of course, with their lurid, mind-rotting covers."* BILL GRIFFITH

the exhibit in the House of Commons, requested, "Pass them over, I should like to read some horror comics," no one came to the defense.

Convinced that a united front was the best way to fight the growing witch-hunt, Gaines rented Wendell Willkie Hall and invited all the major comic book publishers to a meet-

THE MADMEN: *Jack Davis, Will Elder, Wally Wood*

When Harvey Kurtzman created *Mad*, Jack Davis, Will Elder, and Wally Wood were at the top of his list of contributing artists. Each had a different style and strengths, and each made unique contributions to the gestalt that was *Mad*.

Jack Davis, now one of the best-known illustrators in the United States, was one of the original EC artists back in the New Trend comic book days, specializing in the horror comics. His drawings are marked by a loose, active line that is at the same time extremely descriptive and expressive. Davis is also known for his telling caricatures, and although he has become a frequent contributor to *Time*, having created over forty covers, and to other magazines, work for *Mad* remains a favorite assignment. "What I like to do is spontaneous, funny faces and action shots—man, I coast! My wild stuff is fairly grotesque, and it goes back to the horror bit. I'm not a frightening, vindictive, or mean person, but I love to draw things like Frankensteins and monsters," Davis admits. "In *Mad*, I get a chance to do what I like—and I love to make people laugh."

Will Elder had been a friend and collaborator of Kurtzman's since their high school days and had also worked with him on his war comics. In *Mad*, Elder was able to give free rein to his well-developed talent for mimicry. His *Mad* parodies of other comic characters are virtually indistinguishable from drawings by the original artists—no small feat. Elder points out that this authenticity was essential to putting the joke across. "That's part of the

ing. Again, Gaines proposed forming an association to carry out the suggestions he made in his letter.

The other publishers agreed drastic action was needed, and quickly, but their consensus left Gaines reeling: form a self-censoring board and ban the words "crime, horror, terror, and weird, even weird!" Gaines remembers, from the titles of comic books, effectively outlawing most of the EC line. EC was to be offered up as the scapegoat for the entire industry.

By September Gaines announced that he was suspending publication of his horror and suspense comics. Public opposition had grown so strong that Gaines knew that, quite literally, he had to give up the ghost.

Two days later, on September 16, the Comics Code Authority was officially established, headed by the former judge Charles F. Murphy, representing 90 percent of the industry. The code was ruthless: no walking dead or torture was allowed to be depicted, and only "classic" vampires, ghouls, and

"Zippy the Pinhead" Blab!

werewolves were to be shown. Policemen, judges, government officials, and respected institutions could not be presented in a way that created disrespect for established authority, and all "lurid, unsavory, and gruesome" illustrations would be eliminated. Evil could only be used to illuminate a moral issue. The code was apparently modeled in part on the Production Code used for motion pictures, as well as on the self-imposed McCarthy-era restrictions in effect for television productions.

The distributors, who wanted trouble no more than the publishers, agreed that only comic books displaying the seal of the code on

their covers would reach wholesalers, news-stands, and drugstores.

Meanwhile, back in the EC offices, Kurtzman was again growing restless. *Mad* was, by now, a real success, and Kurtzman watched as EC's horror comics, which he personally never liked, but which once supported EC, now jeopardized the existence of the entire company. Except for a fake composition book cover that teachers had hated, *Mad* had not yet drawn the ire of the public; in fact, the mainstream *Pageant* magazine had even run an article on it, one of the few bits of positive press the embattled EC had received lately. Kurtzman had become acutely aware of the vulnerability and limitations of his position as a "lowly comic book" editor when Harris Shevelson, the editor of *Pageant*, offered him a job that would solve these problems in one fell swoop: work on a "slick" magazine as his right-hand man.

Kurtzman told Gaines that he wanted the job. "It was a compound effect that made me get very itchy," Kurtzman recalls. "There was

the political situation, there was *Pageant*, and there was the 'I told you so' situation."

With only *Mad*, *Panic*, and *Incredible Science*

strength of the gag. It's only going to be funny when you can actually fool somebody, when you can actually shock them," he explains. Along with Wally Wood, Elder pioneered *Mad*'s cluttered panel or so-called chicken-fat technique—filling in every fraction of an inch with sight gags.

Wally Wood's early work for EC's science fiction comics gained him the title "Dean of Comic Book Science Fiction" even before his work for *Mad* earned him yet another audience. Wood came to EC with a firm grounding in work on several of the best comics of the day: George Wunder's *Terry and the Pirates*, and Will Eisner's *The Spirit* among others. Having worked on the real thing, Wood was a master at imitating other comics, yet he also developed strong comic and realistic styles of his own, marked by an elegant, uncluttered line, yet telling detail.

Fiction left in the EC line, Gaines couldn't afford to lose Kurtzman, editor of the most successful remaining title. He countered with a proposal to do what Kurtzman had once requested: He offered to allow Kurtzman to turn *Mad* into a slick magazine, a risky proposition that Gaines now realizes was "a piece of luck, because *Mad* comics could never have gone through the [Comics Code] Association."

Kurtzman was ecstatic. "It was a great moment for me, Bill gave me *carte blanche*. And with my *carte blanche*, I went out into the world of newsstands and just bought a bunch of magazines, because I needed a totally original format. It had to have class because we were charging a higher price, and there were no guidelines. Make up the guidelines: now that was a great creative moment for me."

Kurtzman knew that he and Gaines were "stepping out into the void. We didn't have any idea of what the slick magazine business was all about, or where we would wind up." One of the first things Kurtzman had to attend to was to work out how the new *Mad* would be printed. Comic books had always been printed in specific sizes on specialized presses that were also used to print newspapers. The paper used was porous and soft. For *Mad*, Kurtzman wanted to upgrade the printing and paper. The technique "had to accommodate a certain drawing style that didn't exist yet. I knew what I wanted, and if you know what you want, you can create, and that to me is the creative process. I saw the image—I knew where I wanted to go."

Working with the printing broker George Dougherty, Kurtzman found the type of press he needed and invented the package from the ground up. The web press he chose couldn't produce color cheaply enough to be feasible, but since the new *Mad* was not intended to be a comic, this was not seen as a drawback. For the same reason, he made the move from hand-lettering to set type: "That was one of the ways I thought I could give the magazine class."

The new *Mad*, a 25-cent, bimonthly, black-and-white magazine, appeared in early summer 1955. Jack Davis remembers the EC gang trooping to Brooklyn to watch the new enterprise coming off the presses. "We really didn't know how *Mad*, the slick edition, was going to come out. But the people who

printed it were laughing and getting a big kick out of it, so we said 'This has got to be good.'"

This early feedback was on the money—amid the gloom, *Mad* magazine was an immediate success, and EC actually went back

MEETING'S ADJOURNED!

BY GOLLY, CORNED-BEEF AND CABBAGE...

...WITH THE BOYS AT DINTY MOORES...

...NOW IF I CAN ONLY SNEAK PAST MAGGS...!

WHO ♪ THRU THE CHOWDER INTO MRS. MURPHY'S ♪ OVERALLS?

TIP TOE

...SO FAR, SO GOOD...

...OUT THE FRONT DOOR....!!

...NYAAH... WHY KID MYSELF!

xxx xx

...GET UP, YOU WORM, AND LOOK AT ALL THE HAPPY READERS SMILING AT HOW I KNOCKED YOU OVER WITH THE DISHES!

BY GOLLY, MAGGS, THIS ISN'T A VERY FUNNY MATTER!

DAY IN...DAY OUT, YOU THROW DISHES AT MY HEAD AND EVERYONE THINKS IT'S FUNNY! DO THEY REALIZE SOMETIMES A FLYING DISH CAN BREAK OPEN THE SCALP AND CAUSE SERIOUS BLEEDING?

Since the 1930s Maggie and Jiggs's household battles had been taken for granted as a caricature of American life. Jiggs, a first-generation Horatio Alger, is engaged in a perpetual game of sneaking out past his social-climbing wife in pursuit of some low-life male bonding. In their favorite set piece, Maggie responds with a barrage of pottery. Kurtzman couldn't resist satirizing "Bringing Up Father" two different ways. He had Elder draw every second page as a parody in the original style. On facing pages, Bernard Krigstein, who worked little for *Mad*, but whom Kurtzman has called the most outstanding artist in comic books, offered a more realistic rendering. Krigstein's stark, expressionistic drawings are perfectly fitted to tell Kurtzman's message—what's funny in a cartoon can be threatening in real life.
—Kurtzman/Elder, Krigstein, "Bringing Back Father!," *Mad*, #17

to press for a second printing of the first issue. The work of Elder, Wood, and Davis was adapted brilliantly to the new format, as was writing by iconoclastic television personality Ernie Kovacs, the humorist Roger Price, and Bernard Shir-Cliff, an editor at Ballantine Books, all fans of the comic book *Mad*. And because the new *Mad* was a "magazine" rather than a "comic book," it had no problem at all with the distributors or the code.

At the same time, Gaines and Feldstein developed a new line of "clean, clean" comic books that they hoped would be handled by the distributors, despite the lack of code approval. Premiering in April 1955, the "New Direction" comic books consisted of a variety

These two pages from *Mad*'s *Wonder Woman* parody are an encyclopedia of the early *Mad* style. Elder indulges in an orgy of free association: a shooting gallery, the Smith Brothers, beauty queen banners, and football are a partial catalogue of the visual puns depicted. The parody also includes several of *Mad*'s running jokes—Nivlem, the bad guy character, looks like an earlier *Mad* parody of Batman, and his name is "Melvin" spelled backward. In "reality" he is Steve Adore, Woman Wonder's long-suffering boy friend. At one point Nivlem admits that he is a two-dimensional personality as he challenges the plausibility of Woman Wonder's bracelets and steps out of the comic until it becomes more believable.

This *Wonder Woman* parody has all the more resonance when we realize that in the late 1930s, Bill's father, Max Gaines, was responsible for the creation of Wonder Woman. He worked with the psychologist William Moulton Marston to invent a new, psychologically healthy super-hero character. Marston had

of genres: *Aces High*, *Impact*, *Piracy*, and *Valor* were adventure comics; *Extra!* was about journalism; and *MD* and *Psychoanalysis* were based on the medical and psychiatric professions. But the ploy failed, and crate after crate was returned to the distributor unopened by the wholesalers. With EC's money quickly being depleted, Gaines finally realized that he could not wage a one-man war against the upholders of the code. He swallowed his pride

and joined the association, watching aghast and holding his tongue as his new comics were gutted by the censors at the Comic Book Association.

The inevitable confrontation between Gaines and the association took place, ironically, over a story entitled "Judgement Day," a science-fiction morality tale about bigotry on other planets. The censors objected to a detailed rendering of a black astronaut with sweat on his brow. When they demanded that the offensive sweat be removed, Gaines realized that he had had enough. Even though the association caved in when he threatened to sue, Gaines resigned, swearing never to work within the code again.

Guided by the success of *Mad* magazine, Gaines and Feldstein dropped comic books entirely and inaugurated "Adult Picto-Fiction," 25-cent, black-and-white, typeset books

like *Mad*, for which they employed the EC artists to illustrate fleshed-out plots from earlier EC comics. The magazines were instant failures. The new format did not carry the dynamism of EC's comic books, and they lasted only two issues each.

By early 1956 almost all of the profits from earlier years had been absorbed by the abortive "New Directions" and "Picto-Fiction" lines. Although EC was owed $110,000

felt that "from a psychological angle…the comics worst offense was their blood-curdling masculinity." His surprising deduction was that "the obvious remedy is to create a feminine character with all the strength of a Superman plus all the allure of a good and beautiful woman."

Marston's idea of a female superhero met with universal scoffing around Max's office. "Men actually submit to women now, they do it on the sly," Marston asserted. "Give them an alluring woman, stronger than themselves to submit to, and they'll be *proud* to become her willing slaves!"

Kurtzman blew that concept to smithereens as he had Nivlem batter Woman Wonder when she was down, giving vent to just the kind of domineering impulses Marston was trying to discourage. Nivlem, alias Steve Adore, ultimately assumed his "rightful place" as king of his castle in this male supremacist fantasy. — Kurtzman/Elder, "Woman Wonder!," *Mad*, #10

AND STEVE CAN EVEN KNOCK HER DOWN IN BOXING!

by their distributor, Leader News, it was $100,000 in debt to George Dougherty for printing bills.

Mad was a success, but now it was EC's only title, and peace did not reign even there. Kurtzman had been asking for more money for *Mad*'s artists and writers, and in fact had taken a salary cut to help provide the funds. At the same time Kurtzman was plagued by his old nemesis, schedules; he was having deadline problems, with the unplanned re-

sult that *Mad* was now a quarterly. Toward the end of the year Kurtzman had a falling out with Lyle Stuart, and Gaines reluctantly let Stuart go.

Gaines was played out and EC was broke. As he pondered his dilemmas he received a phone call from another publisher: Leader News had gone bankrupt and wouldn't be able to pay their debt to EC, leaving Gaines's company with only a $100,000 debt to Dougherty.

...AND NOW...AN ACTUAL LOOK AT 3-D IN ACTION! SINCE WE SUPPLY NO 3-D GLASSES LET US SUGGEST YOU MAKE YOUR OWN BY PAINTING MOTHER'S READING GLASSES RED AND BLUE... OR PERHAPS YOU MIGHT PAINT RED AND BLUE RIGHT OVER YOUR EYEBALLS... IN ANY CASE...

...YOU WILL BE ABLE TO FOLLOW OUR STORY IN THESE CAPTIONS!...NOW... SOME SAY 3-D CAUSES EYESTRAIN!

...SOME SAY 3-D MAKES YOU SEE GREEN SPOTS IN FRONT OF YOUR EYES! WE OF **MAD** ASSURE YOU THEY ARE **WRONG!**

Three-D comics were all the rage when *Mad* ran this deep-space extravaganza. Kurtzman and Wood wreaked havoc with the conventions of comic books in their depiction of a typical comic book writer and two-headed 3-D artist giving an exposition on the 3-D technique. The second page of the story explored the effects on the eyes of viewing 3-D.
— Kurtzman/Wood, "3-Dimensions!," *Mad*, #12

WHEN THESE PARTIES TELL YOU THAT 3-D MAKES YOUR EYES BURN AND SEE REDDISH... **DON'T BELIEVE THEM!**

...DOCTORS HAVE PROVEN TWO-TO-ONE, THAT 3-D CAUSES NO EYE-STRAIN... NO REDNESS OR FATIGUE!

...IN FACT, DOCTORS HAVE PROVEN THAT 3-D IS BENEFICIAL AND HELPS TO GIVE THE EYEBALLS NEEDED EXERCISE!

LOOK AT THESE 3-D DRAWINGS!... LOOK AT THE CLARITY OF THE PICTURE BELOW... THE FINE DETAILS OF THE FACES... **PROOF POSITIVE THAT 3-D CAUSES NO EYESTRAIN!**

THERE, NOW! LET'S GET BACK TO NORMAL PICTURES... AND IF ANY OF THESE SCHEMING NO-GOOD BUMS TELL YOU 3-D DISTORTS YOUR VISION, YOU JUST TELL THEM HOW SHARP YOU CAN REALLY SEE WITH YOUR EXERCISED EYEBALLS!

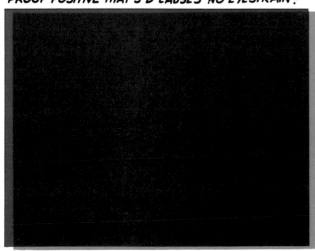

1957

There seemed to be no choice. Gaines laid off Feldstein and the rest of his staff and notified Kurtzman that he was going to shut down EC — he hoped only temporarily — until he could come up with a way to pay off the outstanding printing bill. Kurtzman didn't want to let his hand-picked staff and

THE MADMEN: *Al Feldstein*

Attacked by righteous parents and educators for most of their existence, comic books have been defended for just as long by those who argue that they are nothing more than harmless entertainment. For Al Feldstein, editor of *Mad* for almost thirty years, the truth is somewhere in between.

"When I took over the magazine and guided it through the sixties and the seventies I was really excited," Feldstein says of the time when he came into his own as editor of *Mad*. "I was getting a great deal of satisfaction because I thought that I was performing a kind of service for young people in my own way as a liberal, in at least alerting them to what was going on around them in the areas of advertising, politics, manufacturing, packaging, etc. I knew that I had helped to form some of the militant, liberal young people's minds in terms of the draft card burning, the Vietnam war, and the brassiere burning, at least I was part of it."

Feldstein was born in 1925 of a Russian Jewish family in Brooklyn. His father, a dental technician, lost his laboratory in 1938, and Feldstein knew that he would have to make it on his own. The same year he won a poster contest sponsored by the New York World's Fair, and his path seemed clear. He attended the High School of Music and Art in Manhattan, working after school every day for Eisner & Iger, a large comic shop that produced work for Fiction House, Quality, Fox, and Aviation Press. After graduation Feldstein took advantage of a scholarship to the nearby Art Students League, where he attended night school. He continued his comic work, scraping together enough money to attend Brooklyn College briefly.

In 1943 World War II summoned, and Feldstein joined the United States Air Force as an aviation cadet.

After the war, Feldstein returned to comic book work, free-lancing for many companies. He arrived at EC to find that it was being run by a fellow just a little older than himself, New York University student Bill Gaines.

Spurred on by a mutual appreciation of science-fiction and horror stories, and with nothing to lose since EC had been operating continually in the red, Feldstein and Gaines instituted what they dubbed a "New Trend" in

artists go. He convinced Gaines that it would be a mistake to interrupt the publication of *Mad*, and suggested that all that was needed for the rebound of EC was *Mad* and capital.

Together, Gaines and Kurtzman made a trip uptown to visit Bill's mother, Jessie.

Kurtzman used all his powers to persuade her of the wisdom of investment in *Mad*. A deal was struck: Jessie would invest $50,000 and Bill would invest $60,000 — enough to get EC out of debt, but not out of the woods.

There was work to be done. Gaines had to find a distributor for *Mad*, and fast. The wholesalers, one level down the chain from the distributors, were angry with EC about being stuck with unsold, yet unreturnable, copies of *Mad* when Leader News went belly-up, and they would take more copies of *Mad* only from a distributor who would give them credit for old issues. In desperation, Gaines approached American News, a large distribution company that was untouched by the Leader News fiasco because they owned their own wholesalers. A deal was struck, giving *Mad* better distribution than it had ever had with Leader News. Gaines made an arrangement to pay the printing bill over time. Once again, the future looked promising.

The period of well-being was not to last. In April, with the first issue of *Mad* since October on the stands, Kurtzman told Gaines that he wanted a personal stake in the magazine. Gaines offered him 10 percent, but a day

Mad continued to parody comics over the years. Here Wood illustrates "The *Mad* 'Comic' Opera," with libretto by Frank Jacobs. Wood depicts Dick Tracy, Dagwood, and Little Orphan Annie as shaded, three-dimensional beings, presaging the animated work in *Who Framed Roger Rabbit?* Dagwood executes a dramatic final death scene as Tracy, Tarzan, The Little King, and others look on. —Jacobs/Wood, "The Mad 'Comic' Opera," *Mad,* #56

*Sung to the tune of "Old Man River"

or two later Kurtzman, through his right-hand man, Harry Chester, issued Gaines an ultimatum: 51 percent of the magazine or Kurtzman would walk.

Gaines was shocked. He called Kurtzman to verify the demand, then called his lawyer. He wasn't about to hand over controlling in-terest, but he was sure he couldn't continue to publish *Mad* without Kurtzman. Morosely, he called Lyle Stuart, whose response was a surprise: let Kurtzman go, and replace him with Al Feldstein. Gaines's wife, Nancy, concurred.

Gaines was waiting on the Long Island

comic books.

A new trend, indeed. The line contained some of the first science-fiction and horror comic books, as well as suspense and adventure tales. From 1950 to 1954, Feldstein edited, wrote, and sometimes supplied cover art for six of these bimonthly comics. Today, the New Trend comics are considered some of the best ever published, and single copies can command hundreds of dollars from avid collectors.

In 1953 *Panic*, EC's second funny book, was added to Feldstein's editorial duties. Feldstein was no stranger to humor, having incorporated satire and silly, exaggerated ghoulishness in his other comics.

But the attitudes of the McCarthy era fell heavily on Feldstein's comic books, and they ran afoul of the establishment. "The horror to me was all tongue-in-cheek," Feldstein explains, still amazed at the uproar caused by his creations. "We weren't trying to turn children into monsters, we were trying to scare the pants off them, and we were having fun doing it."

Feldstein stuck loyally by Gaines and they attempted several tactics to avoid censorship and trouble with distributors, but by 1955 it appeared that EC had reached the end of the line, and early that year Gaines regretfully let Feldstein go.

Feldstein was not at liberty long. Within months he was back at EC, becoming the new editor of *Mad* after Harvey Kurtzman left over differences with Gaines. Since Kurtzman had taken most of *Mad*'s artists with him, Feldstein had the challenge of rebuilding *Mad* almost from the ground up. He liked the format and look that Kurtzman had created, but felt that the humor was too eccentric and lacked focus. Feldstein thought that these problems limited *Mad*'s audience, and that its sales could be greatly increased beyond *Mad*'s current 325,000 copies per month. Under Feldstein's stewardship, *Mad* built up a new crew of young artists and writers. Many of them have gone on to become famous for other work, yet most of them continue to write for *Mad*.

Feldstein supervised the greatest period of growth in *Mad*'s history. In his time *Mad* went international, being published in thirteen foreign-language editions, and circulation rose to over two and one-half million copies per issue in the United States alone.

On the whole, Feldstein, who retired in 1984, has been proud to have been a member of "the Usual Gang of Idiots." He admits that sometimes he has "had some problems with an occasional social engagement where I'd meet a parent who would be upset." But he tells with relish of talking the same disdaining parents into reading their first copy of *Mad*: "I would invariably meet them again and get a response much like 'I read your magazine—can kids really understand the satire?'"

Railroad platform when Feldstein returned from another day of job hunting. Feldstein enthusiastically agreed that *Mad* would go on.

What Gaines hadn't known was that when Kurtzman made his audacious offer, he had already spoken with a young publishing whiz by the name of Hugh Hefner. Hefner, whose *Playboy* had been on the stands less than three years, had let Kurtzman know that he was a great fan of *Mad*, and that there were great opportunities at *Playboy* if Kurtzman ever decided on a change of pace. Kurtzman leaped at the possibility of full control of his own full-color magazine.

As soon as Kurtzman's "Project X," as it was known around Hefner's offices, started to roll, Kurtzman signed exclusive contracts with Jack Davis and Will Elder, two of *Mad*'s leading artists. Kurtzman had left several completed articles at EC, and art director John Putnam and Jerry De Fuccio remained, but Feldstein had his work cut out for him. It was up to him to develop a new group of artists, and to find his own direction for *Mad*.

"Of course I loved the EC comics. Most decidedly. They came too late to warp me as a tiny child, but bent me pretty good when they got me."

GAHAN WILSON
Blab!

In September of 1956, as Feldstein's first issue of *Mad* was reaching the newsstands, an article in *Time* magazine reported that Hugh Hefner planned to publish a "still unnamed new magazine this winter," and had "hired the whole staff of *Mad*, a short-lived satirical pulp," to create it.

Gaines and Feldstein, forgotten but not gone, realized that, once again, there was nowhere to go but up.

BEETLE BAILEY

Politics finally enters Beetle Baileyland in this 1969 takeoff drawn by Bob Clarke and written by F. Ridgeway. —Frank Ridgeway/Clarke, "If Comic Strips covered the Burning Issues of the Day," *Mad,* #126

A rectangular skull is the mark of a highly-evolved and intelligent individual. Such people are born to lead. They are usually very handsome, and they always have perfect teeth.

A sloping forehead is found on an individual who has not yet completed his evolutionary cycle. Note the protruding lower tooth . . . a telltale indication of this sub-human type.

Here, a lesson in two-dimensional anatomy for the curious comic book reader. Frank Jacobs and Jack Rickard have fun with the exaggerations of characters we take for granted. —Jacobs/Rickard, "A Mad Guide to the Anatomy of the Human Body Based on the Comics," *Mad,* #236

 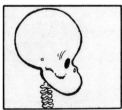

An elongated skull occurs when someone lacks the ability to speak. In such cases, there is also no sign of any mouth. It is not known if this type of individual takes any nourishment.

A round skull with a nose cavity between the eyes, blocking off the mouth from the brain, indicates an underachiever. Speech is not impaired, but sounds bewildered and confused.

***Mad*'s Woman Wonder continues to struggle with the problems of femininity and strength in this cartoon by Sergio Aragonés.** —Aragonés/ Aragonés, "A Mad Look at Super Heroes," *Mad,* #177

NOTES

"a piece of luck . . ." Decker and Groth, "William M. Gaines," 81.

"stepping out into the void . . ." Thompson and Groth, "Harvey Kurtzman," 89.

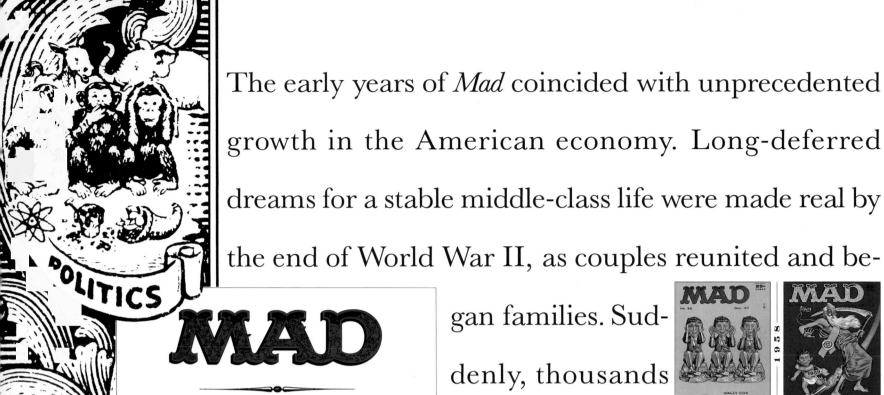

MAD

THE KIDDIN' DISSUADERS, OR THE MADMEN VS. THE ADMEN

The early years of *Mad* coincided with unprecedented growth in the American economy. Long-deferred dreams for a stable middle-class life were made real by the end of World War II, as couples reunited and began families. Sud-

denly, thousands of new products made possible by the technology developed during the Great Depression and World War II inundated the mass markets. This apparent affluence was more than a mirage: postwar American industries produced more and more consumer goods; and from 1940 to the mid-1950s, the gross national product soared more than 400 percent.

By the early 1950s planners and executives knew that they had production problems solved, as factories churned out endless sup-

plies of cars, electrical appliances, and other accoutrements of modern life. Even the baby boom didn't make a dent in the ever-growing stockpiles of goods.

This ad parody was one of the first that appeared in the *Mad* comic book. Found in the "Cut Your Own Throat Department," it was a mockery of an advertisement familiar to any comic book reader. — Kurtzman/Kurtzman, "Comic Book Ads!," *Mad*, #21

A monumental shift occurred in the mind-sets of the top executives, and the focus of their gaze moved from the factory to the consumer. The challenge, the "great unsolved problem of American business," became selling the wares to a populace accustomed to

depression-era lives of frugality. Government economists promoted the belief that a consuming America was a safe and healthy America, and these bigwigs set out to overhaul the buying habits of the nation. They chose to do it not by improving products, but by the arts of persuasion and salesmanship.

Companies eager to maximize the potency of their advertising and packaging consulted psychologists, leading to the development of specialized research firms. One pioneer of this new field was Ernest Dichter, Ph.D., the president of the Institute for Motivational Research, Inc. Motivational, or depth, research is an attempt to discover and control the subconscious urges that cause consumers to buy one product rather than another. Throughout the late 1940s and 1950s, Dr. Dichter and other "depth boys" advised companies like Philip Morris, Procter and Gamble, and General Foods on how to entice the average Joe and Jane to buy products they never knew they wanted, and to buy more of them.

The new advertising developed so quickly that spending on it soared from six billion dollars in 1950 to nine billion in 1955 — fifty-three dollars a year for each man, woman, and child in the United States. The techniques of the depth researchers grew ever more refined. In *The Hidden Persuaders*, a 1957 exposé of the field, Vance Packard outlined the "hidden needs" the researchers had pinpointed, and to which the manufacturers pitched: emotional security, reassurance of worth, ego gratification, creative outlets, love objects, a sense of power, a sense of roots, and, if that's not enough, immortality.

These emotional tie-ins solved a company's problems of selling products like gasoline,

BUT... WITH PRACTICE... HE WAS SOON ABLE TO DO PAINTINGS PEOPLE DID NOT UNDERSTAND!... HERE IS HIS FIRST ABSTRACT PAINTING TITLED *"CHICKEN-FAT"!*

THIS IS HIS SECOND ABSTRACT WHICH IS INTENDED TO CONVEY THE FEELING OF A FINGERNAIL SCRITCHING ON A BLACKBOARD AND IS ENTITLED SIMPLY..."*ECHH*"!

THIS THIRD ABSTRACT CONVEYS A FEELING OF WEATHER... WEATHER IT'S GOING TO BE HOT... WEATHER IT'S GOING TO BE COLD... AND IS SIMPLY ENTITLED *"HURRICANE CAROL"!*

The "Special Art Issue" was devoted to the life of artist Will "Chicken-Fat" Elder, and marks a breakthrough in comic book design. With a conglomeration of imagery that anticipates the pop art movement of the late 1950s, this excerpt described the development of Elder's formative years. — Kurtzman/ Kurtzman, "The Young Artist!," *Mad*, #22

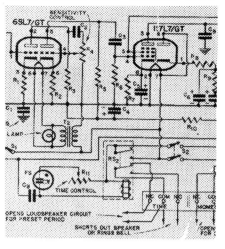

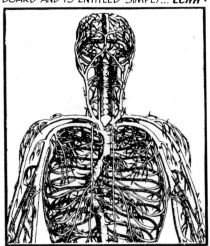

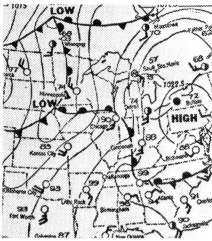

NEXT, YOUNG ELDER WAS INTRODUCED TO THE TYPE ART WHERE YOU DISTORT AN IMAGE TO GET TWO VIEWS AT THE SAME TIME AS IN THIS, HIS FOURTH ABSTRACT... *"GIN"!*

HIS FIFTH, BY THE CLEVER USE OF FLAT PLANES, CREATES AN ILLUSION OF DEPTH!... BESIDES PLANES IS USED SAWS, HAMMERS, NAILS, ETC... AS IN THIS ONE CALLED *"LEVITTOWN"!*

HIS SIXTH CREATES A FEELING OF CLASHING HARMONY, YET AN INNER TRANQUILITY!... IN OTHER WORDS, BUFFERIN ACTS TWICE AS FAST AS ASPIRIN IN THIS ABSTRACT CALLED *'URP'!*

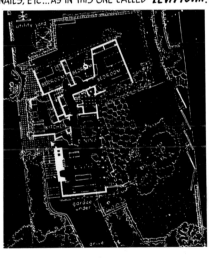

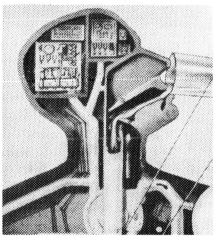

EXPERIMENTING ROUGHLY ALONG THE LINES OF MARCEL DUCHAMP'S *"NUDE DESCENDING A STAIRCASE,"* YOUNG ELDER PAINTED THIS SEVENTH ABSTRACT ENTITLED, *"I DREAMED I DESCENDED A STAIRCASE IN MY PLAYTEX UNDERWEAR"!* AFTER A WHOLE SERIES OF SUCH BRILLIANT ABSTRACTS, ELDER SUDDENLY COMPLETELY CHANGED HIS ART STYLE... SUDDENLY TOOK A TURN THAT CHANGED HIS WHOLE OUTLOOK... HIS WHOLE *LIFE!* THIS TURN HE TOOK WAS INTO A ONE WAY STREET THE WRONG WAY!... WHAT A WRECK!... STILL PAYING!... CHANGED HIS WHOLE LIFE!

3

HEADACHE? COLD MISERY?

Why wait for old-fashioned cold relief? Go Kill yourself!

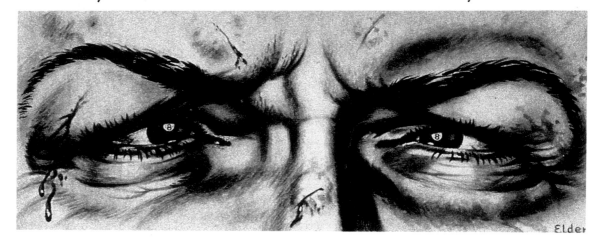

GET FASTER PAIN RELIEF WITH

BOFFORIN

Acts twice as fast

Won't upset your gaskets!

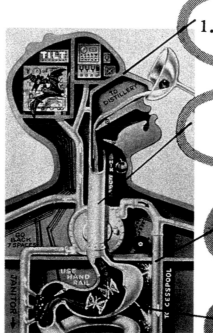

ASK YOUR PLUMBER ABOUT BOFFORIN

1. Medical science knows a pain reliever has got to go through these here pipes and valves and faucets and like that.

Bofforin gets through these things twice as fast and the reason why is that Bofforin combines axle-grease with a tested, proven rust solvent.

3. That way the pain reliever gets into the blood stream and once it reaches the blood stream . . . Boffo! Bofforin acts twice as fast!

4. And all your motors and pumps will go humming along like a sewing machine. You'll work wonders with a "button-hole stitcher" atttched to your nose.

Ask your own doctor about how Bofforin acts . . . how when it goes around in those pumps like in our diagram and how it goes up through them pipes to them switch-boards and lights up the little lights and rings the little bells, and switches the little switches and turns the little dials (they tell you which way is North), I'll bet you never knew you had such little lights and dials and switches in your head.

Ask your own doctor about how Bofforin acts inside those pipes and valves. Better still, ask your own plumber.

NOTE: THOUSANDS have switched from rust preventer to BOFFORIN.

Lesson 1

See the man.
He does advertising work.
He is called an "ad-man".
See his funny tight suit.
See his funny haircut.
Hear his funny stomach churn.
Churn, churn, churn.
The ad-man has a funny ulcer.
Most ad-men have funny ulcers.
But, then, some ad-men are lucky.
They do *not* have funny ulcers.
They have funny high blood pressure.

Lesson 2

See the ad-man run.
Run, ad-man, run.
The ad-man must catch the 8:02.
All ad-men must catch the 8:02.
It is a fast commuter train.
It is never more than two hours late.
And it has a club car.
"All aboard!" says the conductor.
"Chug, chug!" says the train.
"Gulp, gulp!" says the ad-man.
Wouldn't *you* like Bourbon for breakfast, too?

The Madmen introduce the admen in the "Madison Avenue Primer." From the ranch-style suburban house to the narrow tie and horn-rim glasses, Wally Wood drew an impeccable parody of the cultural hero of the 1950s while Larry Siegel explained his exotic lifestyle. — Siegel/Wood, "The *Mad* Madison Avenue Primer," *Mad*, #55

"Us Cigarette-Makers will fight rather than quit!"

Watch the Unquitables overcome the "black eye" of the U.S. Government's latest cancer reports.

You think we're gonna let our billion dollar industry go up in smoke? Sure those Govt. reports linking smoking and cancer gave us a black eye! But just you wait! Our own scientists and public relations men are hard at work and we'll be fighting back with our own reports pretty soon!

COMING SOON!

Carry-on

1964 1965
SALES SALES

LOBBYING   RESEARCH   MAGAZINE, RADIO, TELEVISION ADVERTISING AND PUBLICITY

Breakdown of expenditures* planned for 1965 so
THE CIGARETTE INDUSTRY CAN CARRY ON

*Notice we don't plan to spend a dime to improve the cigarettes!

POTRZEBIE HIGH SCHOOL
To the parents of Melvin Furd
Your son is running around with a teen-age gang ...one of these days, he'll get his teeth knocked out!
— Herman Klotz, Principal

"Look, Mom—no more cavities!"

Crust Gumpaste helps gums take the place of teeth by coating them with a hard white enamel finish! Just the thing for punks who get their teeth knocked out from running around with teen-age gangs.

Crust
GUM PASTE

Fluidsteel is a trademark for Proctor & Rumble's exclusive liquid metal gum-coater.
© 1958, The Proctor & Rumble Co.

Looking back, it's hard to believe that photographs of the wounded could be used to sell cigarettes. Editor Al Feldstein provides the money-burning mug for this parody of the long-running Tareyton campaign. Cigarette advertising has always been a favorite target of the Madmen, and one of few occasions where the product itself is lambasted. — house/Lester Krauss, "Carry-on," *Mad*, #88

Kelly Freas makes a grotesque of Crest toothpaste's fresh-faced child. Readers of *Mad* knew that this juvenile delinquent more closely resembled the boy next door. — house/Freas, "Crust," *Mad*, #43

Mad's antidote to an overdose of schmaltz in the sentimental Parke-Davis campaign to promote doctor worship. This parody, one of artist Kelly Freas's most famous, prompted a number of letters from doctors. One of them congratulated Freas on inventing a disease that could be treated with the instruments shown, one of which is a gauge used in aircraft manufacture. — house/Freas, "Great Moments in Medicine," *Mad*, #48

PRESENTING THE BILL—reproduced here, is one of a series of original oil paintings, "Practising Medicine For Fun and Profit", commissioned by Park-David.

Great Moments in Medicine

Once the crisis has passed . . . once the patient has regained his strength . . . once the family is relieved and grateful . . . that's the time when the physician experiences one of the great moments in medicine. In fact, the *greatest moment* in medicine! Mainly, the moment when he presents his bill! That's the time when all of the years of training and study and work seem worthwhile. And there's always the chance that the shock might mean more business for him!

Park-David scientists are proud of their place in the history of practicing medicine for fun and profit, helping to provide doctors with the materials that mean higher fees and bigger incomes. For example, our latest development . . . tranquilizer-impregnated bill paper . . . designed to eliminate the shock and hysteria that comes when the patient gets a look at your bill. Not only will he remain calm when he sees what you've charged . . . now he won't even *care!*

COPYRIGHT 1959—PARK-DAVID & COMPANY, WITH THE BLESSINGS OF THE AMA

PARK-DAVID

. . . Pioneers in bigger medical bills

* Sung to the tune of: "Get Me To The Church On Time"

* Sung to the tune of: "The Rain In Spain"

SMOKE GETS IN YOUR LIES DEPT.

Some straight Talk about selling cigarettes to a hostile public.

We're R.J. Riddles Tobacco, and we're trying to improve our image.

That's why you keep seeing these drab, black-and-white ads, full of long-winded copy, in which we wax informative on the subject of smoking and try to prove how well we understand and appreciate both sides of the smoking controversy.

We explain the pros and cons of smoking. We present both the smokers and non-smokers arguments. We tell kids that we don't want them smoking, like their parents. We say anything and everything we can think of, so you get the subliminal message that us "bad guys" are really "good guys" and that maybe our product isn't so bad, either.

This isn't as easy as you might think. New anti-smoking laws are popping up all across the nation. Non-smokers continue to argue that "passive" smoking is just as deadly as "active" smoking. The atmosphere is very unfriendly out there right now.

We want to replace this hostility with the trust and confidence the public once had in us—before the ax falls and we get legislated out of business. These double-talk ads were our P.R. firm's brilliant solution.

So, we may be keeping this up for awhile. It's a great way to advertise because—since we don't picture our product—we don't have to include that lousy Surgeon General's Warning.

R.J. Riddles Tobacco Company

WRITER BILLY DOHERTY

cigarettes, and cosmetics that were virtually identical to those of its competitors—don't sell a tract house, sell security. The evocation of these deeply resonant yearnings in advertisements and packaging for everything

from cake mixes to cars made for some very strange ads indeed: men with eye patches modeled shirts, household appliances suddenly appeared in a rainbow of colors, automobiles grew fins, and cigarettes were hawked by a bevy of personality types. This was the opening for the wise-guys at *Mad*, who were beginning to realize that there was more to poke fun at than other comics.

LEGEND HAS IT THAT *MAD* HAD NEVER TAKEN advertising. The truth is even more interesting than the legend. When *Mad* was a comic book, the usual advertisements for BB guns, exercise regimens, and hypnotism manuals appeared on about three pages per issue. Gaines also advertised the other EC comics in *Mad*, with drawings and text that grew more outrageous over the years until the ads became parodies of themselves. In one, a gray-haired doctor gestured to serious-looking charts and contended "extensive tests by the EC research bureau have proven conclusively that *Panic* leads eight other brands in imitating *Mad! Panic* uses more of *Mad*'s printers, more of *Mad*'s potrzebie and furshlugginer than any other *Mad* imitation!"

But it was in the March 1955 issue of *Mad*

that Kurtzman took aim at other advertisers. The cover of the issue imitated a mail-order catalog, crammed with small black-and-white illustrations and fine type. Inside, in the Cut-Your-Own-Throat Department, Kurtzman and Elder parodied the best-known comic book advertisements, offering "Ded Ryder Cowboy Carbine" rifles, "Shmeer's Rubber Bubble Gum," and other bogus products.

Kurtzman was delighted with the effect and the following issue was devoted to a parody of artist Will "Chicken-Fat" Elder's life. This "Special Art Issue" marked a sharp departure from many of the conventions of other comic books. An altered Picasso painting graced the cover, and the inside was chock-full with retouched photographs and found images ranging from popular iconography like Marilyn Monroe to electrical diagrams and reproductions of famous works of art.

The illustrations were a portfolio showing Elder's upward ascent through the ranks of the advertising business. The "clippings" depicted were remarkable imitations of real advertisements. Many seemed to use artwork lifted directly from real ads. The technical limitations of the printing process used for comic books is apparent in the inability of the printing to carry either detail or color photos,

problems that were later solved with *Mad*'s evolution to a more finely printed magazine.

Max Gaines had once sold out a business

I'm the guy who puts eight great tomatoes in that little bitty can!!

All day long – squashing, squooshing, slamming, splattering . . . Yeccch, what a mess! Thank goodness it's my last week at this gooky job! Next week my company starts using a new-type can, and I'll be able to stuff those eight great tomatoes in that little bitty can without ending up looking like I've been attacked with a meat cleaver. Mainly because our new "little bitty can" expands into a "biggy wiggy can" like an accordion.

Concertina

EXPANDING CAN

over advertising differences; perhaps it was a familial distaste for it that led Bill Gaines to allow Kurtzman to run such obviously self-destructive parodies. Maybe advertising contributed such a small part of *Mad*'s income that Gaines just didn't care. Inevitably, Gaines remembers, *Mad*'s advertisers were "very upset." He looked to the past for precedent and remembered a short-lived muck-raking daily from his youth, *PM*. "The basis of the paper was that you can't take an ad from somebody and not be beholden to them," Gaines explained. "In those days there

was no such thing as running an anti-cigarette story because they were terrified of losing their cigarette advertising. So *PM* comes along and tears into everything and doesn't give a shit. And for six or seven years they had a wild time." Gaines, ever willing to rationalize his preferred eccentric business philosophy, picked up the banner *PM* had dropped. Within six months, *Mad* had phased out all advertising.

When Kurtzman declared advertising as fair game for satire, it's possible that he also was remembering the past. A very popular publication of his youth was *Ballyhoo*, a satire magazine that focused on advertisements. At the height of its popularity in 1931, *Ballyhoo* had a circulation of two million, had inspired a Broadway show, and attracted advertisers who paid to be satirized.

In the new *Mad* magazine, Kurtzman was able to reproduce drawings with a much finer level of detail and nuance. The first ad parodies were in Kurtzman's typical surreal, stream-of-consciousness style. Slogans and imagery of wildly different products are conglomerated in the *Mad* version of the melting pot, where even the tiniest detail may be a reference to yet another consumer good or ad campaign.

THE MADMEN: *Bob Clarke, Dick DeBartolo, Tom Koch*

Bob Clarke was a successful Madison Avenue ad man who defected one day to become *Mad*'s preeminent advertising parody illustrator. Although in his early career he worked for Robert Ripley and was encouraged by Gill Fox, an editor at Quality Comics, Clarke had risen to the position of art director at a major Madison Avenue firm when he decided to give it up for the life of a free lance. "*Mad* gave me complete freedom," he says. "There were no taboos, which I had up to my ears in the advertising business." Clarke was able to contribute his clean, slick drawing style to *Mad*'s advertising spoofs, as well as social parodies in general.

At the age of sixteen, Dick DeBartolo had already gotten his first job in mass media, as writer and producer of the 1958 animated program "Winky Dink and You." Perhaps it was only a short step to writing parodies for *Mad*, both of advertising, which DeBartolo collects and revels in, and television and movies. While contributing to *Mad* since 1963, DeBartolo also writes for television comedy and game shows, and has received two Emmy nominations for his work for *The Match Game*.

Tom Koch was writing radio material for comedians Bob and Ray when he first met Al Feldstein, who was publishing work by the team in *Mad*. Although he holds a master's degree in Far Eastern affairs, Koch has always been interested in comedy. While writing for *Fibber McGee and Molly*, George Gobel, and, later, Pat Paulsen's and Jonathan Winters's television programs, he has contributed many works of media and social satire to *Mad*. His television experience has come into play in such articles as "The Evolution of a TV Situation Comedy," and his astute class consciousness in pieces like "How Do You Rate as a Yuppie?" and "The *Mad* Guide to Status Symbols."

When Al Feldstein took over *Mad* in 1955, he honed the parodies, taking advantage of the extended thematic campaigns then in favor. He focused on a single pretentious or

In 1964 the Breck portrait ads caught Nick Meglin's eye. "They were paintings that were like bad photographs, but they weren't great paintings, either. It was that in-between of all these WASPy, bland, Breck-girl faces," he critiqued. "Not one of them had a personality, not one of them looked different enough to have a personality, they were all the same thing." The solution? "The non-Breck boy . . . the ugliest of the Beatles, with a big nose, and the long hair." Meglin commissioned Frank Frazetta to provide the perfect caricature of the newly famous **Ringo Starr.** — house/Frazetta, "Blecch," *Mad*, #90

Make Beautiful Hair

B L E C C H

THERE ARE THREE BLECCH SHAMPOOS FOR THREE DIFFERENT HAIR CONDITIONS

Are you a teenage boy with Beautiful Hair? Well no wonder the girls hardly notice you. Today, you've got to be a teenage boy with Blecch hair. Then the girls will scream with delight, roll on the floor and kick their feet when they see you. So why waste another minute? Shampoo your hair with Blecch tonight. Blecch comes in three special formulas:

● For dry hair—a special formula that takes neat crew-cut type hair and lays it down over your ears. ● For oily hair —loosens up that slick-combing stuff so it spills down over your eyes. ● For normal hair—gives it proper body so it mushrooms all over your head. Get the shampoo that's right for you, and make your hair "Blecch"! Yeah! Yeah! Yeah!

ridiculous gimmick of an ad or ad campaign. Feldstein also began to employ photographs, rather than drawings, for the illustrations for

the satires. While the photos made the parodies more authentic looking, there were a few wrinkles to iron out of the technique. The first ads were shot using professional models

An Advertiser Would Have Us Believe...

...that guests will soon be rushing into our homes, flinging open our kitchen cabinets and subjecting us to humiliation if our glassware has a few water spots.

An Advertiser Would Have Us Believe...

...that a slick, big city announcer becomes more trustworthy when he puts on a grocer's apron, and speaks with a New England twang.

hired by the photographer. The models' limitations were obvious. "Models, don't forget, get paid for what they look like, so they take themselves very seriously," Nick Meglin, then an associate editor, points out. "We'd ask for an expression and they'd give us these wimpy looks—there was no humor in it."

The Madmen found themselves screwing up their own faces to demonstrate the grimaces, frowns, and grins they were looking for, cracking up the models, photogra-

pher, and each other. They quickly realized that they could get the images they wanted cheaper and better by posing for the photographs themselves. "We knew what we wanted, we had written the damn thing, we knew the attitude, and we weren't afraid to scrunch up our faces," declares Meglin. Luckily, the staff of *Mad* comprised a wide range of masculine physical types: Feldstein could pass for a mainstream businessman, Meglin and De Fuccio were younger and good as punks and delivery boys, Leonard Brenner was stocky and wore a beat-inspired goatee, and Gaines was bespectacled and intellectual-looking.

Within a few years, advertising parodies had become a regular feature in *Mad*, and in the fifth anniversary issue in 1957 Feldstein celebrated the trend. The cover illustration by Norman Mingo was designed as a wrap-around and featured Alfred E. Neuman's birthday party. In attendance were almost one hundred guests, all of them from the never-never land of product logos. Betty Crocker, Uncle Ben, and the Smith Brothers cavorted with Bossie and Elmer.

Feldstein went one step up the ladder and began to run satires of the creators of the ads as well. "My Fair Ad-Man," by Nick Meglin, was the first *Mad* musical parody and used the score of *My Fair Lady* to lampoon the lives of Madison Avenue art directors and their ideological opposites, the Greenwich Village beats. The story is a portrait of the adman lifestyle as Irving Mallion was attired in the proper Italian suits, taught to drink martinis at lunch, and to abandon bop talk in favor of the limited vocabulary of the yes-man.

Throughout the 1960s and 1970s ad parodies in *Mad* continued to deflate the most

TO THE SUCRETS CORP.

The Madman version of "Get real!" — Koch/Torres, "Questions We'd Like to Ask Some TV Advertisers," *Mad*, #230

Mad's junk mail maven, Dick DeBartolo, investigates the effects of indiscriminate mailing lists. — DeBartolo/North, "Mixed-up Junk Mail Mailing Lists," *Mad*, #221

For once, every little girl's conspicuous consumers reflect another kind of life. — Raiola, Kadau/Clarke, "Toys 'R' U," *Mad*, #285

No one can say the Madmen weren't thorough in their crusade against advertising and packaging. "We approached *Mad* editorial with the fact that these kids were reading trash, and if they wanted to waste their money on it, okay," admitted Al Feldstein, with the kind of candor that *Mad* readers have known and loved. — Hart/Rickard, "Mad's Packager of the Year," *Mad*, #186

ridiculous excesses of the Madison Avenue masterpieces. In doing so they armed their readers with a crucial weapon against the onslaught: awareness. As Packard pointed out, "In virtually all situations we still have a choice, and we cannot be too seriously manipulated if we know what is going on...when we learn to recognize the devices of the persuaders we build up 'recognition reflex.'"

These days, *Mad* no longer runs as many ad parodies. One reason is that editors Meglin and John Ficarra feel that magazine and other print ads don't have the impact on the public that they once did. Also, the ongoing theme ad campaign has fallen out of favor on Madison Avenue, giving way to one-shot ads; like any moving target, the ads are more difficult to hit. But the biggest reason is that, partly in response to *Mad*'s barbs, advertisements are smarter, wittier, and don't take themselves as seriously as they once did. "Bright young people who were *Mad* fans went on to careers in advertising and wrote funny ads that were satires of themselves," Meglin points out.

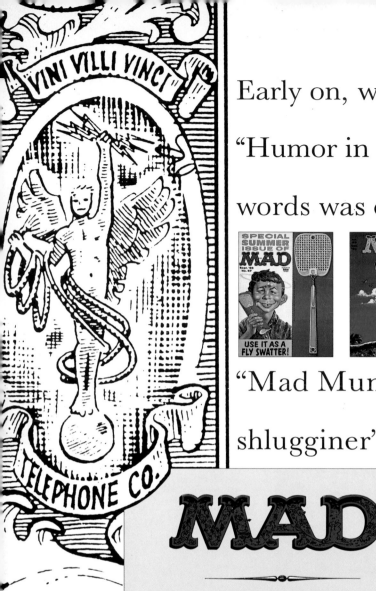

Early on, while *Mad* was still the comic book subtitled "Humor in a Jugular Vein," a particular *Mad* way with words was evident. "What in the world is 'borscht'?"

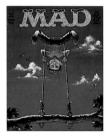

demanded a reader in a letter printed on an early "Mad Mumblings" page. "Please tell me what 'fur-shlugginer' means," pleaded another. And what, indeed, were "potrzebie," "ganef," "veeblefetzer," "farshimmelt," "hala-vah," and the other strange and exotic words that crowded *Mad* comics pages? Other readers un-questioningly joined in on the fun and wrote letters in foreign lan-

MAD

IT'S CRACKERS TO SLIP A ROZZER THE DROPSY IN SNIDE!

guages, pig Latin, dialect, code, bop talk, or backward. To further confuse things, Kurtzman would run whole pages of filler in Chinese, ancient Egyptian, Greek, Russian, and Hungarian.

Doubtless, only a small number of readers must have known that many of Kurtzman's words were based on Yiddish, an especially expressive language with more than its share of words with humorous possibilities. Although Kurtzman has argued that "visually, my stuff is great, but I'm really an illiterate," and that "my sentence structure is labored, clumsy...always falling

apart," he turned the handicap to his advantage. In the early *Mad*s the writing is eccentric and colloquial, and Kurtzman pushed these qualities to an extreme, manipulating words and sentences as if they were the elements in one of Elder's or Wood's surrealist cartoons.

Parodying names was another venue for *Mad* wordplay. Melvin was the favored name for a while, featured on the cover of the first

Mad comic: a mom and dad are in a creepy mansion menaced by something we see only as a shadow. Dad screams, "That thing! That slithering blob coming toward us!" Mom shrieks, "What is it?" Junior, finger up his nose, deadpans, "It's Melvin!" Melvinmania had struck Lafayette Street, for the name subsequently is featured in the parodies "Melvin of the Apes," "Smilin' Melvin," and "Little Orphan Melvin," as well as in the names of the artists, all of whom begin calling themselves Melvin, too, as in Melvin Davis, Melvin Elder, Melvin Severin, and Melvin Wood.

As EC historian John Benson has pointed out, "the syncopation was usually off" in Kurtzman's parody names, gleefully stripping them of any grace they might have had, as in "Superduperman," "G.I. Shmoe" (the G.I. short for "Galusha Iggy"), and "Shermlock Shomes." Other names were inventions of imagination and memory, like Count Amisher Basketball, Mrs. Gowanus, and the Ookabollawonga and Ookabollakonga tribes. "Shadowskeedeeboomboom," used for various heroes and foes, was a name inspired by the Yiddish comedian Aaron Lebedaeff.

"Poiuyt," "frammistan," "moxie," and "axolotl" were all words added to the *Mad* lexicon over the years, as other writers expanded the

styles of writing that appeared. The phrases "It's crackers to slip a rozzer the dropsy in snide" and "I had one grunch but the eggplant over there" upon utterance were able to throw any right-minded fan into fits of unexplainable giggles.

By the end of its first year, poetry and literature takeoffs were beginning to supplement the comic parodies on which *Mad* comics had been based. The first poetry parody to appear in *Mad* was "Casey at the Bat" in issue number 6. The poem, run verbatim over six pages and illustrated with ridiculously literal drawings by Jack Davis, was hailed by readers as "a brilliant satire on America's favorite sport." This was followed by *Mad*ly illustrated versions of "The Raven," "The Face Upon the Floor," "The Wreck of the Hesperus," and "Paul Revere's Ride."

It was not until 1957, after Feldstein had expanded *Mad*'s group of contributing writers and the writing in *Mad* diversified, that Ernie Kovacs contributed the first original verses in the article "Why I write Poetry." "Ode to Stanley's Pussycat," credited to Kovacs's *nom de plume*, Percy Dovetonsils, went in part:

I was a strong child and considered quite manly.
I lived in the suburbs next door to Stanley.
I planned to be a fireman; he planned to be a doctor.
His mother taught psychiatry; honest! I could've
 socked her.

From this modest beginning, Feldstein developed poetry parodies into a regular feature. Great poems, nursery rhymes, greeting card verses — nothing was safe from the satirists of *Mad*.

If only because of its length, most literature was unsuitable to use as it was originally written, and, from the start, the first takeoffs of the classic stories of Tarzan, Robin Hood,

Wordplay has been a favorite feature of *Mad* since the very start. Here, famous names are combined with images that writer and artist Max Brandel felt made for more appropriate logos. — Brandel/Brandel, "A Mad Look at Trade-marks," *Mad*, #106; "A Portfolio of Mad Namelies," *Mad*, #108

and Sherlock Holmes were rewritten and illustrated as complete satires. Partly inspired by the original, partly by movie and other popular culture versions of these tales, literature parodies also became an ongoing genre in *Mad* magazine.

One spoof that upset more than a few parents and educators was a 1959 "Cool School" version of Abraham Lincoln's Gettysburg Address. The one-page piece ran "the old version" in a column on the left and a line-by-line translation (by Paul Laikin) of the Address into what was then known as "bop talk"—the patois of African-Americans as adopted by the beats—on the right. It began:

Fourscore and like seven years ago our old daddies came on in this scene with a new group, grooved in free kicks, and hip to the Jazz that all cats make it the same. Now we're real hung up in a crazy big hassle, digging whether that group, or any group so grooved and so hip can keep on swinging.

Striking a CARELESS POSE

The *Mad* version was quite accurate in content, and the tendency is to compare each

 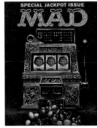  

new sentence with the original—encouraging most readers to spend more time willingly studying the Address than they ever would otherwise.

But it was song parodies that got EC in

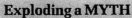

Exploding a MYTH

trouble with the authorities once again, this time in a case that would ultimately be decided by the Supreme Court. *Mad*'s first song parodies were part of the musical spoof "My Fair Ad-Man" written by then associate editor Nick Meglin. The satire was well received, and when Al Feldstein was preparing the 1961 compilation *More Trash from Mad*, Meglin suggested a songbook. Frank Jacobs and Larry Siegel were assigned the project, and within two weeks had churned out forty-six parodies of popular songs, supplemented by eleven more from the *Mad* editorial staff. Entitled "Sing Along with *Mad*," the book was organized by subject matter, with such categories as show business, labor and business, doctors and medicine, and modern-day living. The writers really had fun with the project, transmogrifying "I've Got You under My Skin" into "I Swat You Hard on the Skin," and "When They Begin the Beguine" into "When They Bring in the Machine," and so on.

A hit with the readers, "Sing Along with *Mad*" pointed the way to a new genre of satire for *Mad* to mine. But soon, this parody of "There's No Business Like Show Business" became unfortunately prescient:

HANDY PHRASES FOR TRAVELING IN
RUSSIA

When will I get my camera back?	Спальни—комнаты, принимаютъ гостеи въ которыхъ	Hchoo-vastat lay-dee hchye tsaw yoo veet lest-ni-yit?
Has the chamber-maid finished searching my luggage?	Полъ ея устланъ коврами, и на спятъ люди.	Dyit-yoo hav yoor tsoop too-dyay?
Which corner of the room is mine?	Въ гостинной вис кухнѣ приготовля ютъ кушанье,	Izz dere hay dock-tur hin tzee howze?
What time is the ex-Commissar's funeral?	Столовая-комната, которой кушаютъ.	Vhat har lit-teel gowrls may-de huv?
What time is the new Commissar's funeral?	Около стола	Vhat ist diss tzing corld luff?
Our guide is very friendly.	Въ столовой стоя стоятъ нѣсколько	Tzee cho muz gho hon.
Why was our guide liquidated?	Въ выхъ или въ круглый столъ и высокій буфетъ.	Iz hev-ree budd-hee hap-hee?
Waiter, there's a dictaphone in my borscht!	Въ гостинной при съѣстные припасы хранятся въ	Tsam, hyu med tsee pahntz tu lung!
The handcuffs are chafing my wrists.	Полъ ея устланъ стѣнахъ висятъ пр коврами, и на	Cluz cuh-vor bee-fohr strah-kink.
Do you have a cell with a view?	Спальни ятъ люди; спальняхъ стоятъ кухнѣ пригото	Vye du fahr-menz vhere rähd suz-pëhn-derz?
Will I need my ga-loshes in Siberia?	Въ столовой стоя которой кушаютъ: и ужинаютъ.	Hchow har tzings een Glock-hcha-mohr-hcha?
Is this how you treated Adlai Stevenson?	Около стола	Veel tsöck-tsess spowrl Hchrock Hchun-tahr?
I demand to see the American Consul!	Столовая-комната, высокій буфетъ.	Hchew kent du dzits tu mhee!

Helpful to an extreme, in 1959 *Mad* provided this Cold War–era phrase book for American tourists traveling to the USSR. As writer Sy Reit pointed out: "People who go abroad these days need phrases to fit the situations they'll run into today!" — Reit/Woodbridge, "Mad's Modern Handy Phrase Book for the American Tourist," *Mad*, #46

There's no business like no business
　Like no business I know!
Every day you take another bruising!
　Every day your money worries mount!
Lots of tranquilizers you are using
　When you are losing
A fat account!

Mad was hit by a suit for copyright infringement by a swarm of music publishers representing such heavyweights as Irving Berlin, Cole Porter, and Richard Rodgers. The composers charged that the copyright owners had the exclusive right to make a parody version of their work. Realizing that a precedent was being established, the lawyers for the Music Publishers Protective Association hit hard, suing Gaines, Jacobs, Siegel, the editorial staff, and Jack Rickard, the illustrator. For the twenty-five takeoffs based on works by the composers represented by the association,

IN A RESTAURANT

Hey, Slop Buddy! I have the **Marx Brothers**[1] **bucket-mouthing**[2] for the **50-yard line**![3]

Your **drums** are beating my **ears**,[4] Platter-Spiller! Have they turned on the **green machine**?[5]

Negative, Meal-Dealer! They're **still** on the **curb**,[6] and the **coconuts** are off the **tree**![7]

Are they **neon peons**[8] . . . or at least **housebroken**?[9]

No way, Gravy Splasher! They are strictly **tumbleweeds** in **training pants**![10]

In that case, just **spin their wheels**[11] till the **big hand does its thing**,[12] and then **pull the zipper**![13]

1. A party of three
2. Requesting
3. A good table
4. I hear you
5. Have they slipped you any money?
6. They haven't come across yet
7. My palm is still empty
8. Celebrities
9. Regular customers
10. Tourists here for the first time
11. Make them wait
12. For an hour
13. Tell them that we're closing.

The citizens band radio craze provided the premise for this play on the colorful jargon first used by truck-driving CBers to outwit highway patrolmen, but later adopted by enthusiastic hobbyists. — Jacobs/Coker, "When CB-Type Code Language Is Used in Other Walks of Life," *Mad*, #192

IT'S CRACKERS TO SLIP A ROZZER THE DROPSY IN SNIDE!

ONE BUSY DAY IN A HIGHWAY RESTAURANT

The richness and rhythm of diner jargon boggles a short-order cook when Don Martin visits this highway restaurant. — Martin/Martin, "One Busy Day in a Highway Restaurant," *Mad*, #150

"Though thy crest be shorn and shaven, thou," I said,
"art sure no craven,
Ghastly grim and ancient Raven wandering from
the Nightly shore—

Tell me what thy lordly name is on the Night's
Plutonian shore!"

Quoth the Raven ("Nevermore."

One of *Mad*'s first poetry parodies was this illustrated version of "The Raven." Edgar Allan Poe's tale of grief and paranoia was used unchanged, but for the addition of illustrations drawn by "that Raven maniac" Will Elder. Numerous running sight gags are developed in the series of seven pages, which include nonstop visual puns and other gratuitous oddities as well.
—Poe/Elder, "The Raven," *Mad*, #9

Much I marvelled this ungainly fowl to hear
discourse so plainly,
Though its answer little meaning—little relevancy bore;
For we cannot help agreeing that no living human being

Ever yet was blessed with seeing bird above his chamber door—
Bird or beast upon the sculptured bust above his chamber door,

With such name as "Nevermore."

But the Raven, sitting lonely on the placid bust, spoke only
That one word, as if his soul in that one word he did outpour.
Nothing farther then he uttered—not a feather then
he fluttered—

Till I scarcely more than muttered "Other friends have flown before—
On the morrow **he** will leave me as my hopes have flown before."

Then the bird said ("Nevermore!"

Mother Goose rhymes are fertile ground for commenting on a variety of subjects. "Mad's Medical Mother Goose," by Larry Siegel and Al Jaffee, and "Mad's Updated Modern-Day Mother Goose," by Frank Jacobs and Jack Davis, probably have more pertinence to children's lives than the original rhymes, while Jacob's silly Kipling spoof in all likelihood did more to acquaint kids with "Gunga Din" than all the efforts of their teachers. —Siegel/Jaffee, "Mad's Medical Mother Goose," *Mad*, #117; Jacobs/Davis, "Mad's Updated Modern Day Mother Goose," *Mad*, #134; Jacobs/Rickard, "If Famous Poets Had Written 'Mother Goose'," *Mad*, #113

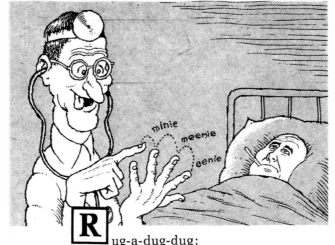

R ug-a-dug-dug;
A man's got a bug
Which puzzles his family M.D.
Bronchitis, Neuritis?
Acute Tonsilitis?
He'll say it's a Virus—you'll see!

Warren Beatty Had A Sweetie

Warren Beatty
Had a sweetie,
   Dazzled and bewitched her;
Warren Beatty
Kept his sweetie,
   For a week, then ditched her!
(*Repeat 81 times!*)

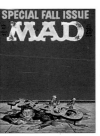  

1962

Lou Silverstone puts words in ex-president and expert yarn-spinner Ronald Reagan's mouth for this spoof.— Silverstone/Clarke, "Famous Stories as Told by Famous People," *Mad*, #268

If RUDYARD KIPLING had written
JACK AND JILL

A Christmas Carol

as told by President Reagan

Ebenezer Scrooge was a hard working businessman. He employed Bob Cratchit as a clerk. Cratchit complained constantly. He wanted "more holidays," and "more money." He was always whining about the office being "too cold," and other such nonsense. It never occurred to Cratchit to roll up his sleeves and do an honest day's work or go to night school and pull himself up by his bootstraps. No, it was easier to complain.

When Christmas time came around the Cratchit family blamed Mr. Scrooge because they couldn't afford an elaborate dinner or expensive presents for their children.

On Christmas Eve, Mr. Scrooge had a terrible nightmare. He dreamt he was visited by his dead partner, Marley, and three ghosts. These ghosts, using Marxist-Lenin propaganda techniques, made Mr. Scrooge feel guilty because he was a success and Cratchit was a failure.

Mr. Scrooge allowed his own good fortune to trickle down by buying expensive gifts for the Cratchit children. He treated them to a fancy Christmas dinner and he paid their medical bills. Even though Cratchit received a fair salary, Mr. Scrooge gave him a raise, which only added to the inflationary spiral. I know this sounds familiar, because it's the same principle as our own welfare system—something for nothing—and it just doesn't work.

Well, we can only pray that next Christmas, Mr. Scrooge will be visited by three Conservative ghosts who will show him the error of his ways.

You can talk of blood 'n gore
When you're in a shootin' war
And the enemy is chargin' for the kill—
But if you're likin' slaughter
Then you oughta haul some water
Like that brave and fearless couple, Jack and Jill.

Well, they had a pail to fill
When they climbed that craggy hill
And they never thought that soon they
       would be dead;
But Jack he took a fall
And he bounced just like a ball
Till he landed in a gulley on his head.

He hollered, "Jill, Jill, Jill!
I'm a-lyin' at the bottom of the hill!"
But poor Jill had plunged as well,
And they died right where they fell.
You've a lot more guts than I have, Jack and Jill.

they were said to be liable for one dollar per song per magazine printed. Since over one million copies of *More Trash from Mad* were sold, the Usual Gang of Idiots was being hit for a grand total of twenty-five million dollars.

It took three years for the suit to come to trial. In 1963 the case was heard by Judge Charles M. Metzner for the United States District Court. The association charged that the songs were "counterparts" to the originals, since readers were informed that they could be "sung to the tune of" the originals. They argued that the lyrics were mostly copied from their clients' creations.

Martin Scheiman and Jack Albert, representing the case for *Mad*, rebutted that only the original titles were printed in *Mad*, that *Mad* was not a music magazine, and that the lyrics were obviously parodies, not the original lyrics.

Judge Metzner delivered a mixed decision.

CHICAGO SUBURB

by Carl Sandbag

Hog Barbecuer for the World,
School Segregator, Mower of Lawns,
Player with Golf Clubs and the Nation's Wife Swapper;
Bigoted, snobbish, flaunting,
Suburb of the White Collars.
They tell me you are lazy, and I believe them; for I have seen your
    women in the super-market parking lots, tipping box boys to load
    their station wagons.
And they tell me you are brutal, and my reply is: At the stations of
    your commuter trains, I have seen old ladies trampled by men in
    quest of seats on the shady side.
And they tell me your soil is rotten and vengeful, and I answer: Yes,
    it is true, for I have seen crab grass killed and rise up to grow
    again.
But still, I turn to those who sneer at this, my suburb, and I give
    them back the sneer and say to them:
Come and show me another town with eight drive-in mortuaries and a
    Colonel Sanders on every block;
Show me a suburb with mortgage payments so high that men worry
    themselves into heart attacks at forty,
    Debt-ridden,
    Overdrawn,
    Embezzling,
    Financing, defaulting, re-financing,
But pleased as punch to be Hog Barbecuers for the World, School
    Segregators, Mowers of Lawns, Players with Golf Clubs and
    Champion Wife Swappers of the Nation.

therapy, and the above-quoted "There's No Business Like No Business." Both songs were found to be too similar to the originals to be considered fair play.

The Madmen were happy with the outcome, being given a clear set of guidelines and a clearly defined field for future satires.

In the 1950s Chicago's famous Forest Lawn development was looked upon as a model for the Promised Land of suburban utopia. Tom Koch assessed its evolution in this early 1970s parody of both Chicago and Sandburg, illustrated with George Woodbridge's overweight housewives and paunchy hubbies.
—Koch/Woodbridge. "Mad Sequels to Famous Poems," *Mad,* #165

"Mad was a puzzle of comedy. You couldn't take it all in one reading, so you'd delve back in. When Firesign started to make records, we wanted to do the same thing—create something so rich in activity that people would want to return to it again and again."

PHIL PROCTOR

New York Times Magazine

While he felt that most of the ditties in "Sing Along with *Mad*" were "completely different" from the originals, he ruled against *Mad* on two of the twenty-five songs: "Always," in a new version dedicated to endless psychiatric

The association was not, for exactly the same reasons. They appealed, and in March 1964 the U.S. Court of Appeals in Manhattan heard the case. Judge Irving R. Kaufman quickly ruled for the rights of *Mad*, noting in

i see the sea
*   and wonder*
if on the other side there is another shore
*   where people stand*
not knowing
i am here
*   confused and short and homely.*

i wait in vain
for you to call
*   just ONE MORE TIME*
beside a phone that never rings
*   unless*
*   i go another place*
and call myself
*   which means that i'm no longer here*
*   to answer.*

A rash of sentimental, overly artistic gift books prompted this *Mad* version, entitled "Sophisticated Swirls in Imagery." The introduction (Goo Unto Others Department) reveals the purpose of these little books: "You're supposed to buy one as a gift to impress a friend, who will then put it on his coffee table to impress his friends." — Koch/Koch, "The Mad Arty Poetry and Fuzzy Photographs Gift Book," *Mad Special,* #16

Always eager to encourage cultural literacy, *Mad* presented this "Shakespeare Primer" for the younger set, in which Macbeth is recast in the more familiar form of an upwardly mobile Organization Man. — Hahn/Wood, "The Mad Shakespeare Primer," *Mad,* #60

his opinion that "through depression and boom, war and peace, Tin Pan Alley had light-heartedly insisted that 'the whole world laughs' with a laugher, and that 'the best things in life are free.'" The suit against *Mad,* he chided, "is an apparent departure from these delightful sentiments." He pointed out that satirists must have an original on which to base their work, or satire could not exist. "While the social interest in encouraging the broad-gauged burlesques of *Mad* magazine is admittedly not readily apparent," he allowed,

MACBETH
Lesson 1.

See the witches stir.
Stir, stir, stir.
What are the witches stirring?
They are stirring up trouble.
The trouble is for Macbeth.
Surprise, Macbeth!
The witches tell Macbeth he will be King.
Macbeth does not want to be King.
Macbeth just wants to be Thane of Cawdor.
Whatever-in-heck that is!
But Mrs. Macbeth wants him to be King.
Wants, wants, wants.
You know the type.
Pushy!

22

MACBETH
Lesson 2.

See the lady.
She is Mrs. Macbeth.
She is washing her hands.
Because her hands are all bloodstained.
Ecch, ecch, ecch!
She has just helped Macbeth kill the King.
Why did Mrs. Macbeth help Macbeth kill the King?
Because the Macbeths always do everything together!
Togetherness, togetherness, togetherness.
"Out, damned spot!" says Mrs. Macbeth.
Mrs. Macbeth has dirty hands, all right.
She also has a dirty mouth!

THE COLLEGE STUDENTS' HOMECOMING MARCH

(Sung to the tune of "When Johnny Comes Marching Home")

When Johnny comes home from school this year—
   Hoo-hah! Hoo-hah!
The neighbors will know that he is here—
   Hoo-hah! Hoo-hah!
The Vietcong flag from the roof he'll fly
While screaming "Pig!" at each passer-by;
How the block will stare when Johnny comes
   home from school!

When Susie comes home from school this year—
   Hoo-hah! Hoo-hah!
She'll swing like a ten-foot chandelier—
   Hoo-hah! Hoo-hah!
She'll offer grass to her ma and pa;
She'll take the pill and she'll wear no bra;
How the town will buzz when Susie comes home
   from school!

When Freddie comes home from school this year—
   Hoo-hah! Hoo-hah!
His parents will want to disappear—
   Hoo-hah! Hoo-hah!
On Monday morn he'll be marching bare
While quoting Mao in the court-house square,
And we all will know that Freddie's come
   home from school!

When Marvin comes home from school this year—
   Hoo-hah! Hoo-hah!
We won't have a single thing to fear—
   Hoo-hah! Hoo-hah!
He'll wear a crew-cut and mow the grass;
He'll go to church and act middle-class;
   What an awful bore when Marvin comes
   home from school!

"we believe that parody and satire are deserving of substantial freedom—both as entertainment and as a form of social and literary criticism." One can almost hear the National Anthem swelling in the background—or something sung to the tune of it.

Mad had won a resounding victory for all

IF YOU KNEW HITLER

The confessions of a publisher who has been making a fortune printing sensational books about Hitler.

Sung to the tune of: "If You Knew Susie"

If you knew Hitler like I know Hitler,
   Oh, oh, oh how he sells!

The world's a patsy for this cute Nazi,
   So, so, I romanticize this ratsy.

I am so noble to tell of his fate.
   But while I'm telling,
Sick folks I exhilarate.

If you knew Hitler, you'd know that Hitler's
   No, no worse than I.

---

their song parodies, one that was trumpeted in *Variety*, the *New York Times*, the *Herald-Tribune*, and other major papers. But the association wouldn't take yes for an answer. They took the case to the Supreme Court, which upheld the lower court decision, refusing the appeal without comment and validating the rights of wags everywhere to satirize and parody to their heart's content.

Over the years, *Mad* has also commissioned and recorded numerous original songs. The first *Mad* record, *Mad Twists Rock 'n' Roll*, was a full-production LP released in 1960. Written and produced by Norm Blagman and Sam Bobrick, the album was "Danccable! Singable! Laughable!" with such searingly apropos songs as "I Saw Someone Else's Dandruff on Your Shirt," "Agnes (The Teenage Russian Spy)," and "Nose Job."

All this, and it had a beat you could tap

Frank Jacobs supplies "Marching Songs for Crusaders, Militants, and Assorted, Sundry Non-Conformists," to a generation that always seemed to be taking their grievances to the streets. Jack Davis depicts the awe and consternation of hometown folks when the students of the 1960s brought a bit of their campuses to the village green.—Jacobs/Davis, "Marching Songs for Crusaders, Militants and Assorted, Sundry, Non-Conformists," *Mad*, #141

A ditty from "Sing Along with Mad," a 1961 parody songbook that landed *Mad* in deep trouble.—Jacobs, Siegel/Rickard, "Sing Along with *Mad*," *More Trash from Mad*, #4

your brother's head to. This album was followed by *Fink Along With Mad*, with even more rock and roll numbers encouraging and admonishing teens of the dangers and delights of the early 1960s. Singles from these collections were pressed on vinyl-coated cardboard and included in several of the compilations *The Worst of Mad*.

Later, more new, original *Mad* tunes were pressed on all-plastic flexi-discs and were bound into the *Mad Specials*. There's a riddle that goes "How many grooves does a long-playing record have?" The answer is "One, that goes round and round and round." True, unless you're talking about "It's a Super-Spectacular Day," a *Mad* flexi-disc by Frank Jacobs and Norm Blagman included in *Mad Special* No. 31. By employing a technical wizardry for which no one else had ever found a use, this "mystery record" was recorded with *eight* grooves running in tan-

THE MADMEN: *Paul Coker, Jr., Phil Hahn, Frank Jacobs, Joe Orlando*

"From the thumbnail sketch to the finished one—it's all downhill," laments Paul Coker, Jr., a man known as being modest to a fault. While working as an illustrator for Hallmark Cards, Coker migrated to New York City, where he began contributing to *Mad*, *Esquire*, *McCall's*, *Playboy*, and other magazines. His drawings encompass a wide range of characters, expressions, and forms, as one look at the series "Horrifying Clichés" will attest.

Phil Hahn, who collaborated with Coker on "Horrifying Clichés," was an old friend from Kansas City. While Hahn contributed to *Mad* from 1959 to 1967, he is best known as a head writer for television, his credits including *Get Smart*, *Rowan and Martin's Laugh-In*, and *M*A*S*H*.

Writer Frank Jacobs can lay claim to several distinctions among the Usual Gang of Idiots. He is *Mad*'s Poet Laureate, being the chief writer of light verse and pop song parodies. Over its entire history he has been *Mad*'s most prolific contributor, having written over four hundred fifty pieces. And last, Jacobs was the official biographer of Bill Gaines; his book *The Mad World of William M. Gaines* was published by Lyle Stuart in 1973.

A review of Jacobs oeuvre leads to the conclusion that the man must *think* in verse. He writes parodies of musicals, poetry, and popular songs. All of Jacobs's work—the song parodies, the movie and television show spoofs, and the wordplays, while often barbed, have in common a sympathy for and understanding of their subject. Jacobs attributes this to "being able to look at the bizarre side, the funny side, the twisted side, the absurd side of everything. Not to lean one way or the other politically and to keep my mind open to everything going on that's worthy of being lampooned."

During the early years of *Mad* magazine, Joe Orlando was one of the most versatile free lance contributors, creating art for advertising parodies, magazine spoofs, and other features. He had been a comic book artist for years, working with Wally Wood and providing art to a number of comic books in the 1940s and 1950s, including EC comics. In the 1960s, he became an editor for DC comics, and is currently a vice president of the company and a director of special projects.

dem, providing eight different surprise endings of the song.

Although reviled by many, *Mad*'s literature and musical efforts have, in fact, sometimes found a place in the halls of the institutions that teach the originals. Not a few teachers have found that recalcitrant students can be interested in the classics through classroom readings of the *Mad* parodies, one of them reporting in an academic journal that "the results were dramatic. Apathy and restlessness were replaced with an attitude of engrossed concentration...." However, the same teacher warned of the dangers of such an approach: "There is one important procedure that I learned in using *Mad* which is a must—number the copies—otherwise they'll all end up stolen."

DON MARTIN DEPT. PART II

As a child prodigy of 3, Don Martin wrote "Fugue for Violin and Rattle". as a father-idiot of 30, he teaches his family —

TOGETHERNESS THROUGH MUSIC

Don Martin's early, even more maniacal, style is seen in this story of family togetherness that gives new meaning to the proverb "The family that plays together, stays together." — Martin/Martin, "Togetherness through Music," *Mad,* #62

NOTES

"visually my stuff is great..." Thompson and Groth, *"Harvey Kurtzman,"* 83.

"the syncopation..." Benson, MAD, vol. 1, notes following issue #4.

"the Yiddish comedian..." Benson, notes following issue #4.

"the results were dramatic..." Sanders, *"Remedial English Class,"* 266–267, 272.

26

69

MAD
THAT'S ENTERTAIN~MENT?

Writer and director Peter Bogdanovich has pointed out that "the influence that the movies have had on every generation since 1910 is amazing. They have told us what to think, how to dress, what to say and do, how to cry, move, fall from a gunshot, act drunk, draw a gun, swoon, kiss." If this is true, then the influence of television on American culture is even more pronounced. Television and the movies constitute a vast lode of mythology, as well as standards against which Americans measure themselves, for better or worse.

Mad talks back to these all-powerful

Hailed as "a carnival of caterwauling idiots in fright wigs," *The Mad Show* was a popular off-Broadway revue that opened in 1965. Props for the innovative staging by the late Steven Vinaver include dangling feet and word balloons. Left to right: Dick Libertini, Marcia Rodd, Jo Anne Worley. —Yale Joel, *Life* Magazine, March 1966, © Time Warner

icons, argues with them, and exposes their imperfect mirrors. For many years, the anchors of *Mad* have been lampoons of motion pictures and television programs. A movie parody almost always begins the magazine, and a takeoff of a popular television show usually falls on the last black-and-white pages. Scattered throughout the magazine are one- or two-page quickie spoofs—"Scenes We'd Like to See," or other short satires poking fun at celebrities, awards, cartoons, and other aspects of the entertainment industry. And *Mad*'s movie and television misnomers like "Balmy and Clod," "Flawrence of Arabia," "Star Blecch," and "Henna and her Sickos"

stick to the mind like Krazy Glue and tend to pop out disconcertingly even in the most serious discussions.

The first issues of *Mad* comics contained no movie or television takeoffs—in fact, the form had yet to be invented. No one knew what one would look like, or whether it could be done. Issue 2 had a Tarzan piece ("Melvin!"), although it drew more from Edgar Rice Burroughs's books than from the Tarzan movies. "Dragged Net!," in issue 3, was the first parody of a program broadcast on television, but Sergeant Friday and his sidekick "Saturday" look nothing like their TV counterparts, and it's likely that Kurtzman and Elder based their parody on the popular, and older, radio version of *Dragnet*.

Kurtzman slowly felt his way through

rather vague and generalized spoofs of *King Kong*, *High Noon*, *The Lone Ranger*, and *Shane*, until he arrived at a full-fledged parody style, in a second installment of "Dragged Net" (in issue 11) and in a lampoon of *From Here to Eternity* (in issue 12). In these, the characters are actual caricatures of the actors playing the roles, and the plots resemble those of the original. Background detail, in true *Mad* style, abounds with running jokes, visual puns, and one-liners, related or unrelated to the plot line. Clichés of the genre are fully exposed and mercilessly poked and prodded.

Although superficially television and motion pictures closely resemble each other, in structure they are quite different, and these organizational differences have profoundly affected the evolution of each medium as well as what is shown. Since 1934 and the creation of the Production Code Administration (also known as the Hays Office), the motion picture industry had been "self-censoring." The code, instituted in the wake of the infamous Fatty Arbuckle sex scandal, kept government censors out of the industry, but the effect on pictures was the same; in the end, it was worse. Most sex, violence, and vulgarity were made taboo (the code forbade even "excessive and lustful kissing"), resulting in movies that were tame, safe, and predictable.

Television, a much younger medium, became just as insipid, but for different reasons. Television is taken for granted as entertainment, but most of us fail to remember, or realize, that the real product of television is not the programming—the product is *us*, the viewers, and we are being sold to the actual consumers of television, the advertisers. In the late 1940s and early 1950s, television shows were written not by professional script-

One of *Mad*'s first television parodies takes on one of television's first children's programs. Harvey Kurtzman was still working out the formalities of illustrating TV images; early parodies are in black and white with rounded panel corners, and some had a pattern of horizontal lines overlaying the image. Shown here is Buffalo Bob, played on TV by Bob Smith, and the Peanut Gallery.

writers, but by advertising executives, with plots—or rather, formulas—tailored to the products that sponsored the shows. This structure was based not on the movie industry, where independent companies produced movies that were distributed to theaters and then paid for directly by ticket purchasers, but on the structure of radio, the other broadcast medium. Advertisers paid for programs in order to pitch their products.

This led to television programs with ludicrously skewed directives. For example, *Man*

reputable person smoking a cigarette. Do not associate the smoking of cigarettes with undesirable scenes or situations plotwise." Fires were not allowed, nor was coughing (difficult to enforce on live TV).

In addition, there was a strict formula to be followed concerning the plot line. Ideally, someone was to be murdered early on in the program, with the threat of additional violence throughout. A beautiful woman must appear and the action had to rise to a cliffhanger just before the middle commercial. A

Against Crime, a show that premiered in 1949, was wholly sponsored by Camel cigarettes. The ad agency in charge gave its writer/executives these instructions (phrased in adman lingo): "Do not have the heavy or dis-

"search" or "chase" scene at the end could be lengthened or shortened on the spur of the moment to help the live production fit its time slot.

If these types of restrictions, common then

In the "Mutt Ado About Nothing" Department in 1960 appeared this takeoff of the long-running CBS series *Lassie*. In the incarnation parodied, June Lockhart played Ruth Martin, her husband Paul, George Chandler, Uncle Petrie, and Jon Provost, the ever-saccharine Timmy. In *Mad*'s version, "Lizzie" has many adventures, chasing a stick into the woods and returning with 112 lost people and winning the Nobel Prize for "Exceptional Canine Brilliance." She is eventually revealed to be a forty-year-old cigar-smoking midget in a dog costume; the parody ends with a testimonial by Mrs. Martin alluding to the game show scandals of the late 1950s—"If Congress would only let TV clean its own house, we'd have better shows, sounder programming, and much more professional rigging in the future!" — Siegel/Drucker, "TV's Wonder Dog Lizzie," *Mad*, #59

Children's television shows always seem to be hosted by men with titles, like Captain Midnight, Captain Video, Captain Z-Ro, or Captain Kangaroo. "Uncle" is another popular prefix; here, Uncle Nutzy (who looks suspiciously like Phil Silvers) takes kids through a game of make-believe in the kind of nursery school program syndicated from coast to coast since the 1950s. — Siegel/Drucker, "Mad Looks at a Typical Kiddie Show, *Mad*, #93

for most programs, were not enough to kill off any creativity or innovation, there was, as of 1950, an industry-wide blacklist of writers, directors, and actors. The list was included in *Red Channels: The Report of Communist Influence in Radio and Television*, published by an extreme-right company called American Business Consultants, which warned of infiltration of the broadcast media by American Communists eager to sell out the United States to the Soviets. The indictment seems incredible today; the list included over one hundred fifty of the most talented people in the industry, including Leonard Bernstein, Oscar Brand, Lena Horne, Gypsy Rose Lee, Dorothy Parker, Edward G. Robinson, Orson Welles, and even Burl Ives. The effect on television and radio was devastating.

Also implicated in this Red Scare was any television show that depicted rich men, businessmen, bankers, or government officeholders as wrongdoers. As the logic went, such hard-core capitalists were public servants in the fight against communism.

Added to these inhibiting factors was a growing realization among the executives that quality programming like *Philco Television Playhouse* and *Goodyear Television Playhouse*, which were anthology series created by noted writers and performed by serious actors, were actually bad for business. Typically, such programs dealt with complex human problems

JOHN-BOY WALTON SLAYS OWN FAMILY, THEN KILLS SELF

John-Boy Walton, 25, murdered his father, mother, six brothers and sisters, and his grandparents today, then turned his revolver on himself.

Residents of Walton's Mountain were stunned after the mass slaying, Walton being described as "a model son," "a fine student and hard worker," and "as good a young man as you'll ever find."

According to Perry Mason, a retired investigator living nearby, young Walton's act was a classic example of "repressed hostility."

"It's the typical case of a goody-goody kid always having to live up to his reputation," Mason said. "He bottles up all his aggression and frustration until, one day, everything explodes inside him and he turns psycho and goes crazy."

JOHN-BOY WALTON

A search of young Walton's personal belongings turned up several knives, a number of crime magazines, and other items too lurid to mention.

of love, work, and social principles. In contrast, most sponsors usually depicted their products—mouthwash, beauty creams, and the like—as magic solutions to life's more tragic dilemmas. Pairing sensitive program-

ming with these commercials revealed the products' claims as ludicrous. As a result, scripts were watered down, and these programs went into a decline from which they never recovered.

Granted, the writers at *Mad* were unaware or unconcerned with some of these specific influences. But as critical viewers and satirists, they were driven by the gut feeling that both movies and television programming had a strange lack of depth, and portrayed a world that was far from what most viewers recognized as reality. Such offerings often lacked even internal logic.

In *Mad* comics and in the first issues of *Mad* magazine, parodies appeared occasionally, but lacked consistency. The quality of the artwork improved as the editors discovered which artists had a feel for caricature, then encouraged them to develop their talent. Jack Davis, Will Elder, John Severin, and Wally Wood were the first artists to try their hands at the form. All had the ability to capture a likeness of a performer—the hard part was depicting the character in a variety of situations, responding with exaggerated facial expressions and postures that would never occur in reality. Davis and Wood were able effortlessly to portray well-known performers doing the most unusual and crazy things. Mort Drucker, who began contributing in 1957, became the most skilled caricaturist of all, the backbone of the team.

At the same time, the editors cultivated a group of writers who had a feel for irreverent satire and an awareness of the clichés of the medium that most people took for granted. Frank Jacobs, Tom Koch, Arnie Kogen, and Larry Siegel began contributing in the late 1950s. They were joined by Dick DeBartolo,

Psychologists tell us that we each have two different personalities: One which shows our true feelings, and the other which we present to the outside world. The latter is called a "personna" or mask. Now, suppose we could see behind these masks into people's real feelings? Interesting, no? Eugene O'Neill did it in a play called "Strange Interlude", but there were hardly any laughs in it. That's because he wasn't looking behind the masks of people we all know. Now, MAD lets you take a look behind the masks of some people . . . some pleasant people . . . some sickeningly pleasant people that we all know—in this . . .

STRANGE INTERLUDE
with HAZEY

ARTIST: MORT DRUCKER   WRITER: STAN HART

Stan Hart and Mort Drucker do some interesting layering in this 1964 parody of the CBS television show *Hazel*. Hart, a scholar of the theater, incorporates the use of masks from the Eugene O'Neill play *The Great God Brown* to give us an idea of what's really on everyone's minds, and allows the former stage actress Shirley Booth to return to the stage. The top right illustration pays homage to Ted Key, the original creator of Hazel as a cartoon character for the *Saturday Evening Post*. Below, Don DeFore as George Baxter, Whitney Blake as Dorothy, and Bobby Buntrock as Harold join Booth in a typical sugary scene from the program. The contrasting pairs of facial expressions constitute a *tour de force* for Drucker—all is revealed, even Harold's pet fish's true identity. The use of subdialogue anticipates Woody Allen's internal dialogue subtitles in *Annie Hall*. — Hart/Drucker, "Strange Interlude with Hazey," *Mad*, #85

zey, your pot roast is delicious! I can't stop eating it!

Georgie certainly adores your cooking, Hazey!

Oh, for Pete's sake, Messy and Mr. G....It's my pleasure!

Actually her cooking stinks, but I need her to solve all my problems! Last week I fired my lawyer! Why should I pay someone $25,000 a year when I can get the same legal advice plus my house cleaned for $45 a week?

I wish George wouldn't eat so much! His face is beginning to lose even the little shape it once had!

It's so uplifting for a Broadway star like me to work as a menial servant for two bit players from Grade "B" pictures!

Responding to a strong civil rights movement, programmers began in the early 1960s to include more ethnic minority characters in television shows, sometimes with a marked lack of sensitivity to the varied lifestyles of those minorities—to most writers and producers, America was one big melting pot. Because there were few minorities working behind the cameras, the credibility gap was sometimes particularly wide. In 1984 when this parody was published, there were, oddly, two television programs starring diminutive, cute, African-American children being raised in white homes, *Diff'rent Strokes* and *Webster.* Here, Alex Karras and Susan Clark, playing the adoptive-parent roles, explain the television facts of life to Emmanuel Lewis, as the orphan Webster. — Siegel/Torres, "Web/Star," *Mad,* #251

In the early days of television, programs were often written not by screenwriters, but by advertising executives, who tailored the content of the program to suit the product. By 1959, programming had become a bit more sophisticated and written by professional writers, but still not immune to product-inspired action in an industry rife with special favors and payola. — Reit/Wood, "Spot that Plug!," *Mad,* #50

Stan Hart, and Lou Silverstone in the early 1960s.

The editors, writers, and artists together worked out a variety of formats to spoof both television and the movies. "Scenes We'd Like to See" was a favorite form for a takeoff of any type of short sequence. Arnie Kogen came up with the idea of a look into the wallet or purse of a celebrity, a series that offered *Mad* readers an insider's peek at the lives of Frank Sinatra (photos of himself in war movies, and his draft deferment card), Elizabeth Taylor (a receipt for a wash-and-wear wedding gown), and others. Another strategy was to combine a show with something else, creating a funny hybrid, like "Hullabadig Au Go Go" (a combination of three programs: *Hullabaloo, Shindig,* and *Hollywood a Go Go*), "Strange Interlude with Hazey," or "TV Game Shows Based on Newspaper Headlines." Writers continue to create "one-shot" articles, like "Academy Awards for Teen-age Films" or "The *Mad* Movie Rating System."

But a third form, and most consistently successful, has been the narrative takeoff of a specific television show or movie. This allows

the writer five to seven pages to do a point-by-point, merciless dissection of plot, characters, and acting, often including references and comparisons to other shows. The artist opens the satire with a dramatic, page-size drawing known as a splash panel, then depicts the action in recreations and interpretations of a variety of scenes.

From the 1950s through the 1980s, *Mad* artists and writers were going to the mov-

The engaging J. Fred Muggs, mascot of the early *Today* show, apes Dave Garroway, *Today*'s original host, in this exceptionally detailed rendering by Jack Davis. Garroway always ended the program with this peculiar hand signal and the word "peace." In the background can be seen an array of clocks, dials, and gizmos that early television executives thought would give viewers something to look at while they listened to what was essentially radio—spoken reports of news items. Muggs was added to the cast of on-camera personalities for the same reason, and was not especially liked by the others. —Kurtzman/Davis, "The Dave Garrowunway Show," *Mad*, #26

Good evening, ladies and gentlemen! Tonight—**live** from New York— **THE WALT CRONKITE SHOW!** And here he is— **Walt Cronkite!!**

Hello there, my little chickadees! We have a really **big shew** on our stage tonight: That great comedy team from Havana, the **Castro Brothers**—the **Security Council Singers** from the U.N.— Three acrobatic defectors from Bulgaria—and—please hold your applause—making their debut on our really big stage—**six new African Nations!** But first—let's open our show with **"TODAY'S HEADLINES"**, presented by the **CBS Singing Newsboys** . . . **Harry Reasoner, Bob Trout, Roger Mudd** and **Mike Wallace!**

And here they are . . .

* Doctors say Nasser's insane! Six Germans crawl through a hole in The Wall! An earthquake's destroying Peru! Yes, we've got the Big News for you!

Khruschev is hiding in Spain! Eight Vietnamese catch a jungle disease When they seize a Chinese passing through! Yes, we've got the Big News for you!

Sung to the tune of "I Get A Kick Out Of You"

Frank Jacobs had some ideas for the *CBS Evening News* program to help them compete with NBC's charismatic Huntley-Brinkley team. "Huntley and Brinkley throw in lots of quips and funny observations," Jacobs noted, and Walter Cronkite should supply a bit of his own entertainment, too. A farfetched fantasy in 1965, this hybrid of *The Ed Sullivan Show* and the evening news was prescient of the changes in news programs of the 1980s, with their ever-larger casts of brightly dressed, anecdote-trading anchors and flashy graphics. —Jacobs/Rickard, "The Walt Cronkite Show," *Mad*, #97

OVERLY CHEERFUL TV NEWS ANCHORS AND WEATHERPERSON ENDERS

Overly Cheerful TV News Anchors And Weatherpersons are required to attend meetings at which slides of very sad events are screened. Each time one of them is flashed, a painful electric shock is sent thru their bodies until they learn to react properly. TV News Anchors and Weatherpersons who continue to be cheerful as the painful shock is applied must immediately go on to "Masochist Enders."

In 1985 Al Jaffee took on the very type of news program that Frank Jacobs facetiously proposed in 1965. Jaffee, bugged by inanely grinning, telegenic newscasters, felt drastic measures were called for as a solution to the problem. —Jaffee/Jaffee, "Bad Habit Enders," *Mad*, #259

When writer Lou Silverstone proposed a parody of the 1965 television hit *Batman*, Al Feldstein said it couldn't be done—because the program was already a parody. Silverstone went ahead with the idea anyway, telling a story from Robin's, that is, "Sparrow"'s, point of view. Feldstein had to admit that the lampoon worked. Here, Robin, played in the series by Burt Ward, explains the facts of life to his mentor (Adam West). Lots of kids had no idea what the Kinsey Report was, says Silverstone. —Silverstone/Drucker, "Bats-Man," *Mad*, #105

WESTERN DEPT.

AND NOW MAD PRESENTS ITS OWN VERSION OF THE REALISTIC WESTERN TV PROGRAM THAT BEGINS WITH AN UNUSUALLY REALISTIC WESTERN FLAVOR.

MAINLY, THIS PROGRAM BEGINS BY FIRST KILLING OFF THE TV AUDIENCE

For years *Gunsmoke*, television's longest-running western, opened with a shoot-out on Main Street in Dodge City. In the wake of the Kennedy and King assassinations and other public strife, the dramatic opening was canned in favor of milder scenes of Marshal Matt Dillon riding the range. —Kurtzman/Davis, "Gunsmoked," *Mad*, #30

ies and watching television like the rest of us, only they were taking notes and making sketches with the concentration of a serious critic. Reading the older parodies is as entertaining as watching a vintage movie or television show, and the nostalgia quotient is high. But the body of satire found in *Mad* also provides an especially revealing look at the separate evolutions of television and the movies, how the shows fit into the cultural context of the times, and how they were received by those smart-alecks at *Mad*.

The radar of the writers at *Mad* picked up on subtle trends as well as outrageous ones. One example of this is *Mad*'s spotting of unannounced free plugs of products. The prac-

tice was widespread in the industry, and often affected the content of the programming. Viewers were sometimes treated to unexplained close-ups of wristwatches or refrigerators. *Mad* ran an exposé of the racket, and shortly thereafter the FCC stepped up their scrutiny of the practice. A congressional investigation put pressure on the networks to crack down on the problem.

Many *Mad* parodies draw attention to the extreme violence in the late 1950s action programs, violence that became so predictable that it led one producer to complain to his writers, "I wish you would come up with a different device than running the man down with a car, as we have done this now in three

In the early 1950s, crime was just as popular on television and radio as it had been in comic books. *Dragnet*, starring Jack Webb as Sergeant Joe Friday, was one of the first to appear. In the early episodes Barney Phillips played Friday's partner, Sergeant Ed Jacobs. In this excerpt from *Mad*'s second parody of the program, Kurtzman and Elder parody several of the characteristics that set the series apart from its competition. Jack Webb, also the series director, was a stickler for authenticity, and Kurtzman shows no mercy in spoofing his penchant for police jargon. *Dragnet* was also one of the first series to be filmed in Hollywood, rather than broadcast live, allowing for more closely planned camera work and dialogue set-ups—Kurtzman mimics the cinematic melodrama. The outrageous theme music has been used as an excuse to bring in an entire *Mad* ensemble, where characters from several other *Mad* comics can be seen, including Shermlock Shomes and the Mole. —Kurtzman/ Elder, "Dragged Net!," *Mad*, #11

different shows. I like the idea of sadism, but I hope we can come up with another approach to it." The Madmen were not the only ones sensitive to this barrage. Once again, outside scrutiny was brought to bear on the industry, this time in the form of crusading Senator Thomas J. Dodd, a former FBI agent who in 1961 led Senate subcommittee hearings on violence in television. Both the Fed and *Mad* were dissatisfied with the state of the art, but while Dodd reviled violence because he felt it had a bad influence on youth, the *Mad* parodies pointed out that it made for boring and predictable TV.

The year 1962 was a turning point in the history of television. The continuing crusade against the more blatant depictions of violence on TV encouraged the development of alternative programming, but more important, 1962 brought the end of the blacklist.

The besieged industry breathed a collective sigh of relief, and constraints on subject matter for television loosened. But before long, new pressures were brought to bear on this most public of media. By 1963 the civil rights movement had begun to demand that programmers racially integrate their staffs and casts, to reflect more truly television's audience. The networks complied, grudgingly, and token members of ethnic groups began to

appear in crowd scenes and other low-profile settings. Rights groups complained at the slow pace of change, and television was forced to integrate more important roles. *Julia* was the first television series since the early 1950s to star an African-American woman, but NBC, having as few minority group mem-

bers behind the cameras as in front of them, came up with a program that neither acknowledged nor exploited an African-American cultural heritage; instead, Julia was an unbelievably good-looking and well-off single mother. As a character in *Mad*'s parody of the

Remind me to check your **Reassembling Unit!** I think it needs a minor adjustment!

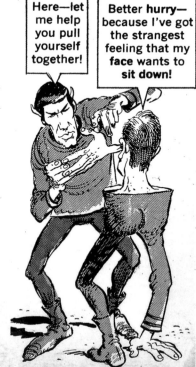

Here—let me help you pull yourself together!

Better hurry—because I've got the strangest feeling that my **face** wants to sit down!

AND HERE IT IS . . . THE BRAND NEW WEEKLY TV SITUATION COMEDY FEATURING THAT GAY, WILD, ZANY, IRREPRESSIBLE BUNCH OF WORLD WAR II CONCENTRATION CAMP PRISONERS . . . THOSE HAPPY INMATES OF "BUCHENWALD" KNOWN AS . . .

Hochman's Heroes

In one of *Mad*'s more controversial television parodies, Larry Siegel tried to show "the idiocy of a program which would have fun with a time when there was such horror going on and make it seem so light." The original program, *Hogan's Heroes*, starring Bob Crane and Werner Klemperer, was a sitcom that took place in a zany prisoner-of-war camp in World War II Germany. Siegel was irked by the attitude of the program: "I resented the fact that they were making the Germans so cute, and these guys were sitting in prison. I was over there, and I saw what it was really like." The last page of his satire is a splash panel depicting what would ultimately come of such insensitivity. — *Siegel/Davis, "Hokum's Heroes," Mad, #108*

Compared to *Hogan's Heroes*, *M*A*S*H* was documentary-like in terms of realism. However, by 1982, when this parody was published, *M*A*S*H* had been on the air ten years—seven years longer than the Korean War itself—and was showing its age. *Mad* had previously parodied the Robert Altman film ("M*I*S*H M*O*S*H," 1970), and the series ("M*A*S*H*uga," 1979), but the temptation for one more swipe at the hit series was irresistible. The genealogy of characters depicted provides a Jack Davis *tour de force*, with virtually all the regular players ever appearing shown. — Kogen/Davis. "M*U*S*H," *Mad*, #234

Hi, there! I'm **Father Nokaypee**, Chaplain of the 4077th M.A.S.H. unit in Korea! Let me **refresh** your **memory** of "The Creation"!

In the Beginning, the **Producers** created a **TV Series**... based on the **Good Book** and the **Hit Movie**! On the **First Day**, They created the **Premise**! On the **Second Day**, They created the **Structure**! And on the **Third Day**, They created the **Pilot Episode**! And They saw that it was **Good**!

On the **Fourth Day**, They went up into Hills of Malibu, and They gazed upon Land and said, "**Let this be Korea!**" it **was**! And They saw that it was **Rig**

And on the **Fifth Day**, They said, "Let there be a **Cast of Characters** played by **Talented Actors** who will be **Funny** and **Facile** and **not Committed** to any other Sit-Com! And thus, They created the **Men of the Series**!

And on the **Sixth Day**, T created the **Women** of Series! And they saw th it was **Good**... and **Fun**

And They said, "Let this Show be **Different** from other Wartime SitComs! Let there be **Brisk, Witty Dialogue**! But, **along** with the Comedy, let us show the **Stark Reality** of War! Let our Show have **Integrity**! And it **did**! And the **Public** saw that it was **Good**! And on the **Seventh Day**, the Creators **rested** ... in the **Polo Lounge** of the **Beverly Hills Hotel**!

And over the Years, the Sh prospered, and became the **Popular Show** in the Land! They were **well-rewarded** w many Statues called "**Emmy**

And They said, "**Be Fruitful and Multiply** into T.V. Syndication!" And it **did**! And They said, "Let there be **Re-runs**!" And there were **Plenty**!

But **lately**, Things have **Changed** in this that was "**Paradise**"! You will see what W in this **MAD Version** that examines the **Si**

M*U*S*H

ARTIST: JACK DAVIS   WRITER: ARNIE KOGEN

Given the multiplication of specialized Emmy Awards bestowed by the Academy of Television Arts and Sciences for things like "Outstanding Host or Hostess in a Game or Audience Participation Show," these Emmy categories invented by Mike Snider seem much more to the point. Other awards proposed include "Most Innovative Use of a Car-Chase Wind-Up In An Action/Adventure Series To Cover Up Bad Writing," and "Best Performance By An Actor Or Actress In a Talk Show 'Plug' For a Failing Series."
—Snider/Michael Montgomery, "TV Emmy Awards We'd Like to See," Mad, #266

series, "Jewelia," pointed out, "It's not an easy life for her, being hated and despised as a member of a Minority Group." "Gee, *we* don't treat her as a member of a Minority Group on the show!" responds someone else. "No... but look at that apartment she lives in, and look at that fantastic wardrobe she's got. She's a member of a minority group as far as the show's audience is concerned—the *majority* of Americans don't live *that* good!!!"

By the late 1960s, television shows were becoming more sophisticated and complex, and the parody writers faced new challenges. Many of the *Mad* writers had themselves "gone Hollywood" and were writing for network television shows. Their insider knowledge was sometimes used to good effect when they wrote articles such as "The *Mad* Automatic Do-It-Yourself Script Writer," or "The Evolution of a TV Situation Comedy," which traced the changes and convolutions of a show through ten seasons, when it ends its run with scant resemblance to its original concept. Often, characters in parodies will lay bare

devices and conventions of television.

It was with true camaraderie that *Mad* printed, in 1968, "A CBS-TV Summer Memo to the Smothered Brothers," an ode by Ronnie Nathan to the innovative, irreverent comedy show that was continually threatened by the network. It went in part:

Three spoofs of that ever-popular primate, King Kong. Kurtzman and Elder based theirs on the original 1933 movie, taking careful aim at the standard motion picture clichés of thick fog and fierce, but unrealistic, African warriors. Dick DeBartolo and Harry North have fun with the 1976 Dino de Laurentiis re-make, where King Kong's famous ascent takes place at the World Trade Center rather than the Empire State Building. Sergio Aragonés's ape is playful, not threatening. —Kurtzman/Elder, "Ping Pong!," *Mad,* #6; DeBartolo/ North, "King Korn," *Mad,* #192; Aragonés, "A Mad Look at King Kong," *Mad,* #192

Playing on the clichés of old Hollywood movies, Earl Doud offers his version of the standard movie – set trade catalogue. —Doud/Woodbridge, "Hollywood Surplus Sale," *Mad,* #77

Don't tweak the beak of Bird-man's mate,
Or bait a certain Southern state.
Don't fool around with Uncle Sam,
And stay away from Vietnam....
Recruitment gags we don't allow,
Lay off the C.I.A. and Dow.

Unfortunately, *The Smothers Brothers Comedy Hour* ultimately succumbed; it was canceled one hundred days into the Nixon administration.

MAD'S ROLE AS A SATIRIST OF MOVIES HAS BEEN a bit different. Since movies are produced by independent studios and, unlike television, are not merely a vehicle to deliver viewers to advertisers, there is the possibility of more variety. Movies are longer, more lavishly produced, and may have more complicated plots than television shows. However, because of the great expense of the productions, movies are subject to similar precautionary

The enforcement of the 1934 Motion Picture Production Code forced movies to curtail sex, violence, and most other things of interest in films until the mid-1960s. One of the most ludicrous results of the code was the use of twin beds, even for married couples. When this satire was published in 1954, EC comics was at the height of its own censorship battle. — Kurtzman/Davis, "Book! Movie!," *Mad*, #13

BEFORE WE LAUNCH INTO OUR STORY, WE'D LIKE TO NOTE THAT IN UNDERTAKING THIS FEATURE, **MAD** FACED THE PROBLEM THAT **IF** WE DUPLICATED A TYPICAL MODERN NOVEL IN THIS COMIC BOOK... WE'D BE RUN OUT OF TOWN ON A RAIL!... SO, IN THE INTERESTS OF GOOD TASTE, US EDITORS HAVE EMPLOYED THE CENSORSHIP STAMP THAT WE PICTURE HERE!... WHEREVER YOU SEE THIS STAMP, YOU WILL KNOW THAT WE OF **MAD** HAVE CANCELLED PORTIONS OF PICTURES WE HAVE DEEMED IMMORAL, INDECENT AND MAINLY BAD FOR BUSINESS!

— *the editors of 'Mad'*

A film of a play by Edward Albee, *Who's Afraid of Virginia Woolf?*, broke ground to new levels of permissiveness in Hollywood films. *Mad's* parody, "Who in the Heck Is Virginia Woolf?" managed to poke fun at the language and sex life of the battling couple (played by Elizabeth Taylor and Richard Burton), while maintaining what would have passed for a "G" rating. Writer Larry Siegel regrets that he was unable to use the word "hell" in the parody title. — Siegel/Drucker, "Who in the Heck Is Virginia Woolf?," *Mad*, #109

efforts by their financiers, leading to the watering-down of extreme plots and the blurring of independent visions, or, contrariwise, the pouring of money and effort into the bloated productions by big-name directors.

In the 1950s, *Mad* had Hays Office movies to kick around, and the contrivances necessitated by the Production Code led to plenty of unrealistic scenes and dialogue. The lampoon "Book! Movie!" explicitly (so to speak) examines the differences between what's allowed in a novel, but not on the big screen. The parody is a savvy breakdown of the effect of the Hays Office on movies as well as an incisive look at the tendency of Hollywood to glamorize and remove any sharp edges from stories—in the "book" version, a low-brow couple tends to the tasks of everyday life, battling, cursing, and making love. In the "movie," polished, upwardly mobile characters drink martinis for breakfast, take

showers in their bathrobes (no nudity allowed), dance, and engage in gunfights with no blood. Kurtzman delivered the crowning, ironic touch in using a blackout technique to indicate the nudity and violence present in the novel.

Readers were treated to a special two-page Drucker panorama of the opening scene of *Hannah and Her Sisters*. The 1985 Woody Allen film was the first of his that *Mad* had parodied. This Thanksgiving dinner is a feast of Drucker caricatures, from upper left, Mia Farrow, Dianne Wiest, Michael Caine, Barbara Hershey, Lloyd Nolan, Louise Lasser (not in the movie, but an old girlfriend of Allen's), Ed Koch (also not in the movie, but supplying essential New York ambience), Maureen O'Sullivan, movie critics Roger Ebert, Gene Siskel, Gene Shalit, and Jeffrey Lyons (obviously not in the movie, but they love to discuss Allen's films), and Alfred E. Neuman. — Debbee Ovitz/Drucker, "Henna and Her Sickos," *Mad*, #265

KNOCK ON WOODY DEPT.

I'm **Woody Alien!** I'd like to introduce you to my **latest film!** I'm very proud of it—it's **new,** it's **different!** Like for instance, even though it's the 14th consecutive film in which I've played a **total neurotic,** this is the **first time** there are **other neurotics** in even **worse shape** than **me,** mainly…

HEN HER

(OR: "PLAY ANNIE HA

I'm **Henna,** and these are my **two sisters, Hollow** and **Loose!** Welcome to our hip, contemporary, utterly *Nouveau York* Thanksgiving dinner! **Let's get started!**

Okay, I'll start with **neurosis** and **guilt!**

Who wants some **angst** and **despair?**

Please pass me a **double helping** of **letching!** And make sure you **lean all over me** when you serve it!

Thank you for the **blessings** we're abo receive—the **turkey,** the **stuffing,** th **cranberries,** and the **one-liners** abo **Franz Kafka, Nazis,** and **psychoanaly**

Listen, everyone—Melissa just said her **very first word!** Say it **again,** Melissa!

Depression!

Isn't she just **darling!**

ARTIST: MORT D

A AND SICKOS

("...NHATTAN MEMORIES AGAIN, SAM!")

Can I make a wish?

If it's appropriate...

I wish for world peace!

That won't do...

Okay, how's this—I wish to attend a Gestalt Therapy summer camp so I can work through my anxiety crisis!

That's much better, dear!

This is a veritable masterpiece! Woody has certainly grown as a filmmaker!

What brilliant touches! Instead of Gershwin music, he's using Rodgers and Hart! And instead of Diane Keaton talking in overlapping dialogue, he has Mia Farrow doing it!

HOW AM I DOIN'?

I ♥ to HATE N.Y.

THANKSGIVING ISSUE MAD A REAL TURKEY!

He shows real maturity as a Director since "Manhattan" and "Stardust Memories"!

Right! Woody's finally learned where to buy color film!

By the late 1960s the Production Code began to ease its grip on the content of films, and in 1968 the code was lifted and replaced by the current rating system, which regulates movie attendance by age. *Mad* lampooned *Who's Afraid of Virginia Woolf?*, *Bonnie and Clyde*, *Midnight Cowboy*, and other movies that most of its readers were too young to see. *Mad*'s takeoffs were as clean as a G-rated movie (the "Midnight Wowboy" sold his kisses), but the parodies did allow underage readers at least a peek and a clue to what they were missing.

THE MADMEN: *Mort Drucker, Stan Hart, Arnie Kogen, Larry Siegel, Angelo Torres*

When Mort Drucker answered a want ad placed by *Mad* in the *New York Times*, he was unprepared for the reception he received. Associate Editor Nick Meglin was impressed with the portfolio of hundreds of comics Drucker had created and illustrated, including war comics, westerns, and humor comics, and quickly took it in for review to Bill Gaines and Al Feldstein, who were engrossed in a Brooklyn Dodgers game. "If the Dodgers win, you're hired," Gaines gleefully informed Drucker. Luckily, they did, and Drucker was enlisted on the spot.

After joining the Usual Gang of Idiots, Drucker's talent for caricature came to the fore. The editorial staff at *Mad* encouraged him to develop his own style, combining the forms of continuity illustration and caricature for television and movie parodies. This challenged Drucker not only to capture a recognizable likeness of a subject, but to show that person realistically engaged in various activities over a series of panels. Drucker's portraits have also frequently occupied the cover of *Time* magazine—over fifteen have appeared since 1970—and seven of the original drawings have found a home in the National Portrait Gallery of the Smithsonian Institution.

One might be surprised to find a man with a Columbia University master of arts degree in Elizabethan theater writing "Top Gunk" or "Strange Interlude with Hazey" for *Mad* magazine, but for Stan Hart it seemed natural. Throughout his life, Hart has concentrated on performance—live, filmed, broadcast, and parodied. He was the co-author of *The Mad Show*, and has written other plays and several movie screenplays as well. He received two Emmys for his writing for *The Carol Burnett Show* in the early 1970s. With so many other interests and talents, what keeps Hart writing for *Mad*? "For me, *Mad* is an outlet for the insanity I see going on in the world today," Hart

THE REACTIONS OF THE TARGETS OF *MAD*'s satire have varied. Early on, Ava Gardner threatened to sue over "The Barefoot No-Countessa." Universal Pictures once made nasty noises about a cover featuring the Frankenstein monster putting together an Alfred E. Neuman doll. Nothing came of either complaint. More recently, when the character Yoda appeared on an issue containing "The Empire Strikes Out," George Lucas's legal staff threatened suit. *Mad*'s bemused editors simply forwarded to the lawyers a letter just received from Lucas himself calling Mort Drucker and Dick DeBartolo "the Leonardo da Vinci and George Bernard Shaw of satire."

Like Lucas, most of *Mad*'s victims have taken the spoofs in good humor, most likely subscribing to the truism that any publicity is good publicity. In fact, to many, it has become a mark of true success to be in a television show or movie lampooned in *Mad*. Celebrities send photos of themselves grimac-

ing while reading the parodies, and the editors run the shots on the letters page.

On several occasions, the influence has gone the other way and *Mad* has found itself

In the *Mad* version of the 1966 movie *Fantastic Voyage*, the trip in miniature through the human body is arranged by advertising executives rather than scientists. — Siegel/Drucker, "Fantastecch Voyage," *Mad*, #110

Stanley Kubrick took a classic Arthur C. Clarke science-fiction tale and interwove it with his own obscure symbolism to make *2001: A Space Odyssey*. *Mad* knew what to make of it, however, having a field day with its many obscure references and product plugs. — DeBartolo/Drucker, "201 Min. of a Space Idiocy," *Mad*, #125

involved with, or appearing in, the media. *Mad*'s first "guest" appearance (*Mad* never pays "product placement" fees) was a copy of *Mad* used as a prop on Ernie Kovacs's 1954 television special *Between the Laughter*. Since then, the magazine has cropped up in *A Hard Day's Night*, John Waters's *Hairspray*, Steven Spielberg's *Goonies*, and a number of other movies and television shows where directors use it to establish attitude and character (or lack thereof). For the 1959 television special *Another Evening with Fred Astaire*, Astaire gained *Mad*'s permission to dance disguised as Alfred E. Neuman.

After fourteen years of give-and-take, *Mad* itself entered show business in a big way with *The Mad Show*. One day in late 1965, Bill Gaines was approached by Mary Rodgers, a young composer and the daughter of Richard Rodgers, and Marshall Barer, another writer.

says. "It takes the far ends of the political, cultural, and religious spectrums and shines a light of sanity on them."

Arnie Kogen is another contributor who likes to have it both ways: for over thirty years Kogen has been one of *Mad*'s most consistent contributors of television, movie, and celebrity satire, and for almost as long he has been one of the most active television comedy writers in the business. Kogen was selling typewriters on the Lower East Side when he was introduced to Gaines and Feldstein by Paul Krasser, who published *The Realist* in an office adjacent to *Mad*'s at 225 Lafayette. Kogen's start at *Mad* led to writing for a number of prominent standup comedians and performers, including Carol Burnett, Sammy Davis, Jr., and Ronald Reagan. He's also received many awards for his television writing, including three Emmys.

Larry Siegel has been writing for *Mad* since 1958, and over the years Siegel has contributed some of *Mad*'s more controversial articles, like "Hokum's Heroes," "Stokely and Tess," and the magazine parody "Passionate Gun Love." Siegel feels that a certain fearlessness is a prerequisite to the type of writing in which he specializes. "If you're afraid, then forget the satire business. I think anything is fair game if you do it right." Like several other *Mad* TV and movie parodists, Siegel writes for television himself, including *Bob Newhart* and *Mary Tyler Moore*, and has received three Emmys, a Writers Guild Award, "a dozen or so" other Emmy and Writers Guild nominations, and "a solid gold Little Orphan Annie Shake-up Mug." He was co-writer of *The Mad Show*.

Angelo Torres's history with EC goes back to the New Trend comic books days in the early 1950s. For several months Torres assisted Al Williamson with his work for EC science fiction comic books. But by the time he was beginning to receive solo jobs the censors at the Comics Code Authority were circling: the only job he completed fell prey and was never published. Since 1968, Torres has been contributing art to *Mad* for TV and movie satires. Luckily, Torres is an "insatiable movie fan," since he sometimes sees the target of a parody three times while at work on it. "First and foremost, I try to get the characters—that's the number one problem.... It's very easy to trace a head, but you can't just make it photographic, you have to cartoon it up," says Torres. "After that, you must make the figures really humorous, and then tell the story."

Rodgers and Barer proposed to produce a revue based on stories from *Mad*, to be performed for a short run at the off-Broadway New Theater.

To everyone's surprise, Gaines readily agreed to the plan and assigned Larry Siegel and Stan Hart to write the script for the show. Siegel, Barer, Steven Vinaver, and Stephen Sondheim (under a *nom de plume*) wrote lyrics to Mary Rodgers's music, for five then little-known actors: Linda Lavin, MacIntyre Dixon, Dick Libertini, Paul Sand, and Jo Anne Worley.

Vinaver played an even more influential role as director of the production. He designed the show so that there were constant wild happenings on the stage, which was

filled with cut-out figures of comic strip characters and blank word balloons upon which were projected one-liners ("Ronald Reagan call your agent." "In case of atomic attack the Hadassah meeting will be canceled." "Good night, David.") Actors crisscrossed the stage, changing costumes and characters, props appeared and disappeared—nothing stopped moving.

The general manager of the show, Mike Brandman, got into the spirit of the production and sent out announcements in the form of ransom notes tied to bricks to New York's theater critics. A concession stand in the lobby was set up to sell hair cream, Drāno, Ex-Lax, and painted rocks. Opening in January 1966 with performances strangely scheduled at three in the afternoon and midnight, the show was a hit with both critics and public. "Even 'wild' is too tepid a word to describe

With the rise of a new generation of directors in the 1970s the satirists at *Mad* began to face a challenge they hadn't anticipated—moviemakers who had grown up reading their satires. George Lucas, director of *Star Wars*, has admitted that *Mad* movie parodies have influenced his films.—Siegel with DeBartolo/North, "Star Roars," *Mad*, #196

A superhero's modern-day troubles are the subject of this Don Martin ditty published to coincide with the movie *Superman*.—Edwing/Martin, "A Mad Look at Superman," *Mad*, #208

STAR TREK 12— ▶
THE SEARCH FOR GEORGE AND JUDY

The Starship Enterprise picks up The Jetsons, who have been wandering through space after losing their home due to the business failure of Spacely Sprockets. While William Shatner tries to help George fight his arch competitor, Cogswell's Cogs, Leonard Nimoy has other problems—the Vulcan has fallen in love. Unfortunately it's with Rosie, the Jetson's robot maid, whose lovemaking is, at best, mechanical.

The combination of *Star Trek* sequels run amok and the animation technology used in *Who Framed Roger Rabbit?* add up to one bizarre movie in this flight of fancy by Stan Hart.—Hart/Clarke, "When Roger Rabbit Technology Takes Over All of Hollywood's Films," *Mad*, #285

these goings-on," one critic raved. "This is uproariously funny stuff—brash, satirical, and merrily defiant," wrote another. "Thoroughly enjoyable," pronounced Stanley Kauffmann, in the all-important *New York Times* review.

The Mad Show ran for over two years, almost nine hundred performances, after which it was taken on the road, with bookings in Los Angeles, Pittsburgh, Chicago, Boston, San Francisco, and Detroit. Steve Vinaver's innovative staging is said to have been George Schlatter's inspiration for television's groundbreaking comedy show *Laugh-In*. An LP was made of the production, which is still occa-

sionally updated and performed around the country.

In the years since *The Mad Show*'s success, Gaines has been approached numerous times with proposals for *Mad* television shows and movies, but the deals have seldom worked out, in part because Gaines has insisted on scriptwriter approval. "You've got to love *Mad*

to do something like that successfully," he insists, and apparently few have loved up to Gaines's demanding standards. Finally, *Mad* went Hollywood with *The Mad Movie*. It was announced in 1979 that the Warner Brothers film was nearing production, but in the end executives felt that the film, written as a series

of vignettes, was too expensive and risky, and the project was canned.

Mad's second foray into movies was even less successful. On the strength of the screenplay, Gaines agreed that *Mad* would lend its endorsement to *Up the Academy*. *Mad*'s name was to be used in advertising, and a statue of Alfred E. Neuman would appear in the film. Robert Downey was hired to direct the movie, but by the time it was released in 1980, *Mad*'s editors and Gaines felt it had become very different from the script they had read, and too crude for even *Mad* to endorse. "We were all so ashamed of it," Gaines comments, ruefully. *Mad* paid to have all references to the magazine removed from the video release.

In the 1970s *Mad*'s material was the subject of an animated television special produced by Focus Productions. The half-hour program, which included characters by Berg, Drucker, Jaffee, and other *Mad* favorites, was completed, but never aired. The rumor around the *Mad* offices was that a major car manufacturer slated to sponsor the program was uncomfortable with the "Car Manufacturer of the Year" sketch.

What happened to **you**?

I was attacked in the boat coming over.

By whom?

Sea gull!

Siegel!? Who would ever have thought that nice, quiet Mr. Siegel would attack a strange girl in a boat! Shows you—you never really **know** your neighbors!

No! No! A **sea gull**—a **bird**—swooped down and bit me on top of my head!

Really? So how come you're **bleeding** on the **side** of your **face**?

You're just a silly, hysterical kid! Now calm down and meet my family. This is my kid sister—and this is my jealous, possessive mother. Folks, this is wealthy Miss Headrinse who intruded on our weekend for the purpose of making a tremendous **play** for me!

How do you do, Miss Headrinse? Is that **ketchup** on your face? Such a sloppy girl to come visiting us! I **don't like** her, son! Send her away!

THERE'S GOING TO BE AN INVASION, I CAN FEEL IT!

Arnie Kogen pokes fun at the labored conversation and contrived romance in *The Birds*. Melanie Daniels, a sophisticated socialite, has, on a lark, dropped in on Mitch Brenner and his family. Drucker's caricatures capture likenesses of Rod Taylor, Tippi Hedren, Veronica Cartwright, and Jessica Tandy. — Kogen with Silverstone/Drucker, "For the Birds," *Mad*, #82

Shame on you, Hollywood, for making such a lousy picture like this!

And mainly, shame on **you**, the American public, for spending good money to **see** a lousy picture like this, when you could have stayed home and read a **GOOD BOOK!**

More recently, another *Mad* television special was produced by Hanna Barbera for CBS. *Goin' Mad* is a compilation of favorite sketches and scenes, from "The Lighter Side" to "Spy vs. Spy" and movie parodies, but the network has been holding off on airing the program, for unknown reasons.

MOVIE AND TELEVISION DEALS ASIDE, THE REAL grist of *Mad*'s mill is still the parodies that appear on their own pages. What does the fu-

1968

ture hold? "The future of movies is so bleak that for our three hundredth issue we're doing parodies of *Casablanca*, *Gone With the Wind*, and *The Wizard of Oz*," quips editor John Ficarra. "If they work out, we're doing *Potemkin*."

— Sid Caesar/Wood, "The Jackie Talented Story," *Mad*, #55

NOTES

"the influence that movies . . ." Webb, Hollywood, 47.

"Do not have the heavy . . ." Barnouw, Tube of Plenty, 132.

"I wish you would come up . . ." Barnouw, 263–264.

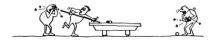

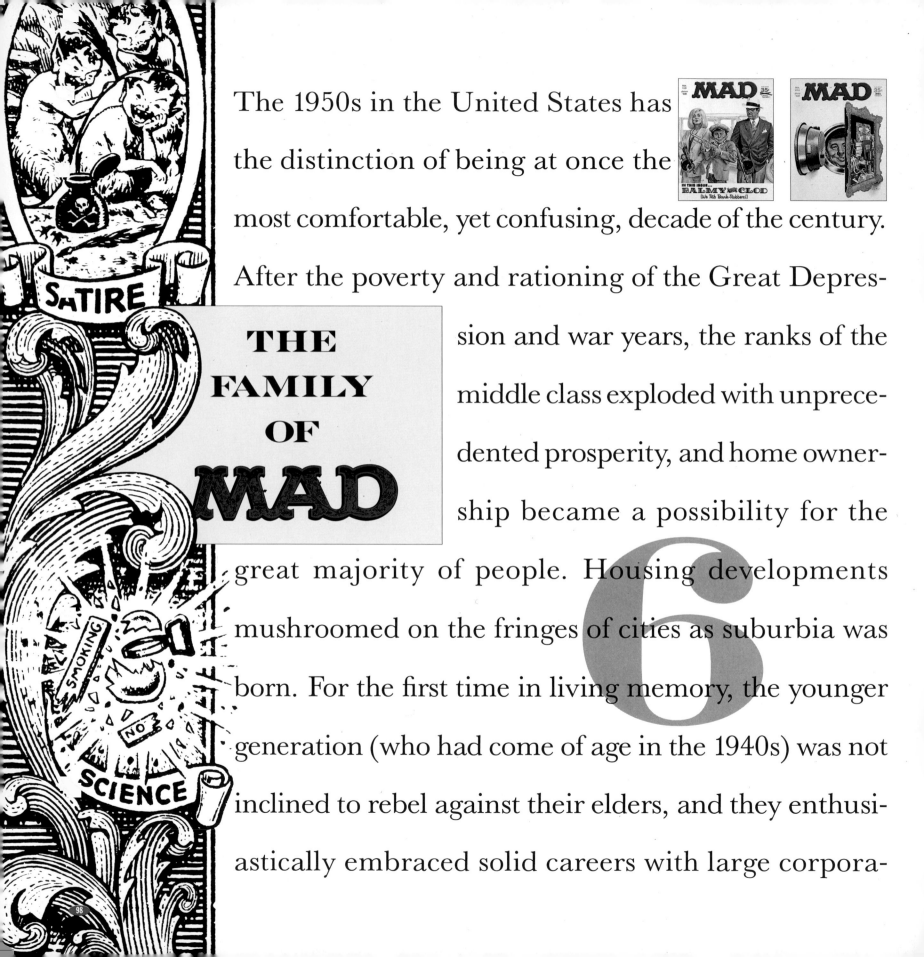

THE FAMILY OF MAD

The 1950s in the United States has the distinction of being at once the most comfortable, yet confusing, decade of the century. After the poverty and rationing of the Great Depression and war years, the ranks of the middle class exploded with unprecedented prosperity, and home ownership became a possibility for the great majority of people. Housing developments mushroomed on the fringes of cities as suburbia was born. For the first time in living memory, the younger generation (who had come of age in the 1940s) was not inclined to rebel against their elders, and they enthusiastically embraced solid careers with large corpora-

Belch-Not
STRAINED
BABIES

PACKED
IN
EAST
AFRICA

BY
CANNIBALS
FOR
CANNIBALS

"Babies are our only business!"

tions, taking jobs that they hoped and planned to keep for the rest of their lives, as they settled down to establish their own families. New technology, much of it developed in wartime, promised lives of grace, novelty and leisure, with a TV in the living room, a washer and dryer in the basement, and a shiny car in the garage of every new split-level from Maine to California.

Still, there were roadblocks and detours on the highways to success, so new that directional signage was either missing or obscured by massive numbers of billboards. Increasing numbers of young couples found themselves moved by the corporation to a new, strange, modern house, its mud lawn embellished with perhaps one sapling, and more closely resembling the moon than any hospitable landscape. Many were the first generation of their family to attend college or to move from blue-collar or farm work to white-collar work, and they didn't know how to live up to their new class status. While they expected upward mobility, they remembered sharply the depression, and were terrified of losing the little ground they had gained.

Pressures to conform were intense; at work Dad was given barrages of personality tests to see how well adapted he was to rising up the hierarchy; at school kids were treated to instructional films on how to be a teenager, and sent home with warnings against too much introversion and lone play. In order to be accepted in the new neighborhood, homemakers performed an intricate balancing act, keeping up with the Joneses, yet not leaping so far ahead of the pack as to become isolated and rejected from the daily Kaffeeklatsch. They were cut off from family, church, hometown, and most traditions they had come to

take for granted. These suburbanites were considered to be in the vanguard of American life. In short, they had made it. But where were they?

Suddenly, there was no dearth of "helpful" advice for the honeymooners from television, magazines, and advertisements, eager to promote what social historian Thomas Hine has dubbed the "populuxe" lifestyle. "Father knows best," Buicks "make you feel like the man you are," and "Blondes have more fun!" were just a few of the directives of the day. "Little boxes made of ticky-tacky," sneered composer Malvinia Reynolds from the sidelines, echoing the sentiments of many intellectuals and social critics of the time, and jabbing the rising middle class just where it hurt.

Mad also had advice for the new generation, but it was a bit more sympathetic, as in this excerpt from "How to be Smart":

Now many people are under the impression that the world is a pretty dumb place and there aren't many smart people around nowadays. To foolishly say whether there *are* lots of those dumb people will not be the purpose of this article.

To *help* all those millions of dumb people will be the purpose of this article.

And with smartness in the minority, let's face it . . . you are probably one of "those" . . .

Especially since you're reading this magazine.

However, cheer up. You too can be smart. It's easy.

The big general-interest magazines, with polished illustrations and articles, were perfect targets for *Mad* writers, who point up the disparities between image and reality. "Field & Scream" reveals the terrors of hunting small game and also contains an article on increasing one's catch of bass by using hand grenades, while "Gook" warns in a special report that "Teen-agers Are Running the Pentagon." — Koch/Wood, "Gook," *Mad*, #45; B. Johnson/Clarke, "The New Yorker," *Mad*, #189; Koch/Clarke, "The Saturday Evening Pest," *Mad*, #39; house/Davis, "Field & Scream," *Mad*, #31

The pride and joy of any self-respecting suburbanite is his house, or, in the lingo of real estate salesmen, his "home." Jaffee and Clarke have gotten this couple's castle just right, neither too big nor too small, with an impeccable lawn kept crewcut short. —Jaffee/Clarke, "Signs of Status," *Mad*, #127

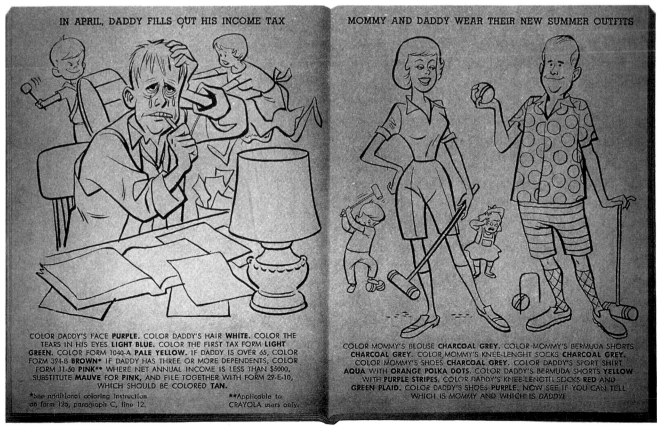

IN APRIL, DADDY FILLS OUT HIS INCOME TAX

MOMMY AND DADDY WEAR THEIR NEW SUMMER OUTFITS

COLOR DADDY'S FACE **PURPLE**. COLOR DADDY'S HAIR **WHITE**. COLOR THE TEARS IN HIS EYES **LIGHT BLUE**. COLOR THE FIRST TAX FORM **LIGHT GREEN**. COLOR FORM 1040-A **PALE YELLOW**. IF DADDY IS OVER 65, COLOR FORM 394-B **BROWN*** IF DADDY HAS THREE OR MORE DEPENDENTS, COLOR FORM 11-50 **PINK**** WHERE NET ANNUAL INCOME IS LESS THAN $5000, SUBSTITUTE **MAUVE** FOR **PINK**, AND FILE TOGETHER WITH FORM 29-E-10, WHICH SHOULD BE COLORED **TAN**.

*See additional coloring instruction on form 126, paragraph C, line 12.

**Applicable to CRAYOLA users only.

COLOR MOMMY'S BLOUSE **CHARCOAL GREY**. COLOR MOMMY'S BERMUDA SHORTS **CHARCOAL GREY**. COLOR MOMMY'S KNEE-LENGHT SOCKS **CHARCOAL GREY**. COLOR MOMMY'S SHOES **CHARCOAL GREY**. COLOR DADDY'S SPORT SHIRT **AQUA** WITH **ORANGE POLKA DOTS**. COLOR DADDY'S BERMUDA SHORTS **YELLOW** WITH **PURPLE STRIPES**. COLOR DADDY'S KNEE-LENGTH SOCKS **RED AND GREEN PLAID**. COLOR DADDY'S SHOES **PURPLE**. NOW SEE IF YOU CAN TELL WHICH IS MOMMY AND WHICH IS DADDY!

By the 1950s the people had more leisure time than ever before, and new activities to go with it. Filing income tax was one, croquet another. Sy Reit started a trend with this realistic coloring book, soon followed by the best-selling **John F. Kennedy coloring book** and others. — Reit/Clarke, "The Mad 'Down-to-Earth' Coloring Book," *Mad*, #58

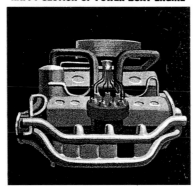

Here, Madman Dick DeBartolo, who for many years has written a regular column in a boating magazine, shares his expertise with readers. —DeBartolo/Clarke, "The Mad Guide to Power Boating," *Mad*, #89

Keeping up with the Joneses had been a crucial element of the suburban lifestyle. Dave Berg points up the importance of appearances and the use of the front lawn as a showcase. —Berg/Berg, "The Lighter Side of Home Owners," *Mad*, #87

With all the wise-guys at advertising agencies and pundits in academia telling them what to do, lots of middle-class people *were* feeling pretty stupid. Following all of the conflicting directives would have torn them apart. But the extreme claims made by both sides were like rocket fuel for the *Mad* satirists, mostly middle-class men who were facing the same pressures themselves. The Madmen not only satirized the mores of the times, but also offered alternatives that were as ridiculous as their inspirations.

For instance, in "How to be Smart," the writer asserts that maintaining an *image* of smartness is what's important, and gives simple tips to accomplish that. "Odd clothing, a strange textured jacket, cleverly fastened drop seat, create smart impressions" and "cultivate a withering sneer" are two hints offered in the article.

"How to be Smart" pokes fun at self-styled intellectuals, but in fact, the quest of the middle class throughout the 1950s and early 1960s was to be "normal," and *Mad* contained a plethora of articles providing antidotes to the images of perfect normality espoused in the mass media. A manifesto, of sorts, is to be found in humorist Jean Shepherd's 1957 article "The Night People vs. 'Creeping Meatballism.'" "The American brags about being a great individualist, when actually he's the world's *least* individual person," Shepherd wrote. "The guy who has been taken in by the 'Meatball' philosophy is the guy who really believes that contemporary people are slim, and clean-limbed, and they're so much fun to be with...because they drink Pepsi-Cola." But Shepherd also offered hope: "Once a guy starts *thinking*, once a guy starts *laughing* at the things he once thought were very real...he's making the transition from 'Day People' to 'Night People.' And once this happens, he can never go back!"

In *Mad*, as in real life, fathers sometimes came home drunk, mothers were lousy cooks, and sullen teenagers hung out on corners looking for trouble. By not only mentioning these unspeakable events, but chortling, guffawing, and belly-laughing at them, *Mad* helped alleviate the stresses of modern living.

Mad put things in perspective. In "Young Men's Spring Fashions for 1956," an illustra-

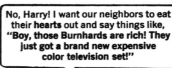

how to look smart

What a college education accomplishes in years, a well-chosen adornment can do in minutes . . .

if a loutish look is yours, the condition can be reversed by plain use of heavy black eyeglasses. (glass not necessary.)

with heavy black eyeglasses, loutish looking clod becomes intelligent looking clod.

you can rise above all the other scrub-women with a simple device.

a slender nickel-plate cigarette holder whipped out at the coffee-break will give you that smart look.

don't be ordinary, (a sure sign of feeble-mindedness). like for instance, don't wear ordinary cuff-links.

wear cuff-links made out of out of old coffee grinders.

if you have the ignoramus look of the rest of the pool-hall crowd, an intelligent gleam is yours for the taking.

grow a well-trimmed beard. it will get you out of that pool-hall class . . .it will get you out of that pool-hall. they'll never let you back in.

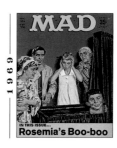

1969

IN THIS ISSUE...
Rosemia's Boo-boo

Kurtzman pokes fun at intellectuals and other wise-guys with these audacious tips for "dumb people." According to Kurtzman, " 'Fantastic' is a high-class smart word" and "fabulous" is also good. Then as now, "smartness is accented by strange objects in your home" like hard-to-understand paintings, arty coffee tables made from Zuni gravestones, and "plenty of books." — Kurtzman/Wood, "How to be Smart," *Mad*, #27

tion of a group of models in the typical conservative fashions of the day is stricken out with the editor's note "Who dresses this way? Big city models? Big shots? Who? What? Where? Let's face it! Let's show how people *really* dress!" The following spread features men in T-shirts and black leather jackets, tattoos and bowling shirts.

"Frightening as it may seem," Gary Belkin pointed out in 1961, "the rebellious adolescent of the present will someday become the mother-symbol and the father-image for the rebellious adolescent of the future." In "Tomorrow's Parents" he tells the story of Fred and Ginger Typical as they become parents in the 1970s. Fred and Ginger give little Tuesday Sandra and Kingston Trio everything they themselves were deprived of as children: "their own rooms, their own phones, monogrammed bongos, subscriptions to *Mad*, and a fifth-rate education."

Mad was there when the 1950s generation left behind the churches and temples of their childhoods and faced the challenge of choos-

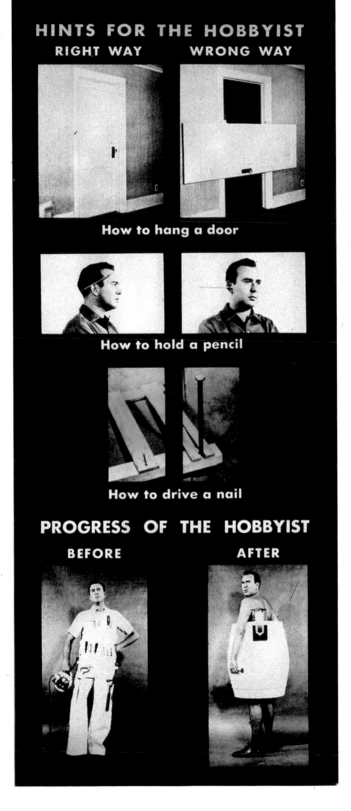

ing their own faiths, be it in a god or in the new, scientific ministers of the day, psychologists, psychoanalysts, and psychiatrists. "The *Mad* Psychoanalysis Primer" helped pave the way. "See the group therapy session," explained Stan Hart. "If you are in group therapy, it is important that you attend every session. Because if you are absent, guess who the others talk about!" Tom Koch offered "Psy-

Carl Reiner gives tips to the do-it-yourself kind of Dad in this excerpt from "A Saw Screams at Midnight."
— Carl Reiner/Reiner, "A Saw Screams at Midnight," *Mad*, #30

THERE IS A GREAT DEAL OF CONFUSION about what is progress. I think one of the fine examples of the difference between "Night People" and "Day People" can be observed when they both watch Betty Furness do a commercial for Westinghouse. You know the one where she says "Another new miracle has been wrought! Mankind once again progresses! The new Westinghouse refrigerator for 1957 opens from *both sides!*" Well, a "Day People" sitting there says,

"By George, we really *are* getting ahead!" And he feels great. He can see Mankind taking another significant step up that great pyramid of civilization. But a "Night People" watching this thing can't quite figure out what's the advantage of a refrigerator which opens from both sides. All he wants to know is, "Does it keep the stuff cold?"

He's not quite sure there's been any great mark of progress, while there's still wars and stuff going on!

PLASTI-SHAM CADILLAC TAIL FINS
($4.98 per pair)

BOGUS-BOARD ATTIC DORMER
($3.99 each)

PLEXI-FRAUD AIR CONDITIONER
($2.49 each — De Luxe Model $2.69)

Full-scale plastic replica — will fool sharpest eye. Assemble as directed and place so tail fins extend impressively several feet past edge of garage door. End embarrassment of having to drive beat-up old '49 car. Rich, successful people always have beat-up second cars!

Sturdy, weather resistant — will hook easily to any standard house roof, and gives home that "finished attic" look. Invite mother-in-law for lengthy stay to enhance effect. Serves dual purpose by impressing neighbors and irritating mother-in-law who ends up on old couch.

Easily assembled — made of laminated shirt cardboards. Useful for both city and suburban dwellings. Place one unit per window for best impression. Place two units per window for sensational impression! De-luxe model has built-in sponge which drips water realistically.

choanalysis by Mail" for those too timid or poor to visit with an analyst. The quiz included such encouraging yes-or-no questions as "Are you humiliated beyond all reason because the ink blot above looks like nothing more than an ink blot to you, while you think that we think that you should think it looks like sex?"

Meanwhile, all the babies born in the decade after World War II were growing up and becoming consumers in their own right. Suburbia became more settled and civilized, and the populace began to take for granted the cornucopia of goods that twenty years before would have been inconceivable. Against

this complacency, trouble loomed on the horizon. Once the pioneering was done, couples looked at one another and often realized that they didn't remember why they got married in the first place: the divorce rate soared. Suburbanites who had come to believe that their housing developments were harbingers of a classless society were discomfited to admit that they'd rather keep out African-Americans than risk living up to their purported beliefs. True to Belkin's prediction, the children of the 1950s generation rebelled heartily against their straitlaced parents, taking up first with Elvis Presley and other rock-and-rollers, then moving on to involvement in leftist politics and experimentation with psychedelic drugs.

During the 1960s and early 1970s *Mad* continued to plot these and other changes rocking American culture. Unlike most publications of the time, *Mad* made fun of both sides of the increasingly polarized society. "The *Mad* Blow-Your-Mind Drug Primer" by Sy Reit was neither an homage to spiritual transcendence through chemistry, nor the type of fear-mongering tract put out by "the establishment." Instead, it was a clear-eyed look at drug use by Americans. "Nice, middle-class parents do not approve of pot. No, no, no," explained Reit. "They are against young people using drugs. The whole idea of their son using drugs is very upsetting to them. It is so upsetting, they will have to double their usual dose of tranquilizers and sleeping pills today."

In the years since the 1960s society has grown more pluralistic, and upward mobility is no longer taken for granted as the middle-class growth levels out and poverty increases. Lifestyles considered radical twenty years ago have entered the mainstream as unmar-

THE MADMEN: *Dave Berg, Al Jaffee, Harry North, Sy Reit, George Woodbridge*

It may come as a surprise to many readers, but Dave Berg, creator of "The Lighter Side," was once the artist of the comics *Death Patrol* and *Combat Kelly*. His "Lighter Side" series got its start in the late 1950s when he played some home movies for Al Feldstein. Berg had filmed his family and neighbors acting out short sketches of everyday situations that he had written, and Feldstein suggested that he do the same thing in cartoon form. All along, Berg's work has been distinguished by an eye for detail, a knack for drawing unique people who somehow look just like the folks next door, and a wry sensitivity to the foibles of life in the United States today.

Al Jaffee's love of cartooning has unusual and deep roots. At the age of six he and his three brothers were taken by his mother on a visit to her homeland in Lithuania. The village in which they stayed was small and backward, like "going into the eighteenth century," Jaffee says. Every couple of months a "huge roll" of daily and Sunday funnies would arrive from his father in New York, as the visit extended to a stay of over six years. The comics, reread countless times, were Jaffee's link to English and to life in the twentieth century. On his return to the United States he entered high school with Kurtzman and Elder, and contributed to some of the earliest *Mad* magazines. He has become *Mad*'s resident specialist in elaborate gimmicks and gadgets, his best-known being the fold-in, which first appeared on the inside back cover of *Mad* in 1964.

Harry North is the only artist to have contributed original work to both the

For years, the nation's educators have been howling about the evils inherent in such big time college sports as football and basketball. They contend that there's too much professionalism, that not enough boys have a chance to participate, etc. But no one really lifted a finger to correct the situation until MAD's Athletic Council went to work—and he's come up with a brand new sport that promises to provide good, clean amateur fun for all. Here, then, are the rules for this great new national pastime of the future. Digest them carefully and be the last person in your neighborhood to play . . . as . . .

MAD MAGAZINE
introduces
43-MAN SQUAMISH

ARTIST: GEORGE WOODBRIDGE   WRITER: TOM KOCH

A Squamish team consists of 43 players: the left & right Inside Grouches, the left & right Outside Grouches, four Deep Brooders, four Shallow Brooders, five Wicket Men, three Offensive Niblings, four Quarter-Frummerts, two Half-Frummerts, one Full-Frummert, two Overblats, two Underblats, nine Back-Up Finks, two Leapers and a Dummy.

THE DAGMAR FRACTURE

One of the commonest of modern auto accidents being reported, this mishap usually succeeds in shattering the kneecaps, fibula, femur, and shins. Shorter people report having teeth knocked out, and also being stuck in the ear.

THE TAIL-FIN GORE

This mishap usually occurs when unwary pedestrians accidentally back up into parked cars. Also, an increasing number of ruptured stomachs are being reported, too, especially from areas where the lighting facilities are very poor.

THE POWER-WINDOW STRANGLE

An increasing number of mishaps caused by this latest innovation in labor-saving devices has been reported, especially among those younger auto passengers who hang out windows. Can be serious if not remedied in reasonable time.

12

This article by Tom Koch outlining the rules for 43-Man Squamish sat on Al Feldstein's desk for over two years until it was finally published—an event which led to the formation of Squamish teams on campuses across the United States and even in Canada. The game, played on a five-sided field known as a Flutney, has devilishly complicated rules. "The offensive team, upon receiving the Pritz, has five Snivels in which to advance to the enemy goal. If they do it on the ground, it's a Woomick and counts 17 points. If they hit it across with their Frullips, it's a Durmish, which counts 11 points. Only the offensive Niblings and Overblats are allowed to score in the first 6 Ogres." "It's a completely impossible game to play," says Koch. "I don't know how in the world they were ever able to get teams together." Twenty-five years later, students are still requesting reprint rights for the rules. — Koch/Woodbridge, "Mad Magazine Introduces 43-Man Squamish," *Mad, #95*

Extremes of auto design in the 1950s prompted Al Jaffee to point out potential hazards. Fins, wraparound windshields, and Dagmars (named after the Vanna White of the day) were all based on modern jet design. — Jaffee/Clarke, "Modern Auto Accidents," *Mad, #46*

Chapter 1.

See the Man.
He is a Hypocrite.
He looks just like you and me.
Doesn't it make you wonder
About you and me?
This Hypocrite hates injustice.
He worries about equal rights for Minority Groups.
Right now, he is worrying about his new neighbors.
His new neighbors are members of a Minority Group.
They have just moved in.
They are looking for equal rights.
Of course, that's fine with him . . . BUT
He worries that they may be uncomfortable in this neighborhood.
He worries that they may suffer from prejudice in this neighborhood.
He hopes they will be happy in this neighborhood.
But he will never know.
Because he won't *be* in this neighborhood.
He is moving out!

Suburbanites believed that they were pioneers of a new, classless way of life—until African-Americans and other minority groups took them at their word and asked for a share in it. Government lending practices helped keep minorities out, since, according to government calculations, by merely buying a house they made the neighborhood property values drop. — Hart/Clarke, "The Mad Hypocrite Primer," *Mad, #103*

Pampered pets are in for a treat with this absurdist mail-order scheme from the fiendish mind of Paul Peter Porges. — Porges/Porges, "A Gift Catalogue for Spoiled Rotten Pets," *Mad, #282*

F. Bone of the Month Club—Imagine the happy sight of your dog salivating uncontrollably as a mailman delivers a new assortment of gourmet bones to his doghouse every month! Here's what you get:
Jan: Imported Himalayan Yak Bones
Feb: Choice Selection of Bullfight Losers
Mar: Glorious Bouquet of Spring Bones
Apr: Hickory-smoked Ham Bones
May: Bones of All Nations
June & Summer Special Assortment of
July: Bone Jams and Jellies
Aug: Succulent Ostrich Leg Bone
Sept: Supreme Bone Meal à la Pekinese
Oct: Six-Year-Old Aged-in-Dirt
         Marrow Bone
Nov: Vermont Turkey Dinner Leftovers
Dec: Holiday Cheer Moose and Elk
         Bone Feast
#Woof-2020 Choice of any six months ..$150.00
#Woof-2121 Full Year ..$299.99
#Woof-4032 Ten-Year Order .. $1,999.99

U.S. *Mad* and the British *Mad*. Art director John Putnam discovered his work in René Goscinny's *Pilote* comic book, and recommended his work to *Mad*'s editors. Since the 1970s, North has contributed art for everything from movie parodies to social satires, which are especially memorable for North's skill with caricature.

Sy Reit has contributed to *Mad* some of the most memorable social satire it has contained. Writer of such articles as "America's Dream Car," "Spot That Plug!," "Antiques of the Future," and many others, Reit is an astute observer of the contortions of American culture at its best and worst. Reit is also known in other fields; he wrote the first "Casper the Friendly Ghost" cartoon, and contributed artwork to "Popeye" and "Betty Boop" animated shorts in the 1940s. He is an active writer, having written over eighty books for adults and children, many about historical subjects.

George Woodbridge had planned to be an illustrator when he was introduced by childhood friend Nick Meglin to many of the artists in the old EC crowd, and later began contributing artwork to *Mad*. Trained as a conventional illustrator, Woodbridge found himself becoming quite interested in the range of subject matter "beyond the limits, or even choices of straight story illustration." At the same time, Woodbridge developed into an historical and military costume authority and has illustrated a number of books on military history, some of them standards of the field.

ried couples live together, increasing numbers of workers are self-employed or work at home, and gay, lesbian, and women's liberation movements bring important issues out in the open and into the courts. The Madmen, ever-willing guides through these times of changing mores, have responded with a number of articles, both gentle and explicit. "The marks of status have changed," Tom Koch noted in a 1974 "*Mad* Guide to Status Symbols." "Suddenly the whole neat orderly garish system has been upset." Among other signifiers, Koch clues readers in that "Dressing poor when you're rich is a status symbol. Dressing poor because you really are poor isn't."

Throughout these years, *Mad* has celebrated the truly ordinary and mundane events that make up most of life. "Everyday Guts," a magazine parody by Larry Siegel, featured "He-Man Adventures of People Who Don't Get to Do Much More Than Hang Around," like "A Terrifying Trip into the Basement of Death!" and "Terror in the Wilds of Philadelphia: I stood by helpless, while my husband bent, folded, spindled and mutilated an I.B.M. card!" Stan Hart contributed a travel series of "Specialized Tours for You and Your Neurosis." And E. Nelson Bridwell immortalized the usual office characters in "New Movie Monsters of the Business World." These included "The Creatures with the Office Collections" ("with their palms outstretched, they kept coming...and coming...") and "The Goldbrick That Walked Like a Man" ("It hovered at the water cooler! It haunted the coffee breaks! It lurked in the restrooms!")

Petty annoyances have been given their due in a number of articles. "Consumer Revenge Bills," proposed by Al Jaffee, were created to retaliate for "crummy service or shoddy merchandise." He included forms for bills to inconsiderate doctors, auto repair garages, and bankers, with calculations for time wasted and aggravation received. Tom Koch made heroic spectacle of common tasks in "*Mad*'s Modern Olympic Games," which includes the 1500 meter taxi cab dash, the 8:14 commuter hop, step and jump, and the do-it-yourself decathlon, while Dick DeBartolo took on rewriting the 1040 income tax form. "If big businessmen can deduct big losses," DeBartolo reasoned, "it seems only fair that us little guys should be allowed to deduct our little losses." His "Minor Personal Losses Schedule" includes deductions for "Losses from Vending Machines," "Losses

We **moved** into this area because my husband **switched jobs**! And I just **love** it here!

The **house** is very comfortable! It's **beautifully situated** near schools and shopping! The **taxes** are low and the **neighbors** are nice! All in all, it's the **best** place we've ever lived!

Here comes my husband! It was his first day at the new plant, so I've been working like a **dog** to get everything cleaned and put away before he got home! **Now**, at last **we're** settled!

I HATE THE JOB!

In the heyday of the organization man, turnover in suburban housing developments had approached 33 percent a year, as families were uprooted and moved by the corporation. Such transfers usually followed a promotion, but sometimes backfired. — Berg/ Berg, "The Lighter Side of Moving," *Mad*, #99

Biggest problem facing the American people is: how does one watch TV and eat dinner at same time without having to look down to see what to scoop up next, thereby missing what happens on screen? Answer: shovel food direct from MAD's

NO-LOOK-DOWN TV TRAY

END

Mad anticipates "couch-potatoism" with this combination plate, bib, and trough. Note the zombielike look in the viewer's eyes. — Laikin/ Orlando, "Mad Eating Utensils," *Mad*, #35

from Pay Phones," and "Product Deficiency Losses." DeBartolo also came up with a scheme whereby those enrolled in frequent flyer programs would be awarded bonus points for such things as damaged bags, bad food, and flight delays. It's about time.

All along, *Mad*, like most of us, has retained no consistent ideology. Articles may chide readers for the foibles of bigotry, gullibility, lust, greed, and other deadly sins, but they just as often show sympathy for readers who have had to adapt to more change than any generation in history. Above all, *Mad*'s social satire reassures us that we are not alone.

THE POGO-STICK-ACTIVATED HIGH-SPEED BLENDER

HANDLE

LOCK-ON LID

FOOT REST

BLADES

CONTAINER

SPIRAL SHAFT MOUNTED ON BALL-BEARING BASE

COIL SPRING

SCHMUCK ON BOARD!
(A MAD CAR WINDOW SIGN)

A car window sign that tells it like it is. — Kadau/house, "Schmuck on Board," *Mad*, #267

Mad's ideas for accomplishing household tasks were much more fun than those to be gleaned from women's magazines or newspaper columns. This combination pogo stick and blender concocted by Paul Peter Porges appears as if it would actually work. — Porges/Clarke, "Some Mad Energy-Saving Devices," *Mad*, #181

QUESTION: WHICH IS THE PROPER MANNER FOR DISPOSING OF SCRAPS, (A) OR (B)?

ANSWER: SCRAPS THROWN ON FLOOR CAN CAUSE WAITER TO SLIP WHILE BRINGING DESSERT. PROPER MANNER, SHOWN IN (B) IS TO SHOVE SCRAPS INSIDE SHIRT. YOU MAY GET A GREASY ABDOMEN BUT YOU'LL SAVE ON NEXT MEAL.

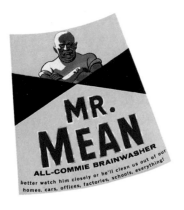

Ever-helpful, *Mad* provides solutions to those ticklish social problems. — ?/Wolverton, "Dining Etiquette Quiz," *Mad*, #29; Jacobs/Clarke, "The Mad Book of Etiquette and Good Manners," *Mad*, #130

Unimpressive Setting For A
High-Class Formal Dinner

Impressive Setting For A
High-Class Formal Dinner

CHOOSING A HOUSE OF WORSHIP

Suburban pioneers often used the move away from family and hometown as an opportunity to choose a new religion. Madman Larry Siegel and William H. Whyte, author of *The Organization Man*, concur: they often based their choice on social criteria rather than on differences in doctrine. — Siegel/Rickard, "Comparison Tests in Everyday Life," *Mad*, #206

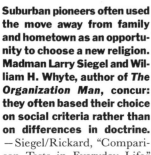

Well, Mrs. Farber . . . you've spent an hour in **both** of these **Houses of Worship!** And you don't know which is which, right? Now . . . which **one** do you prefer . . . ?

Oh, there's **no doubt** about it! I found the one under that cloth much more uplifting! I mean, I was real depressed when I walked in, but **that** one really raised my spirits! Yes, I definitely prefer that House of Worship!

Are you surprised to see which one you chose?

Wow! A Catholic Church! *Shriek . . . laugh . . . giggle!* I don't believe it! I mean, I've been using **Synagogues** all my life . . . but it's the **Catholic Church** for me from now on! Yes, sir, I never experienced a miracle like that before!

Would you care to tell us about the miracle, Mrs. Farber?

You bet! I mean . . . there I was with a lousy card with nothing across, nothing diagonal, and only two numbers down! And then, all of a sudden—WHAM! Three numbers down in a row, and **BINGO!** I tell you, that was some miracle!

IS THIS THE END OF THE LINE?

TICKETS

No, it's the **beginning!** We're all **facing backwards!**

No, it's the end of a freight train, and **I'm** the **caboose!**

No, it's a group of **casual strollers,** who, by some **fantastic coincidence,** have come to stand one behind the other at this **one spot!**

18

For years Al Jaffee has given vent to his, and our, crankier moments in his ongoing series "Snappy Answers to Stupid Questions." Jaffee always included a blank balloon so that readers could write in their own snappy answers, probably articulated around midnight the night after the incident. —Jaffee/Jaffee, "Mad's Snappy Answers to Stupid Questions," *Mad*, #98

A helpful tip from *Mad*'s handbook on how to fish. —Jaffee/Drucker, "Fishing," *Mad*, #57

From the 1950s to the 1970s, a newly fashionable alternative to religion was psychotherapy. *Mad* helped explain the unfamiliar discipline in this "Psychoanalysis Primer." —Hart/Coker, "The Mad Psychoanalysis Primer," *Mad*, #112

Lesson 6.

The Psychiatric Consultation

This Patient is emotionally disturbed.
He has a serious Sex Problem.
He tells the Psychiatrist everything—
All of his strange sex fantasies and wild dreams.
The Psychiatrist keeps all of these admissions
In strict confidence.
He repeats them to no one.
Except, perhaps, to another Psychiatrist
During a consultation.
And during this consultation, both Psychiatrists
Giggle a lot.

RIGHT WAY TO MOUNT A FISH

WRONG WAY TO MOUNT A FISH

YUPPIE EATING HABITS

AWARD YOURSELF THE FULL TEN POINTS if you maintain that everything one eats should first be pulverized in a Cuisinart —including steak, grape nuts and peach cobbler a la mode.
DEDUCT FIVE POINTS if you actually use your microwave oven and metric kitchen scale, instead of eating out every night with other Yuppies who also have fully equipped kitchens at home.
DEDUCT EIGHT POINTS if you serve all the "in" foods, but buy domestic brands instead of imported so you'll have enough money left to pay your rent.

Eating habits reached new extremes in the 1980s as the rich got richer and the poor learned to call ketchup a vegetable. — Koch/Coker, "How Do You Rate as a Yuppie?," *Mad*, #269

DADDY-O KNOWS BEST DEPT.

Much has been written about the teenager of today—but in every article we've seen, one important fact has been overlooked or ignored: namely, that the teenager of today is the parent of tomorrow! Yes, frightening as it may seem, we cannot escape the fact that the rebellious adolescent of the present will someday become the mother-symbol and father-image for the rebellious adolescent of the future. So with this horrible thought in mind, MAD presents an article which sneaks a peek into the future for a glimpse of what it will be like when today's teenagers become . . .

TOMORROW'S PARENTS

ARTIST: WALLACE WOOD   WRITER: GARY BELKIN

In 1961 Gary Belkin predicted what home life would be like in the future in "Tomorrow's Parents." We witness Fred and Ginger Typical's struggle to imbue their kids with their own hip values. To Fred and Ginger's dismay, the kids grow more and more conservative. Finally, the killing blow: the kids have won full scholarships to universities. "Like, don't cry baby!" consoles Fred. "Let's face Truthsville! Our son is a square!" "He's not my son!" Ginger wails. "My son wouldn't want to be a doctor! Like, I HAVE NO SON!"—Gary Belkin/Wood, "Tomorrow's Parents," *Mad*, #62

41
wood.

PAPER SHREDDER/PASTA MAKER

In one easy step this handy, handsome appliance allows you to shred confidential documents *and* add bulk to your family's diet! The stainless steel cutting edges never need sharpening and each unit includes settings for making rigatoni, ravioli and fettucine, as well as destroying photos, blueprints and other top secret memoranda.

COMPUTER TERMINAL/MAKEUP MIRROR

Finally, a way to apply your morning makeup *and* word process at the same time! Each of these powerful 20 megabyte PCs is connected to a central mainframe and comes with a highly reflective monitor screen with adjustable makeup lights. Peripherals include the disk drive/nail polish dryer and the cosmetic tray/letter quality printer.

DIVORCE SURVIVAL MERIT BADGE

REPLACES: GENEOLOGY MERIT BADGE

1. Do not tell your father which one of your mother's "friends" is sleeping over, even if it is one of *his* friends.
2. Agree with your father that the silly, young lady he is dating is "real swell, and a lot of fun."
3. Convince your *father* that you look forward to visitation day; convince your mother you look forward to coming home when visitation day is over.

Al Jaffee comes up with gizmos for changing life-styles. A glimpse of the future?—J. Rios/Jaffee, "Dual-Purpose Office Supplies for Working Mothers," *Mad*, #277

Increasing divorce rates inspired this "Modern Merit Badge," which more realistically recognizes the challenges that today's children face. — Hart/Woodbridge, "Modern Merit Badges," *Mad*, #248

Kids' activities have become all-important to parents who are determined to give them what they never had, as pointed out in Dave Berg's "The Lighter Side of Little League." — Berg/Berg, "The Lighter Side of Little League," *Mad*, #88

Son, I've waited **years** for this day! Now you are old enough to join that **great American Institution—LITTLE LEAGUE!** Now you can officially play that **great American game—BASEBALL!**

Your teammates will be **other All-American boys!** You'll be participating in a **clean healthy sport**—helping to make America a **stronger, more physically-fit nation.**

But, Daddy—I **don't** like to play Baseball!

The kid's a **COMMUNIST!!**

ALFRED E. NEUMAN ANSWERS YOUR QUESTIONS

In his "Shadow Knows" series, Sergio Aragonés contrasts appearances with true feelings, often to hilarious effect. It's not hard to tell here who the doting parents are.
—Aragonés/Aragonés, "The Shadow Knows," *Mad*, #131

The upheavals in the 1960s led to shifting balances of power and some awkward and unprecedented social situations. Here, the Black Power advocate is just what he seems to be, but the white man's shadow reveals his uneasiness. —Aragonés/ Aragonés, "The Shadow Knows," *Mad*, #131

The first Don Martin cartoon to appear in *Mad*, before the name Alfred E. Neuman was taken by the gap-toothed boy. Helpful readers wrote in to correct the instructions for tying the noose. —Martin/ Martin, "Alfred E. Neuman Answers Your Questions," *Mad*, #29

PROBLEM:

Two weeks ago, I was laid off my job . . .

I came home to find my wife in the arms of another man . . .

As I stumbled from the house, I saw my children being carried away by some fiend . . .

On the way to summon the police, I was beaten and robbed . . .

I am cold, hungry and thoroughly depressed. I sometimes say to myself, "If I knew how to tie a hangman's knot, I would end it all!" What should I do?—Anxious

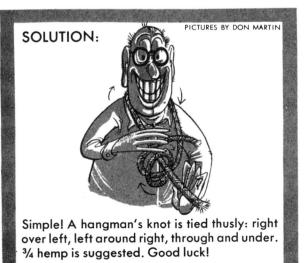

PICTURES BY DON MARTIN

SOLUTION:

Simple! A hangman's knot is tied thusly: right over left, left around right, through and under. ¾ hemp is suggested. Good luck!

you read it in **MAD**   Why not revive "Flat Foot Floogie"?   23

Hey, there goes Keen again. He's wearing a new outfit, too! And it comes complete with matching luggage and a one way ticket to Canada. Looks like Keen is making a *last-ditch effort* to keep from becoming a "G.I. Joey"!

Chapter 6
THE PRIEST

This is a Catholic Priest.
His church believes in many things.
It believes in the Holy Trinity.
It believes in the Pope's infallibility.
It believes in miracles.
The Priest helps Catholics in time of need.
He helps them solve business problems,
Even though he has never been in business.
He helps them solve marriage problems,
Even though he has never been married.
He helps them solve sexual problems,
Even though he has never had sex.
Now you know why the Catholic Church
Believes in miracles!

Chapter 3
JUDAISM

Judaism is the oldest of the three religions.
It is broken down into three major groups:
The first group observes ancient traditions to the letter.
These are known as Orthodox Jews.
The second group believes in combining ancient traditions
With modern conditions.
These are known as Conservative Jews.
The third group hardly observes any traditions at all.
These are known as Reform Jews.
To the other two groups,
Reform Jews have another name.
They are known as "Christians"!

Funny labels for funny products. —House/Clarke, "More trash from *Mad*." #2

In 1969, writer Harold Morrison took a "Mad Look at Realistic Dolls." Morrison pointed out that Keen's girlfriend "Boobie" came "equipped with everything that a young girl of today might wish for: personality, good looks, and pure femininity. Too bad!" he admonished. "She'll have to *change* all that if she expects to be accepted today!" — Harold Morrison/ Schild, "A Mad Look at Realistic Dolls," *Mad*, #127

***Mad*'s idea of Sunday school was depicted in its interdenominational "Religion in America Primer."** —Siegel/ Coker, "Mad's 'Religion in America' Primer," *Mad*, #153

Mad *ESP*

An occupational hazard of social satirists is the possibility that their wilder fantasies may come to pass. In fact, a number of *Mad* articles published over the years have been remarkably prescient. Dave Berg anticipated post-modern architecture by a good ten years in two articles from the 1950s. "Functional Architecture" (from the Edifice Complex Department) proposed that buildings should "look like what they are" and was illustrated with libraries built of books, banks shaped like piggies, and frozen food factories shaped like igloos. It wasn't until the 1960s that leading postmodern theoretician and architect Robert Venturi suggested the same thing in his famous essay about a building in Long Island called the Montauk Duck. The "Highrise of Homes," an unbuilt 1980 project by James Wines and his architectural firm SITE, is virtually identical to Berg's 1958 solution to the overgrowth of suburbia.

Al Jaffee, *Mad*'s resident gadgeteer, probably holds the record for the number of contraptions he facetiously proposed that have actually gone into commercial production. Word processors, locking clothing display racks, inebriation-sensitive cars, telephone autodialers, garbage compactors (Jaffee's gift-wrapped it), television commercial-zappers, and talking toilets are just a few of his "inventions" that later appeared on the market. In 1966, Jaffee proposed selling advertising space on postage stamps as a solution to the annual U.S. Post Office deficit—six years later Pritchard Advertising Inc. suggested the same thing. In 1980 the idea was again revived when Barry Goldwater, Jr. introduced his Free Enterprise Postage Stamp Act. So far, the post office has resisted temptation.

Standard Post Office Dept. stamps could become highly desirable advertising spaces for certain companies because of their clever "message tie-in" value:

"IDIOT-PROOF" TYPEWRITERS

—Berg/Berg, "Functional Architecture," *Mad*, #49

—Jaffee/Jaffee, "Postage Stamp Advertising," *Mad*, #104

—Jaffee/Jaffee, "Idiot-Proof Products," *Mad*, #109

—Berg/Berg, "The Suburbs Are on Their Way Out," *Mad*, #39

Ordinary typewriters are only as good as the people who use them. Above, we see a typical, poorly-typed letter. Note mistakes in spelling, phrasing, syntax, etc.

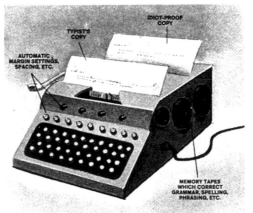

The Idiot-Proof Typewriter will include memory tapes that store millions of words, phrases and correct grammatical expressions. As writer types, two letters will be produced simultaneously: the usual stupid one and instantly-corrected version.

Recipient of letter will find it easy to understand. Of course, a few people will be nostalgic for the old personal style, but isn't perfection better than sentiment?

To his chagrin, Sy Reit has also scored a number of hits. In the 1959 article "A Best Seller Hits the Commercial Trail," Reit took the idea of licensing, then in its infancy, to extremes. In Reit's fantasy, *Doctor Zhivago*, already a book and movie, is spun off in a dizzying number of products: record albums, radio serials, cocktail napkins, bubble gum cards, hats, and jigsaw puzzles. Such a trail of consumables wouldn't raise an eyebrow in these days of Batman kerchiefs and *The Care Bears* TV shows. In 1968 Reit predicted air pollution problems from aerosol cans, which he dubbed "sprog." Other future pollutants he foresaw—"spritz" (from soda cans), "smaft" (from burning draft cards), and "shpiel" (hot air emitted by politicians)—have not posed so dire a threat. In 1972, when James R. Schlesinger, chairman of the Atomic Energy Commission, proposed blasting nuclear waste into outer space, several longtime *Mad* readers thought they had heard the idea before. True enough—in 1960 Reit had pointed out that undeployed ICBMs could be used to rid the earth of accumulated garbage. The article also contained an admonishment: "*Mad* urges its readers not to write their congressmen about this plan.... We're already shooting enough garbage into space as it is!"

Mad has predicted *Time* magazine's "Man of the Year" (Pac Man, 1982), advertising on spaceships, and even "new car scent" in a can; with the thousands of satirical articles published in *Mad* over the last forty-odd years, perhaps it's not surprising that some have come true. But we can count ourselves lucky that other fantasies from the pages of *Mad*, such as "basebrawl" (the bat becomes an offensive weapon), corporate summer camps for kids, and "Cabbage Patch" ashtrays, have not come to pass. At least, not yet.

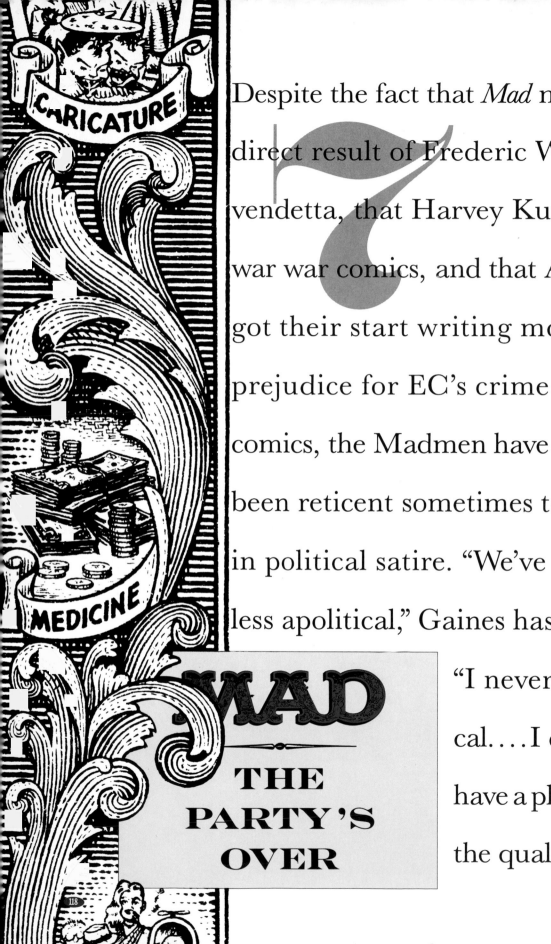

MAD
THE PARTY'S OVER

Despite the fact that *Mad* magazine was born as an indirect result of Frederic Wertham's anti–comic book vendetta, that Harvey Kurtzman's forte was his anti-war war comics, and that Al Feldstein and Bill Gaines got their start writing morality tales of racism and prejudice for EC's crime comics, the Madmen have

been reticent sometimes to admit *Mad*'s involvement in political satire. "We've tried to keep *Mad* more or less apolitical," Gaines has claimed. Kurtzman adds: "I never regarded myself as political....I don't think the fact that you have a platform necessarily gives you the qualification to make a speech."

These statements to the contrary, *Mad* had made the leap into political satire in a big, and potentially dangerous, way, with a 1954 attack on none other than feared and powerful demagogue Joseph R. McCarthy. "What's My Shine!" was a hybrid of the long-running television guessing game and the so-called

Army-McCarthy hearings, the culmination of Senator McCarthy's witch-hunt for Communist infiltration of United States institutions. The daily, live broadcasts of the hearings had riveted the nation that summer, preempting the usual game shows and soap operas.

"McCarthy was a special case," Kurtzman has pointed out. "He was so obvious. And so evil. It was like doing a satire on Hitler." McCarthy's television exposure that summer helped finally do him in; a formal censure and condemnation of his conduct by Senate resolution followed the hearings. EC had gotten away with their first foray into political satire.

"What's My Shine" really *was* a special case for Kurtzman, and although many of his articles had been implicitly satirical of various institutions, it stands alone as a political parody in his tenure as editor of *Mad*.

By contrast, Al Feldstein felt no such compunctions, and within a few years of his taking over *Mad*, political satire by a variety of writers began to appear regularly in the magazine. The dust of the McCarthy era had settled, and the coast seemed clear for political commentary of a humorous kind. Unfortunately, it was not.

One day in 1961 a letter from an Oklahoma City woman was delivered to Bill Gaines's desk. The woman complained that *Mad* had disappeared from local outlets, the result, she believed, of a campaign by Clyde J. Watts, a lawyer and retired brigadier general. After retiring from the army, Watts had become a crusader, having developed, he proclaimed, "an almost unbelievable apprehension about the Communist threat," against which he advised good Americans to adopt a "strategy for survival." In his speeches, Watts was reported to have called *Mad* "the most insidious Communist propaganda in the United States today." This statement pressured drugstores and newsstands mired in a

"Passionate Gun Love" was Larry Siegel's idea of a gun magazine that made no pretense about the obvious—guns are made for killing. As a result, *Mad* caught flak from National Rifle Association members who felt the takeoff unfairly portrayed gunowners as irresponsible maniacs. —Siegel/Davis, "Passionate Gun Love," *Mad*, #131

In the summer of 1954 Americans were riveted to their newly acquired television sets by the spectacle of Senator Joseph R. McCarthy participating in Senate subcommittee hearings investigating both McCarthy's charges that Communists had infiltrated the United States Army and the Army's countercharges against McCarthy. Harvey Kurtzman and Jack Davis melded the hearings with *What's My Line*, one of the game shows preempted by the live coverage. Special counsel Ray Jenkens became Kurtzman's moderator, Jay Renkins, and panelists were committee members, with the addition of Lana Cheesecake, obligatory sexpot. The actual hearings were marked by McCarthy's endless interruptions of "points of order," Roy Cohn's constant whispering in McCarthy's ear, and of the appearance of the infamous doctored photograph, a picture produced by McCarthy to implicate army secretary Robert T. Stevens. The photo purported to show Stevens and David Schine alone and on friendly terms; one day later a committee member produced proof that McCarthy's picture was originally a group photo that had been cropped. In this parody, the photo is actually a picture of Stevens painting his house; a turkey perches on a fence behind his head.
—Kurtzman/Davis, "What's My Shine!," *Mad*, #17

cold war mentality to remove such unpatriotic material from their racks, as well as inspiring the Oklahoma City Mothers United for Decency to include *Mad* prominently in their touring "Smutmobile," a 28-foot-long trailer truck that identified and warned against the dangers of pornography and subversive literature.

Gaines checked with his distributor and found that, sure enough, sales were dropping throughout Oklahoma, and that stacks of *Mad* were being returned to distributors unopened—a sign that the magazines weren't even being displayed. Gaines uneasily remembered the last time he faced the specter of bundled, returned comic books, during the Wertham crusade, and realized that if he didn't act quickly and decisively, the new scare might spread to other states.

With *Mad*'s lawyer, Martin Scheiman,

Gaines decided to hit back with a $1.5 million suit against Watts for libel and slander. Watts responded with a $250,000 counteraction, also charging libel. Scheiman, Gaines, and

THE MADMEN: *Max Brandel, Antonio Prohías, Lou Silverstone*

Max Brandel's biting political commentary originated in his experiences in wartime Eastern Europe. A native of Austria, he had just begun a career as a cartoonist in Krakow when war broke out; during the Russian occupation of Poland he and his wife were captured by the Germans. He was imprisoned in concentration camps, where he escaped death by amusing the Russians and the Gestapo with his caricatures of them. In 1948, with ten dollars between Brandel and his wife, they emigrated to the United States. Brandel contributed cartoons and word puzzles to a number of newspapers and magazines, including *Newsweek*, the *Nation*, and the *Herald-Tribune*. His work for *Mad* was unusually sharp and hard-hitting. "He had a European sense of humor that sometimes didn't apply to *Mad*'s needs," Nick Meglin explains. "But he made up for that with an amazing eye and memory for graphic images. He saw links between images that few have the talent to see."

Antonio Prohías, creator of one of *Mad*'s best-known regular features, "Spy vs. Spy," was one of the most important political cartoonists in his native Cuba. By the age of twenty-five he had won Cuba's top award for

editorial cartoonists, and was soon offered a position at Cuba's most important newspaper, *El Mundo*. When the paper was taken over by the government in 1960, his anti-Communist cartoons were derided as a lunatic's vision. Although the same year Prohías won an award from the American Society of Journalists, the international recognition was not enough—his cartoons were too well known, and had angered and threatened the Cuban establishment all the way to the top. "Fidel kept sending word to me through different people to stop," he explained. "And I started getting fired from every publication." He left Cuba and came to New York City to start over, and was drawn to *Mad* by its name. **(continued on p. 126)**

Feldstein traveled to Oklahoma City for a pretrial hearing, which turned out to be an inquisition of Gaines, rather than an investigation of his charges against Watts. Gaines was grilled by the defense on his understanding and involvement in Communism, and was questioned by Watts himself on an article that seemed to have particularly irked him, Paul Laikin's "Cool School" version of the Gettysburg Address.

Both sides having had a chance to size each other up, the *Mad* group returned to New York City to prepare their case. Associate editor and resident archivist Jerry DeFuccio put together a collection of supportive letters from various parents, children's counselors, and educators. Meanwhile, Scheiman tried to get the judge assigned to the case, Stephen S. Chandler, to disqualify himself, since he was a close personal friend of Watts. Chandler refused, promising ominously that the case would receive "Oklahoma justice."

By September 24, 1962, the date of the trial, the event was starting to look more like an Old West shoot-out than an exercise by the modern justice system. A local barber had threatened Scheiman, and Watts was declining even to shake hands with him. The *Oklahoma City Times* predicted a "bitter showdown between opposing self-styled American patriots," and promised "airings of such emotion-packed subjects as McCarthyism, international Communism, the John Birch Society, Communist fellow-travelers, freedom of speech and freedom of the press." The *Times* went on to describe *Mad* as a magazine of "grotesque, malformed cartoon characters [which] satirizes such time-honored American institutions as the White House and the home."

Part of *Mad*'s strategy was to try to keep the proceedings light, while establishing *Mad*'s place in a continuum of American satire. "I didn't go quite so far in the army as General Watts did," Gaines told the press, jovially. "But if they're going to call him general at the trial, I think I'll insist on them calling me private first class."

"It will be a knockdown, drag-out fight," insisted Watts, in no mood to be tweaked by the self-described "nutty nonconformists" who had come to town to make trouble for him. "They offered to dismiss it if I apologized, but

I'm going through with the trial…even if they take every dime I have."

The morning of the trial, tensions on both sides ran high. Gaines perceived a lynch mentality in the judge and onlookers, and noticed that Watts looked just as nervous as Gaines himself felt. The *Mad* group knew that they would eventually win, at least on appeal, but what Gaines really wanted was an equitable settlement, then and there. A pretrial conference in Judge Chandler's chambers

"After Mad, *drugs were nothing."* PATTI SMITH   *New York Times Magazine*

ended in a stalemate and both sides seated themselves in the courtroom.

Suddenly Gaines stood up, walked over to Watts's table, and said in a low voice, "Let's not let the lawyers screw this up." He went on to reiterate that all he wanted was a statement that Watts did not believe that *Mad* was Communist, and that he never meant to imply

such a thing. Gaines's timing was on the money; Watts immediately agreed. By 1:30 that afternoon, Watts was reading a statement to the court that went in part: "I publicly state I never referred to the magazine as a Communist-inspired and motivated publication or to its editors as Communists, Communist sympathizers or Communist dupes. If any person or persons so construed my remarks, they were mistaken." The case was closed, each side paid its own legal fees, and once again, Oklahoma was safe for Mom, apple pie, and *Mad*.

Having won a battle, *Mad* will probably never win the war with the conservative and reactionary elements of America. Enemies *Mad* has earned over the years include Wil-

John F. Kennedy was the first president to be a target of the full *Mad* treatment by way of Gilbert and Sullivan. After explaining to little Caroline how he became president, Kennedy plays football with his family, is visited by Eisenhower ("I am the very model of a former U.S. President…"), meets with Nelson Rockefeller, Richard Nixon, and Barry Goldwater ("Three little candidates are we…"), and throws a White House party attended by the Rat Pack and assorted hangers-on. Out of respect for his memory, *Mad* never reprinted this parody in any anthology.
—Siegel/Drucker, "A Day with J-F-K," *Mad*, #67

The Japanese Officer is kind, but misunderstood. He is neat and civilized, and talks impeccable English. His teeth are capped and straight. He looks like Keye Luke.

The Japanese Officer is sadistic and brutal. He jabbers and screams in Pidgin English. He has ugly buck teeth. He is short, fat and bowlegged, and looks like a monkey.

Here, a short course on how international politics influences popular culture. George Woodbridge, an expert on military dress, adds an essential note of realism in his renderings of Japanese uniforms. — Siegel/Woodbridge, "The Two Faces of World War II," *Mad,* #59

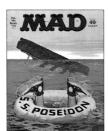

Practically everybody has seen "West Side Story"—which is about a couple of tough gangs on New York's West Side. Well, we think the producers of this show really missed the boat. Like, they went to the wrong side. If they thought the gangs on the West Side were tough, they should have taken a look at those two rival gangs on the East Side — mainly those two rival gangs at the U.N.! Because if they had, they might have come up with a musical called:

EAST SIDE STORY

ARTIST: MORT DRUCKER
WRITER: FRANK JACOBS

When you're a Red
You will sign a peace pact
Which will fool everyone
Till your troops have attacked!

When you're a Red
And you land an assault,
Always shout to the world
It's the other side's fault!

You wear down the West
With every vote you veto!
You're always a pest!
You're like a bad mosquito!
You're not like Tito!

When you're a Red
You're a world racket
Pople get in your way
People soon disappea

Published in 1963 at the height of the Cold War, "East Side Story" was an early, and strikingly successful, experiment, combining drawing with photographic backdrops. Frank Jacobs and Mort Drucker have fully transformed Nikita Khrushchev and other Eastern bloc leaders into a street gang. They look even more hilarious dancing in production numbers than the hoods did in *West Side Story*. Meanwhile, Kennedy's advisers sing a different tune: "Nikita! We've just met a Red named Nikita! He said we ought to know, the world will soon be So-viet!" As in the movie, an inevitable showdown takes place. In *Mad*'s version, the Reds revolt against Khrushchev, and his scolding wife shows up to escort him back to the USSR. How could the Oklahoma Mothers United for Decency object to that?—Jacobs/ Drucker, "East Side Story," *Mad*, #78

1974

"Spy vs. Spy" has, by now, become part of the fabric of American culture. The image and name of the cartoon are often used to invoke any endless, futile conflict. Six originals are in the collection of the Archives of American Art in Washington, D.C.

By contrast, Lou Silverstone cultivated his skeptical outlook from the United States. He studied English literature and fine arts in college, but soon after graduating began developing a career in humor writing. For *Mad* he's written a wide range of satire and parody about movies, television, and politics. Silverstone has also written material for Jackie Mason, Will Jordan, and other Catskill comedians; comic strips, including "Li'l Abner" with Al Capp; and material for radio and television.

Chapter Ten

See the Phony Liberal.
He owns a bank.
He is an "Equal Opportunity Employer".
See the Teller in the bank?
He is a Negro.
He has been with the bank for eleven years.
See the Vice-President of the bank?
He is a White Man.
He has been with the bank for two years.
Some "Equal Opportunity Employers"
Give members of Racial Minorities
A chance to start at the bottom
And stay there.

17

2 PM

9 PM

A tradition of political cartooning shows in this depiction of goings-on at the United Nations from "Diplomatic Immunity" by Antonio Prohías. As one of the leading political cartoonists in Cuba, Prohías was known for his intense, hard-hitting style. — Prohías/Prohías, "Diplomatic Immunity," *Mad Stew*

Without taking sides, "The *Mad* Primer of Bigots, Extremists and Other Loose Ends" tutored readers about the Ku Klux Klan, the New Left, black militants, American Nazis, and other groups capturing the headlines in 1969. — Jacobs with Hart/Davis, "The Mad Primer of Bigots, Extremists and Other Loose Ends," *Mad*, #129

liam F. Buckley, Jr., the Ku Klux Klan, and Major General Edwin A. Walker. Walker was a once-formidable man dismissed from the army in 1961 for his efforts to enlist his troops in the arch-conservative John Birch Society. That same year *Newsweek* magazine reported that Walker's personal dislikes included Eleanor Roosevelt, Edward R. Murrow, Harvard University, and *Mad*. (Coincidentally, Clyde Watts later defended him against charges that he abetted anti-Negro rioting at the University of Mississippi.)

Buckley, a leading conservative known for such statements as "McCarthyism...is a movement around which men of good will and stern morality can close ranks," must

Chapter One

See the Super Patriot.
Hear him preach how he loves his country.
Hear him preach how he hates "Liberals"...
And "Moderates"... and "Intellectuals"...
And "Activists"... and "Pacifists"...
And "Minority Groups"... and "Aliens"...
And "Unions"... and "Teenagers"...
And the "Very Rich"... and the "Very Poor"...
And "People With Foreign-Sounding Names".
Now you know what a Super Patriot is.
He's someone who loves his country
While hating 93% of the people who live in it.

MAD's Great Moments In Politics

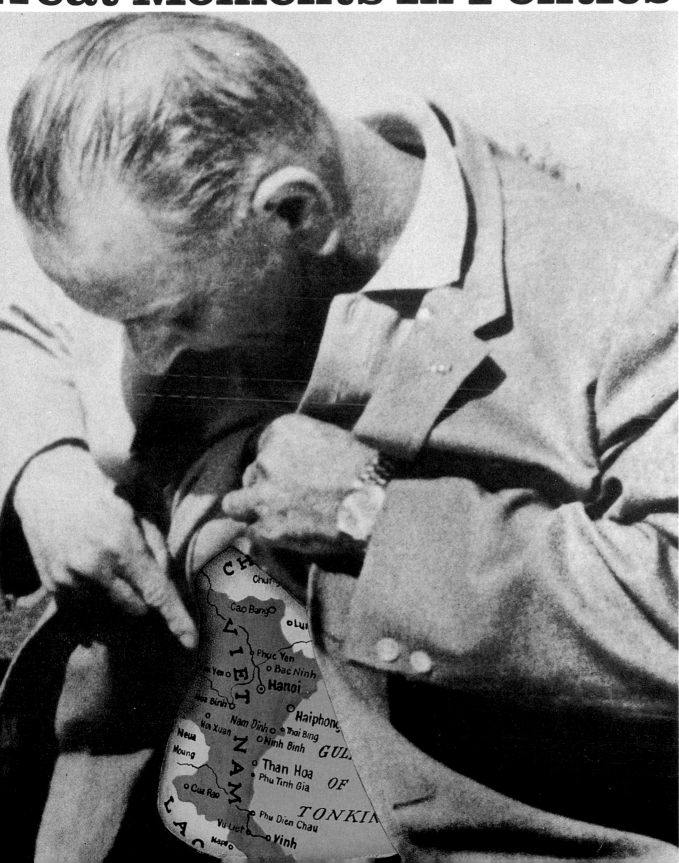

LBJ reveals a sore spot in this 1967 Max Brandel collage. The unretouched photo, widely circulated, was of Johnson displaying a surgical scar. —Brandel/Brandel, "Mad's Great Moments in Politics," *Mad*, #116

The Watergate years remembered in Frank Jacobs's idea of appropriate commemorative stamps. —Jacobs/Clarke, "U.S. Commemorative Stamps that We'll Never Get to See," *Mad*, #179

This harshly ironic assemblage, created by Max Brandel in 1967 when internal tensions threatened to tear the United States apart, was one of the most extreme works of political satire ever published in *Mad*. Brandel, a German concentration camp survivor and no stranger to political upheaval, chose images he found frighteningly similar to those of Nazi Germany thirty years before. — Brandel/Brandel, "The Preamble Revisited," *Mad*, #109

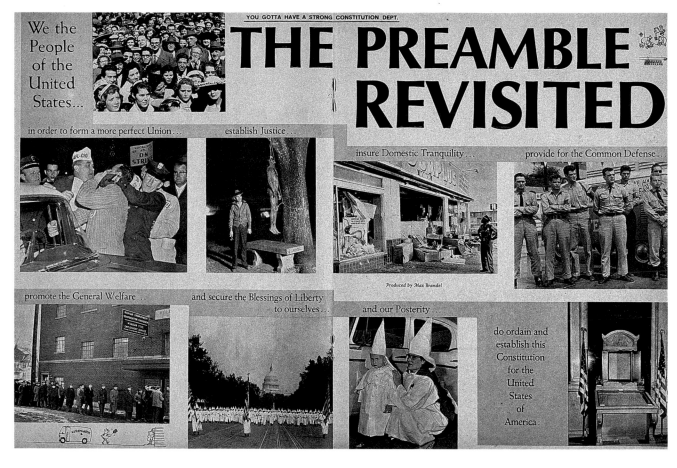

We the People of the United States...

THE PREAMBLE REVISITED

in order to form a more perfect Union...   establish Justice...

insure Domestic Tranquility...   provide for the Common Defense...

Produced by Max Brandel

promote the General Welfare...   and secure the Blessings of Liberty to ourselves...   and our Posterity...

do ordain and establish this Constitution for the United States of America.

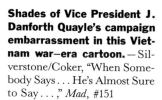

Shades of Vice President J. Danforth Quayle's campaign embarrassment in this Vietnam war–era cartoon. — Silverstone/Coker, "When Somebody Says... He's Almost Sure to Say...," *Mad*, #151

1975

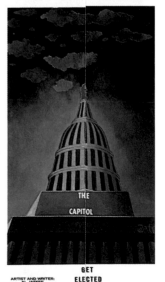

have felt the need to do the same against *Mad* on the occasion of *Mad*'s twenty-fifth anniversary in 1977. In *The National Review*, Buckley sniped at a lengthy article about *Mad* published in the *New York Times Magazine*, which pointed out that many credited the magazine

with shaping a generation of kids that opposed a war. "Wait till their fiftieth anniversary," Buckley threatened, leaving readers to wonder what he might have in store for the celebration.

WHEN JOHNNY COMES MARCHING HOME AGAIN
hurrah, hurrah!

The term "posttraumatic stress syndrome" had not yet been coined when this dramatic miniposter was published in 1971. One look into this veteran's eyes tells of the terrible toll of an unpopular war on those who were called to serve. —Brandel/J. Thurston, "When Johnny Comes Marching Home Again," *Mad*, #149

Bill Wilkinson, Grand Dragon of the Ku Klux Klan, had taken offense at a *Mad* comparison of a fraternity toga party with the Klan, where one student pointed out that both provide a chance "to put on sheets and go berserk!" In a 1979 letter to *Mad*, Wilkinson charged that "You and the jew-communist run MAD Magazine are obviously trying to do away with the great Red, White and Blue and promote radicalism in this country's youth.... The Klan has never done any wrongdoing in their robes as you suggest." The editors reproduced the letter, including the ornate Klan letterhead, on the *Mad* letters page without comment.

While *Mad*'s political satire may tend to favor a liberal point of view, the main targets are extremists of any stripe. "East Side Story," a parody of *West Side Story* casting the Eastern bloc and the Western bloc as opposing street gangs, was a hymn to life in a democracy, ending when Khrushchev is ignominiously dragged back to the Soviet Union by his stout and ugly wife. "A *Mad* Guide to Russia," written by Phil Hahn in 1962, was similarly hard on Soviet rule, pointing out, for instance, that "in America, 'Time for a Change' means the citizens are going to get rid of the current government and replace it with a new one. In Russia, it means the government is going to get rid of the citizens and replace them with new ones. If this sounds unbelievable, just remember what happened in Hungary in 1957." The article provoked quite a bit of adult reader mail, some congratulatory, others disappointed. "Your article on Russia showed what a farce Communism is," commented one reader. It "ran like a chapter from the John Birch Society's *Bluebook*," declared another.

.. as "Dr. Jekyll And Mr. Hyde" ...

I condemn as **immoral** any **Goverment** that denies a Union its **RIGHT** to **STRIKE!**

Of course, that **DOESN'T** apply to our **OWN Government**... and The Air Traffic Controllers Union!!

In "Ronald Reagan Now Starring at the White House," Stan Hart and Mort Drucker point out some inconsistencies in President Reagan's character. Other commentators were noticing that Reagan was retelling scenes from old movies and stories from *Reader's Digest* as if they were fact, giving some credence to *Mad*'s claims. — Hart/Drucker, " Ronald Reagan Now Starring at the White House," *Mad*, #233

GOVERNMENT "LOGIC" is...

...saving other countries from the oppression of left-wing dictatorships...

...by supporting equally oppressive <u>right</u>-wing dictatorships!

Writer Mike Snider received hate mail for revealing flaws in government logic in this **1988 article.** — Snider/North, "A Mad Look at Real-Life Government 'Logic,'" *Mad*, #279

GOVERNMENT "LOGIC" is...

...continuing to promote nuclear power plants as "totally safe"...

...even though no insurance company will insure them—at <u>any</u> price!

"I first came across Mad in 1961 at the tender age of eight and proceeded to baffle and disturb my parents by asking them who Jimmy Hoffa was and making what I believed to be wildly sophisticated, satirical remarks about Fidel Castro and Caroline Kennedy at the tea table, only to be met with blank stares of incomprehension and not a little alarm."

ALAN MOORE
British comic book writer
Watchmen, Swamp
Thing, Blab!

later in the 1960s, *Mad* continued to include topical satire. No president was exempt from

> *"There was a spirit of satire and irreverence in* Mad *that was very important, and it was the only place you could find it in the '50s."*
> GLORIA STEINEM   *New York Times Magazine*

Mad's sledgehammer humor, no movement or institution safe from *Mad* jabbing a finger at its excesses and inconsistencies, laughing fiendishly. If *Mad* ran a satire about policemen, like "Badge and Billy Magazine," it also published "Hippie Magazine" about the other side, then to be followed by "Silent Majority: The Magazine for Middle America," and "Picket and Strike: A Magazine for the Modern Unionist." Satires on religion were not far behind, beginning with "A Mad Guide to Religion in America" and "Mad's Religious Cult Leader of the Year." By 1982, *Mad* came back full circle to politics with "The Model Majority Manual," the cover of which depicted Mom, apple pie, baseball, servicemen, and the golden arches, as well as the more traditional wooden church, all against the backdrop of the American flag.

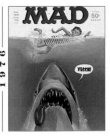

If the tenor of the times got too shrill, there was always *Mad*'s Joke and Dagger Department, with Antonio Prohías's Cold War kids in "Spy vs. Spy." Since 1961, the black spy, the white spy, and the occasional gray spy have enacted their monthly game of challenge and

Founded by Robert Welch, a retired Massachusetts candy manufacturer, the far-right John Birch Society began gaining members and prominence in the late 1950s. Among other things, the society postulated that Dwight Eisenhower was an agent of the Communist conspiracy, that fluoridation of water was also a Communist plot, and that the U.S. was threatened more by Communist Americans than the Soviet Union. Even before this article was printed in 1965, *Mad* was on the hate list of the society's most prominent member, Major General Edwin A. Walker. — Ronald Axe. Sol Weinstein/Orlando, "Mad Interviews a 'John Birch Society' Policeman," *Mad*, #97

Similarly, a controversy was fueled three years later, when *Mad* published a farce interview with a John Birch Society policeman. Written by Ronald Axe and Sol Weinstein, the parody featured a mild-mannered interviewer who followed a bigoted policeman through his day of selective law enforcement. Reader response — again, mostly from adults — ranged from charges that *Mad* writers were "pinko subversive undermining liberals," to suggestions that the article should be "read by every thinking American," to one reader declaring that "your incrimination of the Birch Society smacks of the same infamous tactics of mass-denunciation that *they* employ."

As the political climate entered a hot spell

Antonio Prohías's "Spy vs. Spy" is wild, brutal, and filled with gadgets that would give even Rube Goldberg a run for his money. The Morse Code lettering under the splash panel was always the same, it read "by Prohías." — Prohías/Prohías, "Spy vs. Spy," *Mad*, #95, #111, #102, #67, #89

JOKE AND DAGGER DEPT. PART II

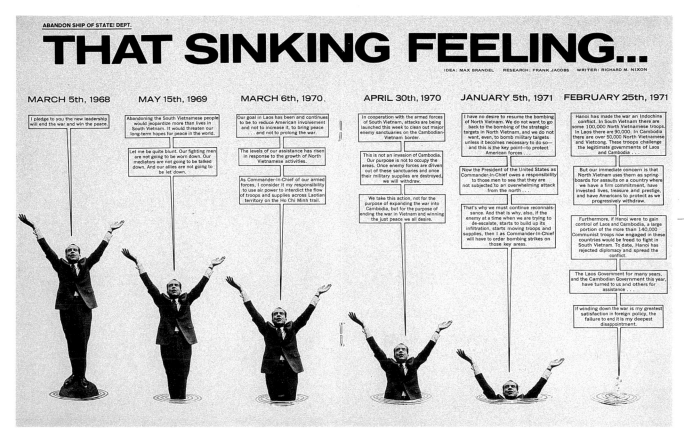

Mad has had a number of well-known contributors over the years, but this is the only *Mad* article ever crediting a U.S. president as writer. 'Nuff said.
—Richard M. Nixon/Brandel and Jacobs, "That Sinking Feeling," *Mad*, #145

"*You were good to remember me in such a thoughtful way. I want you to know how pleased I am by your kindness. Thank you for thinking of me.*"

RONALD REAGAN
note to the editors

deceit, as stylized and ritualized as a Kabuki play. Sometimes the black spy wins, sometimes the white spy; although, his chivalry showing, when Prohías includes the gray spy, she *always* wins.

Mad's editors know that they sometimes walk a fine line in their political satire, and maintaining a balance is important to them. "We've been chastised regularly the last couple of years by some very conservative members of the writing staff that *Mad* has gone too far to the left," John Ficarra admits. "They just don't understand that *Mad* attacks whoever's in office. The more fanatical or more strident they get, the more our criticism heats up, because we always attack extremes. So when they say we've gone too far to the left, it's because Republicans and conserva-

tives have been in control, have owned the White House. If Dukakis had won the election, we would do Dukakis jokes."

The *Mad* party line is perhaps best typified in the issue that appeared on newsstands the morning after election day, 1960. *Mad* was the first national magazine to depict President-elect Kennedy on the cover, quite a trick since, like all other monthlies, *Mad* is printed over four weeks in advance of its distribution. A closer examination revealed the reason: the flip side of *Mad* bore the image of defeated candidate Richard M. Nixon—each magazine had two covers. News vendors simply displayed the side depicting Kennedy, with the Nixon cover to the back. Both covers were emblazoned with banners proclaiming "We were with you all the way!"

NOTES

"We've tried to keep Mad . . ." Goldberg, "William M. Gaines," 75.

"I never regarded myself as political . . ." Benson, MAD, vol. 4, notes following issue #23.

"McCarthy was a special case . . ." Benson, notes following issue #23.

"Oklahoma justice." Jacobs, William M. Gaines, 196–204.

"McCarthyism is a movement . . ." Rovere, Senator Joe McCarthy, 152.

"Fidel kept sending . . ." Montane, "The Minister of Sinister," 16.

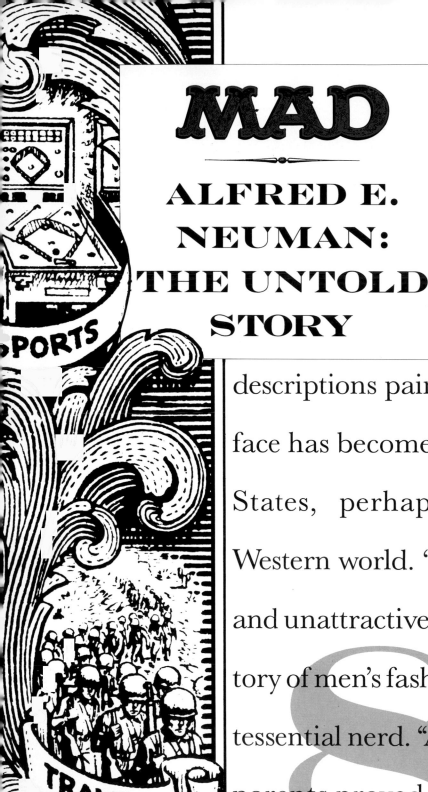

MAD

ALFRED E. NEUMAN: THE UNTOLD STORY

"The guardian gargoyle of *Mad*," a "grinning nebbish," "a shit-eating smile," "more a mental defective than a lunatic," "a vacuous, strabismic, slightly leering face"—none of these descriptions paints a flattering portrait of a boy whose face has become one of the best known in the United States, perhaps in the

Western world. "Unkempt and unattractive," was the verdict of the writers of a history of men's fashion who selected Neuman as the quintessential nerd. "Alfred E. Neuman was everything that parents prayed deep-down their kids wouldn't turn into—and feared they would," noted two other writers

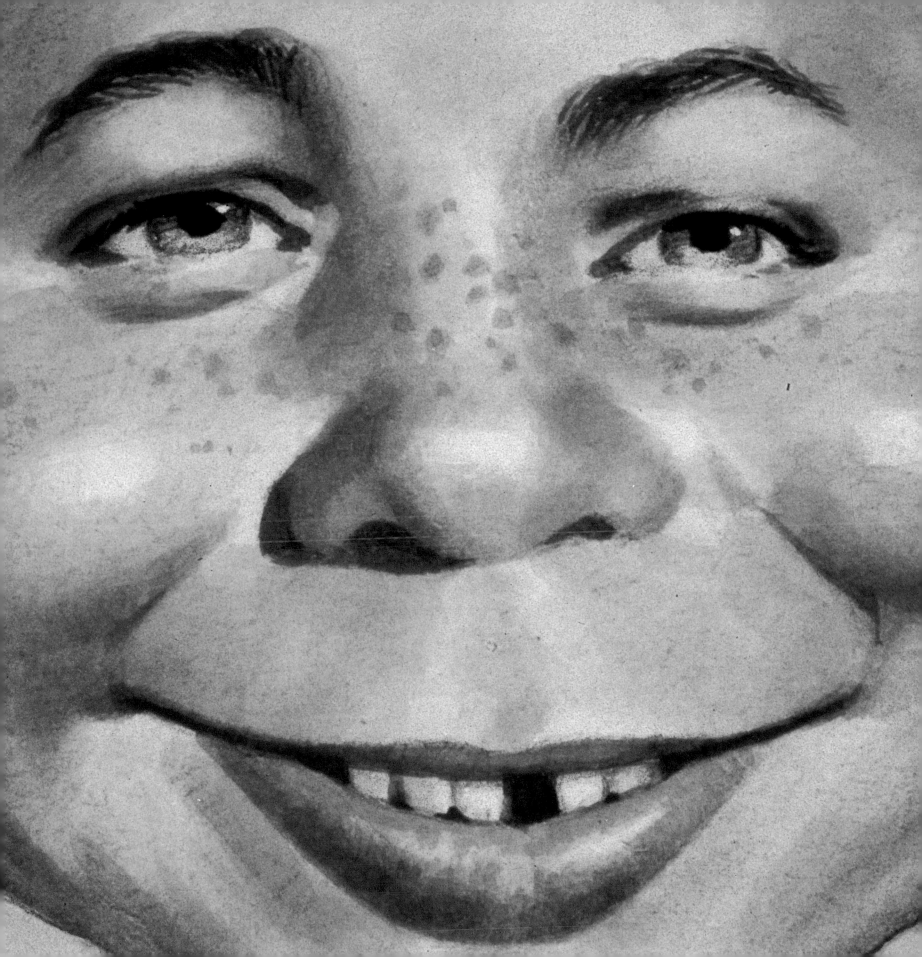

By 1963, Alfred E. Neuman was so well known that a letter mailed from the far reaches of Auckland, New Zealand, by John S. Henry, showing the boy's face but no name or address, arrived intact at *Mad*'s offices in New York City.

in a *New York Times Magazine* article. A writer for *Look* was a little kinder, pointing out that "the lad...always manages to give a daffily Kiplingesque impression that he is keeping his head—a pinhead, to be sure—while all about him are losing theirs."

To all these writers straining to capture in a few words Neuman's unique *je ne sais quoi*, the boy himself would no doubt respond:

"What—me worry?" For over thirty-five years Neuman has been *Mad*'s mascot and spokesperson, having appeared on the cover of virtually every issue since 1955. Over the years, Neuman has played more roles than any but the most prolific actors. His range is astonishing; he has appeared not only as General Patton, Uncle Sam ("Who needs *you*?"), George Washington, and Santa Claus, but also in the younger roles of Rosemary's

From the very earliest days, Alfred E. Neuman's motto has been "What—me worry?" Other than that, he speaks only through short quotations above the *Mad* masthead. These bits of wit and idiocy have helped define the "What—me worry?" spirit. "Most of us don't know exactly what we want, but we're pretty sure we don't have it!" was one pronouncement. "If you want to know what it's going to be like being married to your girl, just watch how she treats her little brother," advised another.

Mad's mascot has cult appeal, and has become so well loved that every year *Mad* receives numbers of photographs from parents of children bearing a supposed resemblance. "Imagine a mother being proud of a kid like Alfred!" Feldstein wonderingly remarks. A number of silly stunts have been inspired by his goofy countenance. Dedicated mountain climbers have planted flags bearing his image at twenty-eight thousand feet in the Himalayas. In 1960, one of the first computers to "understand" English spoke what was dubbed the *Mad* dialect (short for Michigan Algorithm Decoder). In response to mis-

"**Mad** *made me fall in love with people with big ears. That's a good influence, isn't it?*"

ANDY WARHOL *New York Times Magazine*

Alfred E. Neuman has become famous as the ultimate know-nothing. Editorial cartoonists like Don Wright sometimes exploit the broad understanding of this aspect of the kid, using his image to instantly convey the "What—me worry?" spirit. — Don Wright, *Palm Beach Post, 2/11/89*

baby, a hippie, and a high school student. He has not been limited by race or ethnic group, and has played Michael Jackson, an Italian organ-grinder (with King Kong as the monkey), an Indian guru, Tut-Ankh Neuman, Alfred E. Toto, and Alfredo, Teenage Mutant Ninja Turtle. When he's not involved in masquerade, he has been the perpetrator or butt of hundreds of practical jokes. He has been running for president each election since 1956, with the slogan "You could do worse, and always have!"

direction, it printed out a picture of Alfred E. Neuman, complete with motto. Students risked arrest by crashing a 1964 Goldwater campaign appearance bearing placards announcing Alfred E. Neuman for president. In

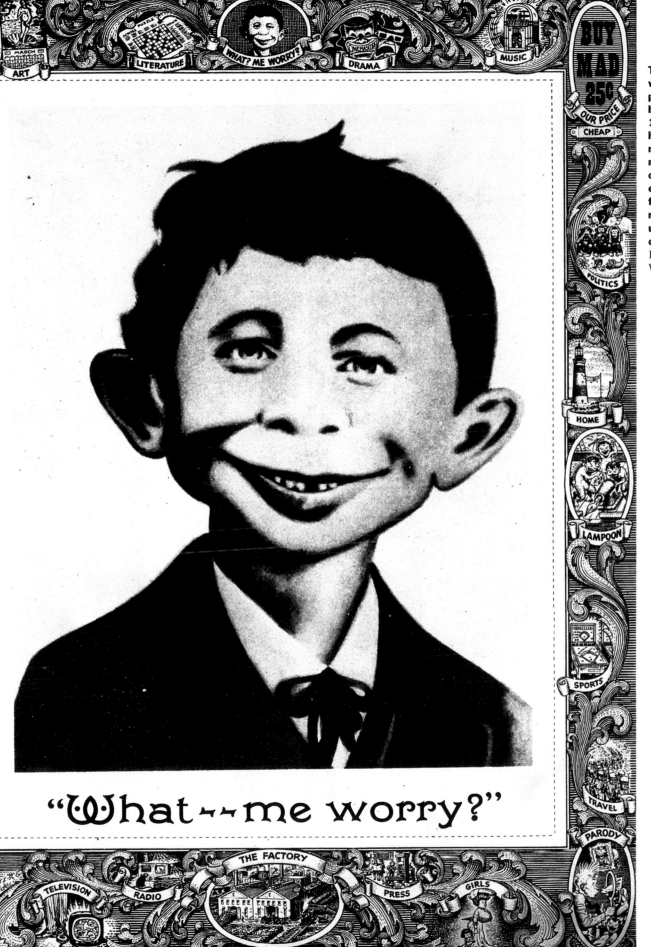

"What --- me worry?"

The original *Mad* "What—me worry?" kid in his first full-page appearance on the inside back cover of *Mad*. In April 1956, when this appeared, he hadn't been named yet. This reproduction is an enlargement from a postcard that caught Harvey Kurtzman's eye; the border was taken from the cover of *Mad*, a more refined version of the one used on the first few issues of the magazine. —border by Kurtzman/Kurtzman, Elder, Wood, *Mad*, #27

THE MADMEN: *Frank Kelly Freas, Norman Mingo*

Frank Kelly Freas, a cover artist and illustrator of many of *Mad*'s most memorable advertising parodies, is even better known as a science-fiction illustrator. In the *New Encyclopedia of Science Fiction* he is called "the most popular illustrator in the history of science fiction." His specialty is a realism unique to the genre: his characters have wrinkles, expressiveness, and a bit of humor. These qualities served him well when he began contributing art to *Mad*'s advertising parodies in 1955: he always seemed to hit just the right balance among realism, warmth, and mockery. By 1957, Freas had mastered the art of rendering Alfred E. Neuman on *Mad*'s cover.

Norman Mingo is the only World War I veteran ever to be included in the Usual Gang of Idiots. He began contributing covers to the magazine in 1956 at the age of sixty after a long and well-established career as an advertising illustrator. Mingo became known for his drawings of elongated luxury cars and beautiful women (he is rumored to have once ghost-drawn for Vargas), and his Chicago firm helped set the graphic style of the day. Because of a business failure, Mingo was beginning his career over when he began contributing to *Mad*. Little did he realize that the next twenty-five years would make him better known than all his work in the previous forty. When Mingo died in 1980, his obituary in the *New York Times*, while noting all his work, identified him in its headline as the "Illustrator Behind 'Alfred E. Neuman' Face."

1983, a man wearing an Alfred E. Neuman mask tried to hold up a gas station in Grand Rapids, Michigan. He couldn't get the attendant to take him seriously, and fled without any money.

When *Mad* first adopted Alfred E. Neuman, featuring his picture on the cover of the *Mad Reader*, the first *Mad* reprint anthology, the boy didn't even have a name. Soon after, he made his first appearance in *Mad* itself as a small tidbit of "clip art" on the *Mad* comics fake mail-order catalog cover of issue 21.

Later that year, *Mad* became a magazine, and a drawing of the boy's face was elevated to top center position in the ornate cover border, and festooned with a banner bearing his famous motto. He was in good company, flanked by drawings of Socrates, Beethoven, and Napoleon on one side, Freud, Alexander the Great, and Marilyn Monroe on the other. All, save Neuman and Monroe, were depicted reading *Mad*. Inside, he played cameo roles in several articles.

Clearly, the boy had tickled editor Kurtzman's fancy; the readers, as well, fell for the imp's strange charms. Queries began to pour in to the mail room. Obliging requests, a full-page black-and-white picture of the What—Me Worry? kid was reproduced on the inside back cover of issue 27, with an opportunity to order additional copies on better paper for fifteen cents.

Up until then, in *Mad* the boy had been called Melvin Coznowski, Mel Haney, the What—Me Worry? kid, but never Alfred E. Neuman. That name *had* appeared in *Mad* and other EC comics as a joke name EC writers had picked up from Henry Morgan's radio show (who had, in turn, swiped it from Alfred Newman himself, a Hollywood musical director). Kurtzman remembers that it was the readers who first referred to the gap-toothed boy as such. In *Mad* the name was first connected with the face in issue 29, Al Feldstein's first issue as editor, in a one-page ad parody that trumpeted "Biggest Year in *Mad* History" and included several ludicrous charts revealing "fantastic comparisons to top selling magazines." The surveys were purportedly the work of Alfred E. Neuman, who was depicted at the bottom of the page.

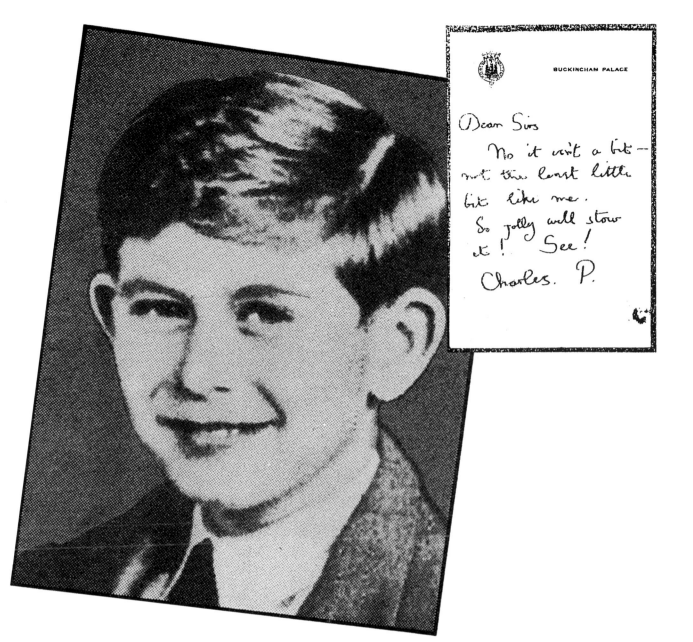

In 1958, a number of readers sent copies of a widely reproduced photograph of ten-year-old Prince Charles. "Am I finally cracking after so many years of enduring *Mad*'s brainwashing, or do I really detect a resemblance?" queried one. Several weeks later arrived a letter of complaint, postmarked London. Having a little fun with their newfound correspondent, a subsequent issue of *Mad* included this Frank Jacobs and Wally Wood spoof on royal life. They succeeded only in arousing the ire of the British press. "We say that it is a cheap and contemptible insult," the tabloids screamed, to the surprise of *Mad*'s editors. — photo of Charles: *Mad*, #48; Jacobs/ Wood, "Comic Strip Heroes (Taken from Real Life)"; Prince Charles letter and envelope

"Mad magazine was a sore point in our house because my brother was terrified of looking at Alfred E. Neuman's face. He had a poster of him on the wall of his bedroom, and one time when he had the flu, he said he saw Alfred's lips moving. So after that he went berserk whenever he saw Alfred's face. I always tried to keep a copy of Mad *around the house because my brother and I were mortal enemies, so it was a good weapon to have."*

Lynda Barry   *Blab!*

BRINGING UP BONNIE PRINCE CHARLIE

Every four years, Alfred E. Neuman gamely throws his hat into the ring. Lou Silverstone and Max Brandel composed this portrait of *Mad*'s ideal candidate for the 1968 election. —*Mad*, #122

As soon as the "What—me worry?" kid began appearing in *Mad*, his past came back to haunt him. Readers sent numbers of postcards, advertisements, and memories of the boy, from before *Mad*'s time. These early pictures were occasionally run on the letters page as the mystery deepened. Soon, several parties emerged who claimed to hold a copyright to the face. The suit filed by Helen Pratt Stuff eventually reached the Supreme Court before *Mad*'s right to their adopted mascot was established. This picture, copyright 1914 by Stuff, was submitted by them as evidence.

"Recently, while converting our spare bedroom into a Juan Peron Memorial Museum, I found this priceless memento of the Depression," joked reader Paul Knbloe when he sent *Mad* this postcard. This card, was distributed by the opposition to a third term for the well-loved president. "My New Deal acquaintances took most Republican propaganda calmly, but this particular item roused some of them to a fury," remembered historian Kenneth Wiggins Porter in a letter to the *New York Times Magazine*. "They considered it not only blasphemously anti-Roosevelt but also anti-Semitic, inasmuch as they profess to recognize the Alfred E. Neuman-to-be as not only an 'idiot' but also a Jewish 'idiot.'"

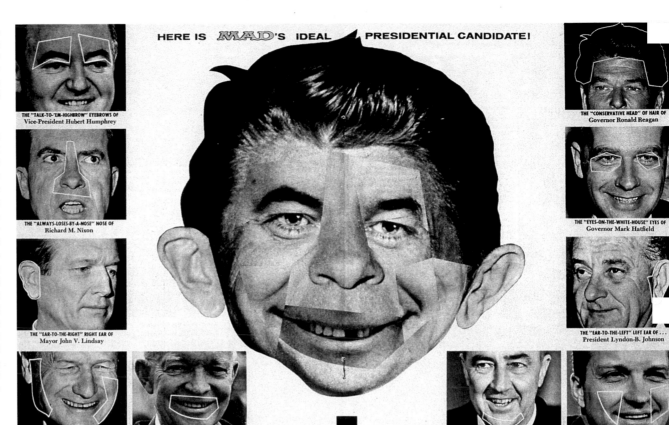

HERE IS MAD'S IDEAL PRESIDENTIAL CANDIDATE!

THE "TALK-TO-'EM-HIGHBROW" EYEBROWS OF Vice-President Hubert Humphrey

THE "ALWAYS-LOSES-BY-A-NOSE" NOSE OF Richard M. Nixon

THE "EAR-TO-THE-RIGHT" RIGHT EAR OF Mayor John V. Lindsay

THE "UNMITIGATED CHEEK" CHEEKS OF ... Governor Nelson Rockefeller

THE "LAUGHING-UP-HIS-SLEEVE" GRIN OF Ex-Pres. Dwight D. Eisenhower

THE "CREDIBILITY GAP" CREATED BY Practically All Politicians

THE "CONSERVATIVE HEAD" OF HAIR OF Governor Ronald Reagan

THE "EYES-ON-THE-WHITE-HOUSE" EYES OF Governor Mark Hatfield

THE "EAR-TO-THE-LEFT" LEFT EAR OF ... President Lyndon B. Johnson

THE "STICK-YOUR-CHIN-WAY-OUT" CHIN OF Senator Eugene McCarthy

THE "SMILING LINES" SMILE-LINES OF ... Senator Charles H. Percy

"Me —Worry?"

.. Sure - I'm for Roosevelt

Feldstein and associate editor Nick Meglin realized that the boy had potential, and one of Feldstein's first acts as editor was to find a special cover illustrator to do him justice. He placed an advertisement in the classified section of the *New York Times*, and a man by the name of Norman Mingo was the first to respond. One look at his portfolio, and Feldstein knew that Mingo had the talent and *have been harder to survive a Republican upbringing."*

CANDICE BERGEN

Mad World of William M. Gaines

style needed for the task. *"Playboy* had the rabbit and *Esquire* had Esky the fat dirty old man. However, the portrait of the 'Me Worry?' kid that we'd been using was from an old print that had been around for years. It was in black and white, very crude, and lacked detail and charm. What I wanted was a full-color, humanized rendition of this face, and I wanted it infused with personality and impish lovable character." Mingo's forte was portrait illustrations, and he set about to create a fully rendered color portrait of the newly named mascot of *Mad*.

Mingo's painting became the model against which all other *Mad* drawings of Alfred E. Neuman were judged. As associate editor Jerry De Fuccio once put it, Mingo "did for Alfred E. Neuman what Leonardo da Vinci had done for the Mona Lisa—created an image that would endure." Neuman's full-color debut took place on the cover of issue 30, in an announcement of his 1956 candidacy for the office of president of the United States. From this point on, the boy virtually disappeared from the inside of the magazine and took a starring role on the cover.

Mingo, Frank Kelly Freas, and Richard

Williams have been Neuman's primary portrait painters, but most of the *Mad* artists have taken their turns, at one time or another. The face is more difficult to render than one might imagine, since each nuance, from the famous smirk to the tousled hair, must be just so. "Alfred's facial charm is that one eye is higher than the other. I have the impulse to 'correct' that, each time I draw him," Bob Clarke once lamented to De Fuccio. "I was constantly putting a little twist to his lips, or lifting an eyebrow or something to make him a real person," remembers Freas. "I felt very—paternal, I suppose—toward Alfie, and I was treating him as a real person all the time."

In more recent times, Alfred E. Neuman has become popular with editorial cartoonists as well. He has been used to personify P. W. Botha of South Africa, Libyan Prime Minister Muamar Qadaffi, former president of the Philippines Ferdinand Marcos, Colonel Oliver North, news anchor Ted Koppel, and, most often, former president Ronald Reagan. Don Wright, an editorial cartoonist based at the *Palm Beach Post*, has used the character several times in cartoons that have been widely syndicated. He says

that "the face, the character itself, has come to epitomize stupidity. It is one of the most widely understood symbols, these days, with the educational system being what it is." Not very complimentary to those so depicted, but a real testament to old Alfred's fame.

The "What—me worry?" kid was playing masquerade long before he became the cover boy for *Mad*. This patriotic envelope was imprinted privately from 1943 to 1945. Other versions with the boy as a sailor and a milkmaid were printed in a variety of colors.

This is not a *Mad* parody, but a real "Peanuts" that appeared in 1973. Charles Schulz finally got back at *Mad* for all the parodies they had run of his comic strip. His Alfred looks a little strange because he didn't make one eye higher than the other. — © 1973 United Feature Syndicate

The boy's devil-may-care attitude must have struck just the right note to fliers serving in World War II, as evidenced by the nose art on this C-47 bomber.

The kid struts his stuff in Miami in February 1948 in this "eat your heart out" type postcard. —Collection of Don and Newly Preziosi

Bob Adamcik's twenty-six-hour café, with a smokehouse and barbecue pit, is fondly remembered by many Texans. During the 1940s the "What—me worry?" kid was the café's mascot and was featured on many postcards given away by them, as well as this matchbook, which testifies to the quality of Bob's taste. —Collection of Don and Newly Preziosi

Two his-and-hers versions of the kid. One, a Kaiser postcard from the 1930s, the others are souvenir cards published by the Kier Company in 1941.

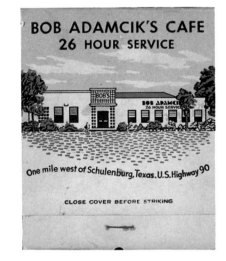

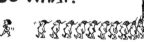

ALFRED E. NEUMAN HAS ALWAYS INSPIRED LOTS of reader mail, and very early in his history with *Mad*, the editors received some surprising letters. In issue 27, a whole page was devoted to a variety of pictures of Alfred E. Neuman in earlier incarnations that took the form of old postcards, newspaper clippings, and other paper ephemera sent by readers. The boy appeared in his familiar dark suit and string tie, as well as with a necktie, glasses, and a mustache, in a plaid suit, in a Canadian Mountie hat, and cross-eyed with a cowboy hat. He had clearly gotten around. The pictures had various captions: "Me Worry?" was most common, but one (the cowboy) said, colloquially, "Da-a-h...Me

Worry?" Another was captioned "Our Grate Founder."

The letters provided a number of reminiscences. "The 'What, me worry?' boy's pen name is Old Jack. He is a newspaper man," revealed one reader. "Your little mascot...was a smiling egregiousness in our high school biology text...an example, as I remember, of a person who lacked iodine," opined another. "He is a Siamese boy named WATMI WORRI," pronounced a third. "The original...was created some 30 years ago by an old friend of mine, the late Harry Spencer Stuff," a best-seller in a series of postcards, remembered yet another reader. One letter claimed that he "first appeared on highway billboards around 1915 advertising a patent

"I wouldn't make too much of the resemblance. Old Alfred E. has survived innumerable assaults on his character, but suggesting that he looks like a journalist (and a television journalist to boot) may be more than even that durable dummy can survive. Personally, I think he looks more like Prince Charles."   TED KOPPEL

It remains a mystery whether this letter was actually from the Prince of Wales. *Mad*'s art director, John Putnam, a connoisseur and collector with an educated eye, pointed out that the paper was triple-cream laid, and that the crest of the Duke of Edinburgh was a copper engraving—in all likelihood the stationery was authentic. The postmark was from an office within walking distance of the palace. The signature was short for Charles Princeps, just the way the prince would have signed his name. Unfortunately, the original letter disappeared several years ago while on loan to a magazine preparing an article about *Mad*, and the photocopies that remain cannot be used by experts for authentication. The response to a recent inquiry sent to Bucking-

ham Palace was regrets and no comment from an older, and perhaps wiser, prince.

For several years Alfred E. Neuman's motley past provided colorful items for the letters page, as readers became adept spotters and sent pictures of the boy's countenance adorning all sorts of old advertisements, postcards, and even World War II aircraft. The editors responded as Kurtzman had to the initial mail-load of items: "What, us worry?"

But by the late 1950s, *Mad* found itself embroiled in a series of copyright infringement charges for its use of pictures of the boy. By 1965, one of the cases, a claim by Helen Pratt Stuff regarding her late husband's copyright

medicine called 'Papaya'" (a use that leads one to wonder whether the boy was an example of "before" or "after"). "As you can see, the source for the 'What, me worry?' picture is becoming clearer by the hour," mused the editor. "What, us worry?"

In 1958 another spate of letters notified *Mad* of an unusual coincidence. A widely published photograph of the young Charles, Prince of Wales bore a startling resemblance to none other than Alfred E. Neuman. "Could it be?" gasped one reader. "No comment," responded the editors, when they ran the prince's picture on the letters page.

Several weeks later *Mad* received a letter from London. The note, handwritten in a childish scrawl on Buckingham Palace stationery, read in its entirety:

Dear Sirs
No it isn't a bit—not the least little bit like me.
So jolly well stow it! See!

Charles. P.

"Me Worry?"

Several versions of the boy from the 1910s and 1920s show a variety of toothedness and garb. Two are virtually identical: a postcard from the studio of Harry Park, an actor who appeared in Thomas Edison's first motion pictures, and a card printed by Andre Papantonio in 1916. The boy in the nightgown is from a correspondence course by the artist Eugene Zimmerman; the baseball fan, from the old *Life* humor magazine, is by the same artist. The 1924 advertisement for Cherry Sparkle soda is a rare three-quarter view.

Just as Cherries are healthy and tasty so, too, is

EXQUISITE Cherry Sparkle

wholesome and refreshing. A rare fine flavor distinctively different and a goodness quickly recognized by a discriminating public. Day by day, more bottlers are being converted from ordinary cherry flavors to

Cherry Sparkle

"The Taste Tells The Tale"

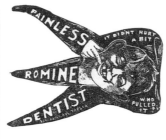

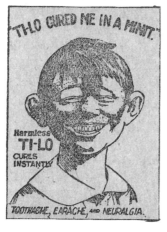

of "The Original Optimist," had moved through a lower court and reached the Federal Appellate Court for New York. Harry Stuff's original copyright had been filed in 1914, and, although the image had not been reprinted after 1920, his widow had renewed the copyright in 1941. The Stuffs had sold about two thousand copies of the popular postcard, and between 1941 and 1948 the widow had won six claims for infringement. Her claim against *Mad* was a strong one, and *Mad* stood to lose not only its beloved mascot, but millions of dollars in damages. *Mad*'s lawyer, Martin Scheiman, went to work. The nature of copyright law is such that if *Mad* could prove that the Stuffs had even once failed to protect their copyright of the boy's image, or if *Mad* could prove that the image existed prior to 1914, the widow's claim would be invalidated.

Researchers were hired to scour the United

States for pictures of the boy not bearing the Stuff copyright. Among the large collection of images compiled for the case were a number of pictures that bore no copyright mark at all, including the postcard from which Kurtzman had originally taken the image. They also found several prints, virtually identical portraits, that had been copyrighted by other publishers. Most interestingly, they found that pictures of the boy existed prior to 1914, and had additional evidence that the image had been published before the turn of the century.

By the time the case was heard, Jack Albert, who had become *Mad*'s lawyer after Martin Scheiman's death, was able to prove that even though the Stuffs had won several cases, they had abandoned their copyright by not contesting every subsequent copyright of the boy's picture, and that they also had no case based on originality, since the picture had been in prior use. In fact, while the Stuff case was going on, *Mad* had been sued by a 1936 copyright holder, William A. Schmeck. Neither Stuff nor Schmeck was told about the other, and Albert was able to use the simul-

taneous claims in court to prove *Mad*'s case. The court found that Harry Stuff "had been most derelict in preventing others from infringing his copyright." The case eventually went to the Supreme Court; all previous copyrights remained invalidated, and *Mad* established its right to its adopted mascot,

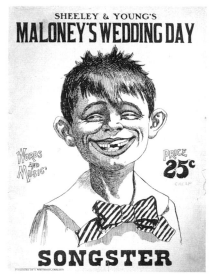

Alfred E. Neuman.

Through evidence collected for this case and through ongoing contributions of readers, *Mad* has accumulated a bulging scrapbook of images and information that has only deepened the mystery surrounding the origins of the boy. The face has been a favorite of artists for well over one hundred years. Here is the kid in a depression-era postcard denouncing President Roosevelt; there, he appears in a 1909 handbill playing the part of a baby in the play *The Newlyweds' Grown Up Baby*. In the years 1901 to 1903 alone he turns up on a promotional button given at the Dunlap, Iowa, street fair, in an obscure ornithological journal, in a Maryland family's parlor and garden, at an itinerant photographer's tent studio that traveled the mother lode area of California, and on a dentist's building in Brooklyn.

Kurtzman admits that he had seen some of these other pictures when he decided to use the face in *Mad*, and that, in fact, was what attracted him to the boy. "Obviously, there were several generations of 'What—me worry?' There was the original, there were the imitations, and there were imitations of the imitations, there had to be," he deduced. "So in wandering through life and picking up on these images, I suddenly saw this thing on

The kid appears as an assistant birdwatcher in this 1901 illustration from *The Condor*, an ornithologist's journal. Although much of the drawing is crudely rendered, the detail of the boy's face is almost identical to other representations of him from around the turn of the century, from which it was probably copied.

This souvenir button was enclosed in a 1956 letter to *Mad* from reader Don Moir. Moir's letter, addressed to Alfred E. Neuman and written with a quill pen on an enormous sheet of parchment paper, took a jovial tone. "Do you ever think of the good times we shared, like the herring-and-knish breakfasts at your cousin's place after our nights on the town...? And do you recall, Alf, the time Susie Higgins quit you cold in the middle of the floor at the Dunlap Hog Breeders' Barn Dance?" Moir soon heard from *Mad*'s lawyers, who were then beginning their research into the origins of the boy.

The boy appears mysteriously as a garden faun. This 1902 photograph was printed from a glass negative found among others in the basement of a house in Takoma Park, Maryland. Legend has it the photograph was the work of a young amateur photographer who once lived in the house.

Bernie Shir-Cliff's wall and I said, 'That's the original! It's got to be the original!'" Shir-Cliff, then an editor at Ballantine Books, kindly gave Kurtzman the postcard of interest, which was the image used by *Mad* until Mingo created his rendition.

But Kurtzman is not the only one to think he had found the original Alfred. Many of those who have contributed pictures to the scrapbook claim to have met the original photographer, or even the boy himself. E. C. Kaeser, president of Kaeser & Blair, Inc. of Cincinnati, thought that one of his employees drew the original in the 1930s. A newspaper once wildly reported that "It is Neuman who created the half-witted boy." Mark James Estren mistakenly stated in his book on underground comics that Alfred E. Neuman was none other than the Yellow Kid, the star of the first published comic strip by Outcault.

One of the most intriguing stories was related to *Mad* by Joyce Widoff in 1958. She had been working on a biography of Harry Park, an actor who was featured in the first motion pictures made for Thomas Edison's Kinetoscope. "In rummaging through his collection I came upon a very old print of the 'What, me worry?' boy," Widoff wrote in her letter to

Mad. Park had explained to her that he had once had a print shop in Los Angeles. About 1903, he bought a photograph taken by a friend of "a simple-minded lad," added the famous motto, and reprinted it for sale. "Mr. Park even TOLD ME THE NAME OF THE BOY, but at the time I did not think it important and therefore did not record it." Park had died before Widoff could complete her biography. Yet another near-miss.

In fact, no story yet told has satisfactorily established the origins of the boy. The earliest known reproduction of the face is from the late nineteenth century, yet he is already unmistakably Alfred. Representations have been found as far afield as England and Germany. In earlier appearances the character is

younger, more boyish, in the later ones, starting about 1910, he appears older and more idiotic, as if he has actually aged.

But he has never had a handsome coun-

he can be quite reckless, often getting into bad trouble himself. Peck's Bad Boy is a more contemporary example of the trickster, according to the writer Harold Schecter. Created in the 1880s, and enduring enough to be known today, George W. Peck's stories tell the tales of a very bad boy who especially delighted in torturing his stodgy old father with an endless stream of nasty pranks.

These antics—practical jokes, disguise, parody, and chaos—sound right up Alfred E. Neuman's alley, but the trickster has another, seemingly antithetical role. Surprisingly, the side effect of the trickster's shenanigans is often creativity, albeit of a random and unintentional sort. In flying in the face of every social contract of politeness and honesty, he opens a window to a state of being free of the tensions that build up in a society as

tenance, and there is a more curious question than his birth: What's the attraction? Why has this face been chosen, time and time again, to inspire and amuse? Why has he been such a perfect mascot for *Mad*? The answer may be that the boy is an archetype of the Jungian sort; he seems to fit, perfectly, the role of the trickster, a powerful character who appears the world over in some of the oldest and most popular folk tales. According to Jungian analysts, the trickster is a sort of malevolent jester, often appearing small and helpless, but capable of causing immense chaos through practical jokes. He is a "shape-changer," known for indulging his love of disguise. The trickster was manifested in medieval times in Church carnivals known as Ass Festivals or Fools' Holidays. On these days, the hierarchic order of the Church was overturned and parodies of the mass were performed, to the horror of the bishops. The trickster loves to see pomposity pricked, but

bound by taboos, hierarchical orders, and organizations as ours. Vicariously enjoying the trickster's activities, one can suddenly breathe again, and with the fresh air come fresh thoughts and new ideas, or at least a good laugh.

Mad's mascot in yet another outlandish get-up, this time dubbed "Train Boy." The character turns up more than once in the cartoons of Fredrick Opper, an Ohio-born artist who contributed cartoons to *Life* and *Puck* around the turn of the century. —Courtesy of the Ohio Historical Society

Whatta mug! The boy turns up on this turn-of-the-century giveaway advertising a "Dental Parlor." —Collection of Dr. Perry F. Levinsohn

Here, boy-Alfred displays salesmen's miniatures of farm plows. This print appeared in the J.B. Lyon's printing company's 1905 sample book of typefaces. The proprietor identified it as a woodcut, and thought that it dated from at least 1890, and perhaps earlier.

Dating from 1895, this is the oldest verified image of the boy. Interestingly, it is from the *Illustrated London News*, an English tabloid that printed a New York City edition. The kid's features are fully developed and unmistakable, and the image was very likely taken from an older archetype that has yet to be found.

NOTES

"Unkempt and unattractive . . ." Martin and Koda, Jocks and Nerds.

"The lad always manages . . ." Flagler, "The MAD Miracle," 46.

"Kurtzman remembers . . ." Kurtzman, My Life as a Cartoonist, 61.

"Playboy had the rabbit . . ." De Fuccio, "Norman Mingo," A47.

Stuff had "been most derelict . . ." U.S. Patent Quarterly, 560.

"Peck's Bad Boy." Schechter, The New Gods, 78.

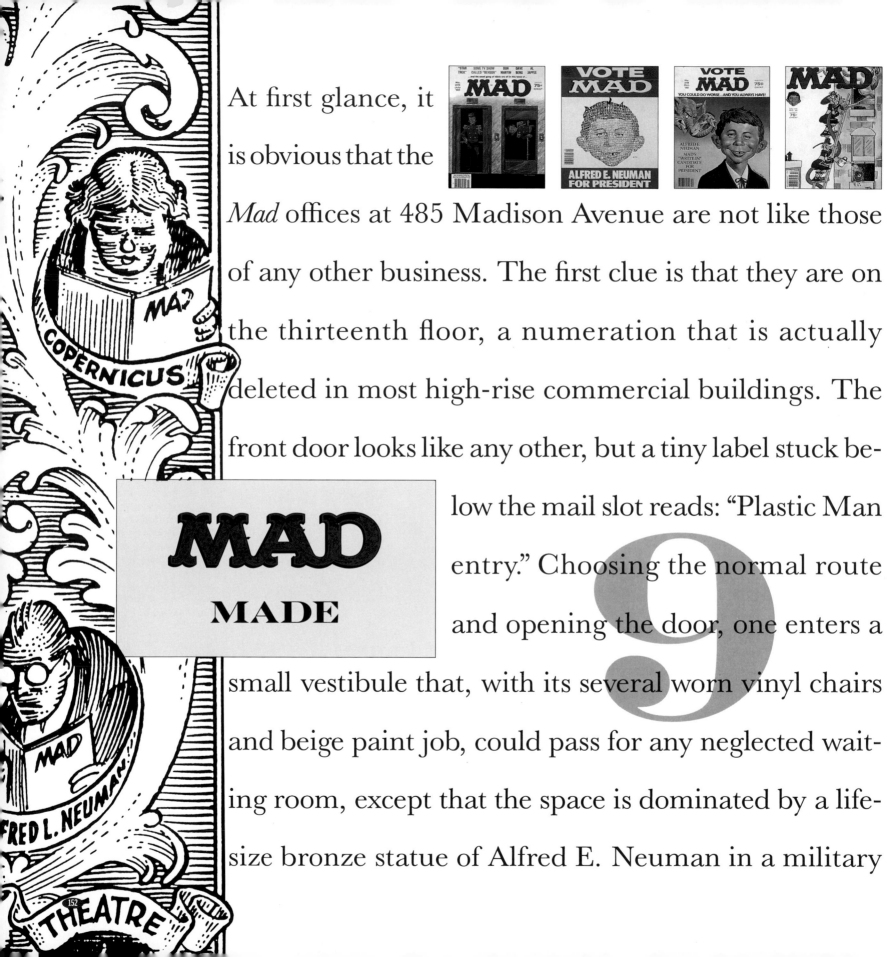

At first glance, it is obvious that the *Mad* offices at 485 Madison Avenue are not like those of any other business. The first clue is that they are on the thirteenth floor, a numeration that is actually deleted in most high-rise commercial buildings. The front door looks like any other, but a tiny label stuck below the mail slot reads: "Plastic Man entry." Choosing the normal route and opening the door, one enters a small vestibule that, with its several worn vinyl chairs and beige paint job, could pass for any neglected waiting room, except that the space is dominated by a life-size bronze statue of Alfred E. Neuman in a military

MAD
MADE

9

school uniform. No matter what the season, there's a fully decked Christmas tree in the other corner. A rack of reading material takes up what space remains: *Mad* magazines in Finnish, Danish, Chinese, and other espe-

Mad *Imitates* Life

Although *Mad*'s first parodies were of comic books, it was a leap for the editors to begin to satirize the more sophisticated print media of magazines and newspapers. *Mad*'s first magazine parody transformed the look of *Mad* itself. For issue 11, Harvey Kurtzman replaced *Mad*'s usual cover, with its distinctive yellow block-letter logo and color cartoon, with an outrageous takeoff of *Life* magazine. Breaking a cardinal rule of marketing, Kurtzman altered *Mad*'s logo, and in a case of *Mad* imitating *Life*, the word "Mad" appeared in *Life*'s typeface in a red box in the top left corner. The rest of the cover mimicked the black-and-white photographic style of *Life*, which often featured a cover photograph of a pretty woman—*Mad*'s cover featured a hideous gorgon by Basil Wolverton. The background was a photo of a grimy skyline, said to have been shot from the men's room window of 225 Lafayette Street.

The effect was startling, and Kurtzman followed it with a series of mimic covers. The next issue resembled the cover of a serious journal, designed to "make people think you are reading high-class intellectual stuff instead of miserable junk." The cover of issue 16 faked a tabloid newspaper. Designed at the height of EC's troubles with the Senate subcommittee, this cover bore "news" of arrests of comic book artists and the article "Comics Go Underground," which told the story of desperate comic book publishers "disguising their books to look like newspapers in order to sneak them onto the stands."

Although Kurtzman was clearly kidding, this was just the transformation that saved *Mad* from the Comics Code Authority less than a year later. Kurtzman took the opportunity to make the form of *Mad* itself a magazine parody, and the graphic style of the first issues was a conglomeration of several different existing magazines. The new *Mad* magazine's cover bore an ornate, slightly stodgy border, like that of *National Geographic*, which on closer inspection was revealed to be made up of busts of historical personages reading *Mad*. The logo resembled old wood type lettering, with odd curved serifs, shading, and strange scribblings. Page one was devoted to a masthead and table of contents, articles were alphabetized and departmentalized, and the whole was embellished with dingbats and other typographical ornamenta-

cially exotic tongues. Welcome to *Mad*.

Lillian Alfonso, acting as receptionist, sits at a desk behind a sliding-glass window; she's the one who unlocks a second door, using a buzzer more suitable to a high-pitched game show than an office. The hallway beyond is cluttered shoulder-high with boxes, framed original *Mad* cover paintings, and, stapled frieze-like to the top of the walls, the front covers of *Mad* special issues, forming a never-completed procession of Alfred E. Neumans. On the right, one passes a closed door, almost

completely obscured by clippings, stickers, photographs taped and glued on, then, another door to the right, this one open, revealing co-editor John Ficarra's small neat office, its lightless window draped. It contains a nondescript couch, a television, desk, bookshelves, a four-foot hypodermic needle, and a drum set. Seated on the windowsill is an anatomically correct life-size rag doll that bears a not-very-flattering resemblance to the office's occupant. Ten feet above the desk, the ceiling tiles support the addition of several dozen pencils, stuck like pins in a pincushion.

The next room on the right, a little smaller than Ficarra's, is crammed with three desks, bookshelves, bulletin boards, and several tall file cabinets. It is the shared office of *Mad*'s associate editors, Sara Friedman, Charlie Kadau, and Joe Raiola. Continuing down the hallway, one passes a stock and mail room on the left, a tiny office with a copy machine

and a computer on the right, used by Dick DeBartolo on the days when he's in the office, and by Rey Cruz, *Mad*'s accountant, on the others. The next room to the right, stuffed floor to ceiling with drawings, files, and office furniture, is that of *Mad*'s senior co-editor, Nick Meglin. Every surface is layered with at least half a foot of papers and other objects, from tennis racquet to coffee machine, and only a tight path leads from the door to the desk and word processor.

The hall ends in a glare of daylight, the first seen since leaving the street below. Stepping through the door, one enters the art department; at about ten by twenty feet, it is the largest office in the warren. The windows make it seem bigger. Large, slanted drawing desks dominate the room. Scattered about are implements of the tasks at hand — colored markers, pencils, rulers, and a bank of large flat files with drawers marked "sex" and "dirty pictures." Beyond the files is a sink, surmounted by a beautifully lettered plaque

tion. The interior design was more modern and emulated the look of *Life*: lettering was now typeset, rather than written by hand, and dialogue balloons were banished, while blocks of text alternated with illustrations that bled off the edge of the page. Following magazine conventions, full-page advertising (parodies) appeared on the inside and back covers, and smaller ads appeared in the front and back of the magazine.

From the start, Kurtzman's aspirations for *Mad* magazine were limited by its budget. He styled *Mad* as a parody of the slick photo magazines, a format that had the advantage of allowing for large illustrations. But *Mad*'s paper and printing, while an improvement over the comic book, was just a little better than that of newspapers.

The layout style worked well in many ways, allowing filmlike sequences of drawings and articles with varying amounts of text. But it, too, had its limitations and, from its first issue, *Mad* magazine began a process of reverting to a more flexible, comic book–like form. Today, the remnants of *Mad*'s early look are seen in the simplified logo, the masthead, the letters page, and typeset article introductions and dialogue.

bearing the words "Nixon Pissed Here." The windowsill near one of the desks is filled with objects of various sorts — a Styrofoam wig stand, a paper cup, a bowling pin — each bears the embellishment of large round eyeglasses above a beard, the signature of art director Lenny "the Beard" Brenner. A grouping of scraggly avocado plants grow in front of another window. A six-foot-long slide rule hangs on an adjacent wall; below it are a slot machine, some strange cardboard sculptures that are a cross between a garden folly and a modernistic skyscraper, and on top of the pile teeters a portable CD player. From its speakers waft strains of Wagner.

Although the art department's relative spaciousness and natural light are inviting, one is inevitably drawn back down the hallway, to the closed door bypassed earlier, for it leads to the office of William M. Gaines. Opening it without knocking, Gaines's preferred etiquette of entry, one is immediately aware

The *Mad* staff in 1963. From left to right: associate editors Nick Meglin and Jerry De Fuccio, art director John Putnam, publisher Bill Gaines, artist George Woodbridge, editor Al Feldstein, production manager Lenny Brenner, and, of course, Arthur.

of the chill and the drone of an air conditioner, kept on high, no matter what the outside temperature. As befits an important publisher, it is a corner office, but the windows admit no light: one is visibly walled in, and the other is filled with the peering, gigantic three-dimensional face of King Kong. From the ceiling hang a dozen-odd airship models and toys, ranging from the earliest dirigibles designed to the graceful zeppelins

In 1960 Bill Gaines called a general meeting of *Mad* staff and free lances to announce that he was taking them all on a vacation to Haiti. The trips became a tradition, making world travelers of all the *Mad* regulars.

of the 1930s, and including a wooden model of the *Mad* zeppelin.

Small file cabinets are scattered about, and every otherwise-unused area in the room is stacked with papers and magazines. The walls are hung with original art from Gaines's days of publishing horror, science-fiction, and war comics. Glass-encased bookshelves house leatherbound volumes of every issue of *Mad* printed. The bookshelves also display varied memorabilia of Gaines's life: a bust of

Alfred E. Neuman, a human skull (Gaines says it is his father's), and a shadow box containing a white shirt, a tie patterned with tiny blimps, and a sign reading "BREAK GLASS IN CASE OF A BUSINESS OR SOCIAL EMERGENCY ENGAGEMENT." In contrast with the rest of the room, the desk is relatively neat. It bears a large "No Smoking" sign, a foot-tall rubber stamp tree holding thirty rubber stamps, a daily calendar, and a large, shabby, old-fashioned desk blotter. Behind the desk is propped, mirror-like, a life-size painting of the back of Gaines's white-haired head.

In these small, strange offices the most successful humor magazine in history is produced. But *Mad* was not always located on Madison Avenue. At first, *Mad* was made downtown at 225 Lafayette Street, in the heart of the Little Italy section of Manhattan. Those offices had been used by Max Gaines since the early 1930s, and when Bill Gaines took over in 1947, he saw no reason to move. Gaines, Frank Lee, Sol Cohen, and later Johnny Craig and Al Feldstein worked out of them, Harvey Kurtzman preferring to work at his home.

In the early 1950s EC was a small operation compared to comic book publishers like Avon, Fox, or DC, but this enabled the editors to spend more time and care with each comic book. Every issue would go through an elaborate process before it was distributed to the outside world.

IMMIGRANT
CASTRO YES...PROHIAS NO!

Mr. Gaines, mi corazón siempre viaja con ustedes
Proh'14, 1969.

Dave Berg's rendition of a *Mad* trip, with Gaines as the *Mad* zeppelin. — Berg/Berg

Cuban artist Antonio Prohías often joined in on the *Mad* trips, but occasionally faced problems with immigration officials. For the trip to Italy in 1968 he got as far as the gates, luggage in hand, before being turned back. — Prohías/Prohías

Harvey Kurtzman wrote every story in the twenty-three issues of *Mad* comics, but he took his editorial powers a step further. He would also lay out the panel patterns and sketch out what each panel was to contain.

The artist would then go back to his studio with the work, pencil in the drawings, show them to the editors, wait for them to be lettered, then ink them.

The "filler stories," two pages of text in each comic book that were required by the post office in order to mail them by second-class rates, were written at first by EC writers and typeset. Later, Kurtzman simply purchased various foreign newspapers and reproduced columns of Greek, Russian, or Egyptian under short introductions. In one fell swoop Kurtzman complied with government regulations, saved money on writers and typesetting, and added to *Mad*'s arcane mystique.

Next, the black-and-white drawings, twice the size they'd be when reproduced, were returned to EC for corrections. Coloring the drawings was yet another process, and comic books are colored in a way peculiar to the medium.

A peek behind the scenes at *Mad* magazine by Sergio Aragonés. —Aragonés/Aragonés, cover, *Cartoonist Profiles* #7

CARTOONIST PROfiles

Issue No. 7 — August 1970 $2.50

Comic books are usually sent to an engraver as black-and-white line art. The engraver has teams of colorists who decide what to color each element in a picture. Comic

THE MADMEN: *Nick Meglin*

Nick Meglin has been on the staff of *Mad* for nearly its entire existence, and before that, he was contributing ideas and writing. His introduction to the EC gang had been through the artist Frank Frazetta, who had worked with Al Williamson on EC comic books. Although trained at the School of Visual Arts as a magazine illustrator, Meglin also possessed a sense of humor and a talent for writing, and he began contributing writing to Al Feldstein's *Panic*. Later, he contributed more writing to *Mad* magazine and started working closely with Feldstein, providing ideas and developing the unique *Mad* sensibility for which it has become best known. No sooner had his name begun to appear on the masthead than he was drafted into the army, although his time was conveniently served in the publicity department at New York City's Whitehall Street Induction Center, making it easy for him to continue to moonlight for *Mad*.

Upon discharge, Meglin returned to a full-time associate editor position, becoming *Mad*'s chief talent scout. Meglin was responsible for finding and cultivating many of *Mad*'s contributors, including Mort Drucker, George Woodbridge, Larry Siegel, Sergio Aragonés, Antonio Prohías, Angelo Torres, Dick DeBartolo, and Stan Hart. He became the main editorial liaison with artists and writers, smoothing feathers that Feldstein occasionally ruffled and developing a painless editorial style.

When Meglin, along with John Ficarra, assumed the chief editorial position in 1985, his easygoing way didn't change. He is still a favorite with *Mad*'s contributors, and Bill Gaines refers to him as the "soul of *Mad*."

Along with his duties at *Mad*, Meglin also manages to work on a variety of other projects. He has written three books: *Pen Drawing* (Pitman Books), *On the Spot Drawing* (Watson-Guptill), and *The Art of Humorous Illustration* (Watson-Guptill Publications), which includes an analysis of the work of several artists who regularly contribute to *Mad*, as well as Norman Rockwell and other notable illustrators. He teaches a course in drawing and illustration at his alma mater, the School of Visual Arts.

book color is flat, and there are no gradations of tone. It is also limited to a small number of color mixtures of the four basic colors. That's

why men in comics wear green suits and buildings are purple. The engraver's colorists would specify a certain color, by number, for each delineated area, which would be translated into print by using special dot screens known as benday dots. Produced this way, comic book color is flat, crisp, brilliant, and predictable.

Early on, EC grew dissatisfied with this assembly-line approach to coloring their comics, so they hired Marie Severin to be their in-house colorist. An artist in her own right, Severin was able to work with the editors to create many special effects seldom seen in the comics of the times. The 3-D parody illustrated earlier is but one example of her work. Severin was also known around EC as the one person allowed to put the reins on the enthusiasms of the staff and artists. "The only self-censorship that we ever had was Marie Severin, the only person we allowed to trample on our creative efforts," Gaines admitted. "No one else could control us without a cleaver." When Severin was faced with a particularly gory or tasteless scene in a suspense or horror comic, she simply colored the area a dark, impenetrable blue. In fact, when the entire run of EC comics was reprinted several years ago in black and white, several surprising new details emerged that would have added more fuel to the comic book burnings of the 1950s.

When *Mad* became a magazine, the process of producing it changed. Since there was type to size and set, and new forms of layout to work out, a production person was needed. When it came to decision-making, Kurtzman was often intuitive rather than logical, and for the staff of the new *Mad* magazine he was looking for the perfect blend of sensibilities. For production he cast his eye to the unlikely personage of John Putnam. Putnam had had some experience in comic books, drawing backgrounds for other artists, but he had never worked on production. A good ten years older than most of EC's crew, he was a bright but shy and eccentric man, having spent much of his childhood in tuberculosis sanatoriums, or traveling around the world with his mother, Nina Wilcox Putnam. Putnam's name came from Robert Faulkner Putnam of the publishing firm, but his biological father was rumored to be the well-known American artist Rockwell Kent. Putnam spent his idle hours in obscure Greenwich Village cafés and bars reading French novels, at the offices of EC comics, building models of historical ships, and writing poetry in French.

When Putnam was approached by Kurtzman for the production job, his first inclination was to turn Kurtzman down, citing his lack of experience and his natural messiness. Kurtzman persisted, sure that Putnam's quiet looniness was just what the new *Mad* would need.

When Kurtzman left *Mad* in 1956, Putnam was the only *Mad* staff member to stay. After Feldstein was rehired by Gaines to take over *Mad*, he regrouped the small staff. Jerry De Fuccio, dubbed by Frank Jacobs "*Mad*'s token gentleman," was a prep-school boy and comic book fan who had studied writing. He was always impeccably attired in a suit and tie, an anomaly at 225 Lafayette Street. His proofreading skills were invaluable, and he was legendary for his ability to sweet-talk secretaries into helping him acquire movie and television stills and scripts for *Mad*'s parodies.

Nick Meglin joined the staff as an "idea

man" soon after. A recent graduate of the School of Visual Arts, Meglin had contributed stories to Feldstein's short-lived humor comic *Panic*.

Soon it became apparent that Putnam's work load was becoming too great. Kurtzman's intuition had been on the money: Putnam had developed an eye for design and was contributing many of the quirky ideas that gave *Mad* its character, from cover ideas to the small details that were noticed only on the second or third reading of the magazine. He had also developed a great talent for mimicry, and was able to duplicate anything from a train schedule to a hair color advertisement, perfectly matching typefaces and design grids. But research for these tasks took time,

and it was clear that if *Mad* was to take advantage of Putnam's creativity, he would need help. A call went out to the School of Visual Arts for someone who could take over production, and Korean war veteran Lenny Brenner answered.

The offices of *Mad* were never to be the same. At first meeting, the bearded, stocky

THE MADMEN: *John Ficarra*

A member of a younger generation, editor John Ficarra grew up reading *Mad* on Staten Island—and he hasn't outgrown it yet. Although he began his college years taking pre-law courses at Fordham University, he soon transferred to New York University and switched his major to journalism, working his way through school with a job selling nickel and by playing schmaltzy piano music at cocktail lounges. Even while a student, Ficarra began selling articles to *National Harpoon*, *International Insanity*, and the local newspapers. He began sending material to *Mad* soon thereafter, but it was not until 1979 that his first article appeared in those pages. By then he was writing humorous material for radio comedy and comedians like Joan Rivers, Soupy Sales, Rodney Dangerfield, and Phyllis Diller. When Jerry De Fuccio left *Mad* in 1980, Meglin recommended hiring Ficarra to replace him and Feldstein agreed.

Ficarra continued to write for *Mad* while holding down the duties of an associate editor. When Feldstein retired in 1985, Bill Gaines appointed both Ficarra and Meglin to the top editorial position at *Mad*. "I'm very uncomfortable in the spotlight," Ficarra says. "When I go to parties, the last thing I mention is that I'm an editor of *Mad*. When I do, I always get one of four responses: 'I read it as a kid,' 'Is *Mad* still around?' 'You should come down to where I work—you'd get enough material to fill *twenty* books!' or they want to compete like crazy with me to be funny."

Ficarra says that his editorial guiding light is "Question everything—trust no one!"

Brenner is an intimidating man, greeting visitors with "What the hell do you want?" or "Get the hell out of here!" On second or third meetings he is just as gruff, if not more so. His favorite snack is raw garlic, and his presence often permeates the offices. He had suc-

ceeded in raising misanthropy to an art, and the rest of the staff liked him immediately. Although he had bluffed about his experience in production on his job interview, he was a quick study, and he and Putnam soon became a closely working team.

Meanwhile, Feldstein was fine-tuning the procedure for creating *Mad*, and through many years and several staff changes, it is still the process followed today. Each issue of *Mad* begins with ideas, either suggested by one of *Mad*'s free lances, cooked up by the staff, or, occasionally, received in unsolicited mail. The ideas, or premises, are circulated among the editorial staff who mull them over, discuss them in meetings, and then decide on which are the funniest. If an idea is approved, it goes back to the writer, who writes the gags or script, and sends it back to *Mad*. In the case of articles that comprise a series of jokes, the writers often write two or three times as many as are needed, and the editorial staff decides which are to be used.

Finished manuscript in hand, the editors and the art department now decide how and by whom the writing will be illustrated. The number of pages, composition of the layout, and artists' styles and schedules all figure in to the decision-making process. The article is laid out by an editor, who also works out a rough idea of the volume and location of the text. If the piece incorporates pictures of celebrities, a television show, or a movie, one of the associate editors compiles an assortment of reference photographs for the artists, known as a swipe file. The text is typeset.

The artist then goes to work, often embellishing the piece with touches of his own, making obscure gags clear, and giving personality to jokes. When the drawings are de-

Jack Davis captures George Woodbridge and Dick DeBartolo going native in Tahiti in the traditional colorful skirts. Meanwhile, Gaines sticks to a sun deck and a mystery novel.
— Davis/Davis

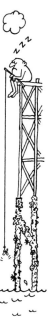

livered, they are examined by the editors, then are turned over to the art department, who send the finished layouts on the road to being printed. The work is first sent out to be photographed, a complicated procedure in which the line work and type are photographed separately from the shaded areas, which are shot through a dot screen called the halftone. This procedure, peculiar to the reproduction of cartoons, gives sharpness to line and intensity to the black or white areas while maintaining subtle gradations in the gray tones. Returned to the art department, examined, then sent back out, the photographs are combined and printed together, and the "boards" are delivered to *Mad* for proofing.

Corrections are made and the boards are returned to the printer, who makes the printing plates and runs off a replica of the maga-

zine called the blue line. The art department and the editorial staff examine the blues for one last proofing, mainly for page order and other problems of assembly. Once the printer receives the go-ahead to roll the presses, the entire run of millions of *Mad* magazines is printed in just a few hours, culminating a process that began about seven months earlier. Of course, since *Mad* comes out eight times a year, there are always several issues of *Mad* in the works at any given time.

George Dougherty has overseen the printing of *Mad* since the very beginning. Besides attending to the details of scheduling, paper supply, distribution, and other technical matters, Dougherty has worked out ways for *Mad* to include many types of special material, such as stickers and records. The freebies were often featured in *Mad*'s special issues, and many of the items were things that had never before been bound into a magazine. A life-size poster of Alfred E. Neuman required special gizmos on folding and binding machines, and a complex, die-cut *Mad* zeppelin model was almost a fiasco, since the perforated card stock tended to stick together in the stacks. "They're all things for which the technology was available, but that had never been applied to the field," Dougherty explains. "*Mad* has always tested the outer limits of printing equipment."

Over the years there has been remarkably little staff turnover. John Ficarra replaced Jerry De Fuccio as associate editor in 1980. When Feldstein retired in 1985, Gaines promoted both Meglin and Ficarra to the top editorial position, which they share as co-editors.

Hired to replace the two as associate editors were Sara Friedman, Charlie Kadau, and Joe Raiola. By the time Friedman was offered the full-time job in 1985, she had already had a long association with *Mad*. As a young girl growing up in Memphis, Texas, she had written Gaines a lengthy fan letter praising the work of Mort Drucker. Gaines wrote back, and the two began an active correspondence, exchanging letters, drawings, tapes, and postcards. "So at the age of eleven, I became pen pals with this man, this publisher in New York City," remembers Friedman. "It was sort of mystifying to my parents." When a position on the editorial staff opened, she became the first woman to work in that department. Her placement made fewer ripples than might be expected in a situation that had been wholly male for over thirty years. "In meetings I think they were restraining their jokes a little," she comments, "but that restraint disappeared in about a month." "We've been holding back all of our sexist articles for when she's on vacation," adds Kadau.

Kadau and Raiola are a sort of comedy team, Kadau fair and portly, Raiola dark and wiry. Together they share the other full-time associate editor position. The two got their first professional writing credits working on several one-shot newsstand magazine parodies produced by Gerry Taylor and Ed Shain: *Cosmoparody*, *Penthouse Parody '85*, *Like a Rolling Stone*, and others. They also began selling their work to *Mad*, and when they joined the staff, they worked out a part-time arrangement that allowed them to work on other projects.

Tom Nozkowski joined the art department in 1980. Nozkowski had been designing *Mad*'s paperbacks on a free-lance basis for several years to support himself as a serious painter, and was a natural for the part-time position. His abstract paintings have been shown in a number of solo exhibitions and have been

A case of mistaken identity on *Mad*'s 1973 trip to Mexico. The poor tourist has made the error of querying *Mad*'s resident misanthrope Lenny Brenner, as captured (or imagined) by Al Jaffee. —Jaffee/Jaffee

Mad cover artist Norman Mingo was an older gentleman known for his dignity, refinement, and mannerliness—in contrast to the rest of the traveling Madmen. Don Martin gives his rendition of a typical meal on the road.
— Martin/Martin

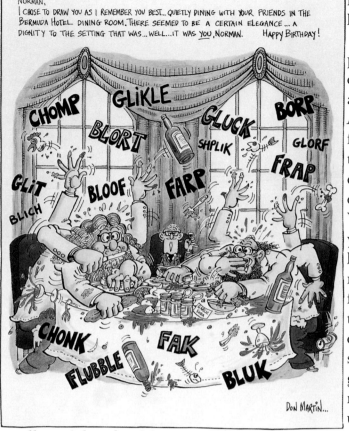

running his company in a way no company has ever been run before.

He has developed an immutable business philosophy of precepts that are, on the face of it, outrageous. Some of these eccentricities are apparent to *Mad*'s readers. For instance, *Mad*'s not a monthly: it's published every forty-five days, and an issue is off the rack by the time it reaches the month written on the cover. After three hundred issues, *Mad* is still on Volume One. Gaines says they'll start Volume Two with issue one thousand (in the year 2078). Other of *Mad*'s unusual practices have more to do with behind-the-scenes business. Virtually all magazines exist as a vehicle for advertising, and *Mad* doesn't take advertising. Neither does *Mad* advertise itself in other media. Gaines has never run a reader survey, and has no concrete idea of the demographics of *Mad*'s readership and doesn't really care, since such statistics are mainly used to sell advertising. At most magazines, subscriptions are usually the core of circulation, and heavily discounted, but a one-year subscription to *Mad* saves the reader only twenty-five cents, once again, because *Mad* has no need to subsidize circulation to attract advertisers. Gaines does not rent or sell the subscriber mailing list, and he doesn't believe in sending out repeated renewal notices to subscribers; instead, a card (with no return postage) is inserted in the subscriber's last issue, a fact that was once reported by a shocked writer for the trade journal *Circulation Management*. Gaines will interrupt whatever he's doing to write a check for a *Mad* freelance artist or writer on delivery of finished work. At other magazines, payment often takes weeks or months. And for the last thirty years, he has periodically shut down the en-

collected by the Museum of Modern Art, the Metropolitan Museum of Art, and the Brooklyn Museum, among others. At first, Nozkowski found his prominent position at *Mad* to be in conflict with his reputation as a "serious" painter. As that reputation has grown, the artist finds the situation has improved. "When I talk in schools about my painting, I used to go out of my way not to bring up this job, because I was afraid that that's all the kids would want to talk about," Nozkowski adds, "but I find it useful now to explain to them about having jobs."

The business end of *Mad* is supervised, as it always has been, by Bill Gaines. Gaines retired from the editorial staff of EC when the last of the New Trend comics went out of print, and has since applied his creativity to

tire office and treated staff and free lances to weeks-long trips around the world.

But *Mad*'s success has shown that there is method to Gaines's madness. In fact, by 1960, Gaines was advised by his tax accountant that no individual could pay income taxes on

the kind of money *Mad* was making. In 1961 he sold *Mad* for several million dollars to Premier Industries, a diversified company that produced battery additives, venetian blinds, and fur coats, among other things. A few years later, *Mad* was sold by Premier to National Periodical Publications, the same company that was once owned by Max Gaines's business partner. In 1969, National Periodical merged with Kinney Corporation, which then acquired Warner Brothers Movies, taking the name Warner Communications, and *Mad* found itself owned by a company whose movies it had satirized for years. As of 1989, Warner Communications became Time Warner, the biggest media conglomerate in the country.

Through a succession of owners, Gaines has managed to retain full authority over how the magazine is run. How has *Mad* survived unscathed, and even thrived, through these many corporate takeovers? There is a well-known street strategy in New York City to avoid an imminent mugging: once aware of being threatened, the intended victim simply throws himself into the role of a raging maniac, acting as crazy and unpredictable as

possible. The surprised attacker will usually abandon the attack for easier prey. This seems to be the strategy adopted by Gaines, and, so far, it has worked. *Mad* is overseen by William Sarnoff, the chairman of Time Warner's trade publishing division. Ask Sarnoff what he thinks about the way *Mad* is run, and he'll answer, cagily, "We know that the fellow that was responsible for [*Mad*'s success] is Bill Gaines, and we knew that if we brought all our expertise to it, we could screw it up. . . . It's a unique and wonderful operation, run by people who would not easily fit into a corporate culture."

Sarnoff is being kind; *Mad* fits like a square peg in a round hole, and its ownership sometimes causes Warner a bit of trouble. In 1981 the publishing house Harcourt Brace Jovanovich realized that Warner was going to

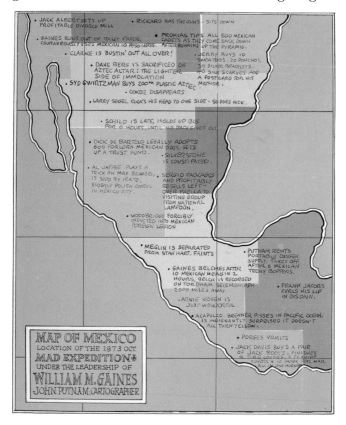

A highly personal map of *Mad*'s tour of Mexico by John Putnam.

attempt a takeover of the company. Harcourt fought back by announcing to the press that "no company that owns *Mad* magazine has any right to try to associate itself with a stable of twenty Nobel prize–winning authors."

Nevertheless, Time Warner has resigned itself to having an anachronism like *Mad* in its midst. Of course, the fact that *Mad* has an estimated net profit margin of 11 percent, compared to the industry average of 9.7 percent, doesn't hurt. "We're happy with something eccentrically run that works," hedges Sarnoff.

If he could only see Gaines filling out his monthly cash flow report, one of the few responsibilities Gaines has to fulfill to *Mad*'s parent company! The object of the report is

means that there's something very wrong. *That's* when you employ the Boogerian Constant—it's the number you multiply this by to get that. It's a simple thing!" He adds, proudly, "I've been faking it for twenty-five years—they've never found the Boogerian Constant!"

Actually, Gaines is quite a serious businessman, and a crack mathematician when he needs to be. After Kurtzman left *Mad* in 1956, Gaines and Feldstein were determined to make *Mad* a financial as well as a popular success. Although *Mad* had been making money under Kurtzman's stewardship, its publication dates had been erratic, and there never seemed to be enough money to produce the kind of work that Kurtzman really

     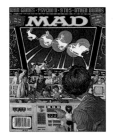  

to predict how much money *Mad* is going to take in during the coming month. The way Gaines runs *Mad*, he already knows the future amount, through calculations not at all like the sort that Time Warner wants to see. So Gaines uses Time Warner's formulas, but employs what he calls the "Boogerian Constant," a technique he developed in his days as a student at Brooklyn Polytechnic Institute. He starts with a beginning and a final cash amount. "You work forwards with all your math to a certain point, then you work backwards to a certain point," Gaines explains. "So there you are, you've got this figure here and that figure there and they're supposed to be the same figure, but they ain't, which

wanted. Feldstein analyzed Kurtzman's *Mad*s, gleaned the most successful concepts and formats, fine-tuned them, added a few of his own, and made the humor broader and more accessible. He developed a procedure for producing the magazine that relied on a number of established formats that work—the magazine hasn't changed much in form since 1960.

Gaines and Feldstein disagreed on the matter of advertising—Feldstein wanted it, Gaines was adamantly opposed. In 1959, Gaines gave Feldstein the go-ahead to try a little experiment. In typical *Mad* fashion, Feldstein chose as his subject Moxie, a little-known, bitter soft drink, the main selling

Nothing can stop Gaines and Brenner in their pursuit of the local specialties of cuisine, as depicted in loving detail by Angelo Torres. —Torres/Torres

point of which was that it had been invented by a doctor. Feldstein got permission from the perplexed president of the Massachusetts company to use the brand name. In that year the logo for Moxie appeared over forty times in the backgrounds of *Mad* illustrations. *Mad*

MADRID · GRANADA · MALAGA · CASABLANCA · MARRAKESH · FEZ
MEKNES · TANGIER · SEVILLE · 1972
Bill.. Another Great trip — thanks JACK RICKARD

received hundreds of letters from sharp-eyed readers, and sales of Moxie rose over 18 percent.

Gaines, however, was not convinced.

But after many years of stubbornly defending *Mad*'s lack of ads to both editors and corporate higher-ups, Gaines was finally vindicated in an article he distributed triumphantly at Warner's next board meeting. In 1984 a lengthy analysis of *Mad*'s success by Vincent P. Norris was featured in the *Journal of Communication*, a scholarly publication pro-

duced by the Annenberg School of Communications at the University of Pennsylvania. Norris pointed out that *Mad* defied two myths of magazine publishing: it didn't carry ads and it didn't charge high prices. In fact, the average consumer magazine ended up costing readers half again as much per editorial page.

(Up to this time, Gaines had been defending *Mad*'s price increases with what he calls the Frankfurter Equation. It goes something like this: in 1955, when *Mad* was 25 cents, a Nathan's Famous Coney Island hot dog—in Gaines's opinion, the ultimate—was a dime. In 1990, *Mad* is $1.75 and a Nathan's hot dog is also $1.75—while the frankfurter is *over seventeen times* what it once was, *Mad*'s price has increased only sevenfold.)

Although *Mad*'s lack of color and glossy paper has often been attributed to Gaines's legendary cheapness, Norris, with copious charts and statistics, showed that in keeping the costs of producing the magazine low, with black-and-white interior pages and a small staff (no one at *Mad* has a secretary), *Mad* was able to compete with slick, color magazines that maintained complete departments of advertising salespeople, who often managed to subsidize only themselves.

A substantial part of *Mad*'s profits also comes from repackaging original material from *Mad*. Special double-size, double-price editions of vintage articles culled from earlier issues appear four times a year, and cost *Mad* little to produce. The *Mad* policy is to make no secret of what the readers are getting: special editions have borne titles like *The Worst from Mad*, *More Trash from Mad*, and (a rare hardcover) *The Ridiculously Expensive Mad*. There are also, at last count, twelve foreign-language editions, all of which use material predominantly from the U.S. *Mad*. Then there are *Mad* paperbacks: over 80 contain republished material; an additional 120 are original books by *Mad* contributors, who split the royalties with *Mad*.

One of the reasons *Mad* is able to reprint material so freely is that, unlike other magazines, *Mad* buys contributions of art and writing outright, as what are called "works for hire," retaining the copyright to the work—when contributors sign the back of their check, they are also signing a rather lengthy rubber-stamped agreement giving up all future rights to the original art and its reproduction. It is this practice that has caused *Mad* to be embroiled in one of the biggest controversies among those in the trade about the way it does business.

Back in EC's comic book days, virtually all comic book publishers purchased work outright from their contributors, printed it once, then either carelessly stored it in insecure warehouses or threw it away. Gaines, on the other hand, from day one, archived the original drawings for all the EC comics, including *Mad* comics and *Mad* magazine. *The Mad Reader*, a paperback book edited by Kurtzman with an introduction by humorist Roger Price, was the first reprint of *Mad* material, and was such a success that in subsequent years Feldstein edited three hardcovers with introductions by Ernie Kovacs, Steve Allen,

and Sid Caesar—big time for a small magazine. Gaines realized that he had a gold mine, and began producing the paperbacks and specials still in print today. Early on, Gaines

THE MADMEN: *William M. Gaines (Part 2)*

In 1955 Bill Gaines married Nancy Siegel; she had been working in EC's subscription department. Together they took an apartment on Manhattan's East Side. Due to EC's political trouble, his new marriage, and perhaps the psychoanalysis he was going through, he began to withdraw from the creative end of production and concentrate on his duties as publisher.

After EC comic books ceased publication and Harvey Kurtzman left the company, Gaines gave new priority to keeping EC financially profitable. Feldstein took over as editor of *Mad* and the two of them kept their eyes firmly on the bottom line, while Gaines cultivated a family atmosphere with the staffers and free lances who worked for him. While gaining the reputation as a very difficult (many say impossible) negotiator, Gaines also became known as one of the most honest, straightforward, and loyal publishers in the business.

As EC became continually more prosperous in the 1960s and 1970s, Gaines relaxed and partook of the spirit of the time, letting his graying hair grow long and his wardrobe become even more casual. He and Nancy had three children, Cathy in 1958, Wendy in 1959, and Christopher in 1961. Although they shared a love of travel and good food, the marriage eventually disintegrated, and they divorced in 1971.

Over the years one of Gaines's favorite duties at *Mad* has been writing personal letters of response to readers. Some of these readers have become pen pals of years' duration. One eventually became Gaines's wife. Anne Griffiths wrote in 1970 requesting a copy of a *Mad* article she was unable to find in her stockpile at home for a college term paper.

The two began a correspondence and the next trip Gaines took to visit relatives near State College, Pennsylvania, he contacted Griffiths in advance. Gaines and his cousin took Griffiths and a friend out to dinner, they hit it off, and the letterwriting continued.

After Griffiths transferred to the University of Colorado, an art course brought her on a field trip to New York City. A romance began, and Griffiths spent the last summer of her college years with Gaines in New York. After Griffiths was graduated with a bachelor of fine arts degree, she moved to New York to be with Gaines. She began working for *Mad* in 1980, and in 1987 she and Gaines formally tied the knot.

The trip to the U.S.S.R. in 1971 included a stop in Copenhagen, where Paul Coker was spotted in the back of a book shop reading a book on chicken sex. Knowing that he was going to be razzed by the Madmen for the rest of his life anyway, Coker has made the incident the motif for his contributions to Gaines's scrapbooks, depicting a camel for Morocco, a bull for Mexico, and an oyster for Tahiti.
—Coker/Coker

decided that it was only proper to share the wealth, so he concocted an elaborate formula based on each artist's and writer's relative contribution of pages to determine end-of-the-year bonuses and, later, participation in annual trips. The bonuses are not contractu-

ally promised; in fact, after Kurtzman left *Mad*, Gaines quit giving him checks for the sales of *The Mad Reader*. Kurtzman sued, and years later the case was settled out of court.

This system has made Gaines both the hero and villain in the comic book world. *Mad* has always paid some of the highest rates in

the business—between $350 and $650 per page—to both artists and writers. This is from two to five times the comic book industry average. Because Gaines has saved the original art, the boards have been available to produce fine-quality reprints for a public increasingly aware of comic books as an American art form; in the 1980s the entire run of EC comics was reprinted in annotated slip-cased editions. Also in the 1980s, the original art was made available to collectors in a series of auctions, the proceeds of which were split with the artists, resulting in quite a windfall for the free lances.

Some artists and writers have been uncomfortable relying on Gaines's largess for a substantial portion of their income, and *Mad* has lost several contributors because of the practice. Perennial favorite Don Martin quit contributing because he wanted to own the rights

to his artwork, going so far as to testify at a congressional subcommittee hearing on the subject of works for hire, increasingly an issue for all free lances in the comic book and magazine world. Even ongoing contributors to *Mad* occasionally grumble about the system, but most make light of it. When Gaines's mother, Jessie, died, Arnie Kogen remarked that he wasn't going to the funeral because he didn't have enough pages.

But Gaines is slow to change. He runs *Mad* as a benevolent dictatorship, and feels entirely justified in his unusual ways. As Kurtzman has pointed out: "Bill has always had a very strong intellectual understanding of the democratic processes. Up to a certain point; then he turns into a monster." Gaines knows that he's sometimes difficult, admitting: "The philosophy of the outfit was to do what we liked, as long as it fit certain compulsive

During the 1980s, Gaines also found himself to be visited by the ghosts of comic books past in the form of Hollywood producer Joel Silver, who approached Gaines with a proposal to make a movie using the plots from EC's horror comics from the 1950s. It took seven years to get the project off the ground, during which it evolved from movies for theaters to half-hour programs produced especially for the HBO cable network. *Tales from the Crypt* premiered in 1989 and was an instant hit, both with viewers and in the industry, becoming the most successful original series the network has yet aired. Silver's special effects staff created a creepy Crypt-Keeper who opens and closes each program with pun-filled patter that any loyal EC fan would recognize.

These days, although Gaines is active as *Mad*'s publisher and a movie consultant, and takes several major trips abroad each year, he is approaching his seventieth birthday and is slowing down. He has given only a little thought to his successor at *Mad*. "I do not plan to retire, ever," he says. "Either I'll die here in my chair, or they'll fire me." For nearly forty years, through *Mad*'s astronomical growth and numerous ownership changes, he has managed to keep *Mad* the way he loves it. He still opens all his own mail, writes the checks, and says goodnight to each staff member at the end of every day.

frameworks which I had...."

Gaines is assisted in running the business end of *Mad* by Gloria Orlando, office manager for many years, who suspects at times that she may be the only sane person in the office. She and Lillian Alfonso take care of the eighty thousand subscribers to *Mad*.

Mad's international circulation is supervised by Dorothy Crouch, who first became involved with *Mad* in 1970 when she was managing editor of Warner's Paperback Library division overseeing the *Mad* paperbacks.

Although he avoided hiring family members for many years, two of the Gaines family are now on the staff. Anne Gaines, Bill's wife, has worked as his personal assistant since 1980, handling *Mad* original artwork and helping Bill with many aspects of his work as publisher of *Mad*. She refers to herself as a "glorified gofer," but Bill Gaines gives her more credit. "I have gotten to the point in life that I could not run this business without Annie," he says of the one person he trusts to help with several crucial tasks. Chris (M.C.) Gaines manages the mail room, shipping artwork and subscription freebies. "I do what nobody else does—they hand me all the lowest jobs," he claims.

Yet another of Gaines's eccentricities is that he has never been enthusiastic about merchandising *Mad*. "A lot of people have one way of looking at it: like 'Peanuts' is merchandised up to its eyeballs," says Gaines. "I don't object to that, except that a magazine like *Mad*, which makes fun of people who do that—it doesn't seem proper for us to do it ourselves." In the early years there were occasional items offered by *Mad* itself—a T-shirt, a bust of Alfred E. Neuman, the *Mad* straitjacket—but

Gaines has almost always turned down offers by companies to exploit the *Mad* name or characters. When Laurie Curran approached Gaines for Parker Brothers with an idea for a board game, she got the predictable answer, but continued to badger him. After she was finally able to negotiate a contract, the *Mad* game became Parker Brothers' most successful board game since Monopoly.

In more recent years, *Mad* has entered

licensing to a limited degree, allowing several items to be produced with modest success. As John Ficarra points out: "Alfred E. Neuman is *not* Snoopy—he's not cuddly, or lovable." Gaines, Meglin, and Ficarra each hold one vote on any merchandising proposal; any of the three can veto any idea, and most are rejected.

One reason that Gaines now entertains licensing proposals at all is that with the teenage population declining, *Mad*'s circulation has dropped from a high in 1973 of 2.4 million to one million or so. This slide at first caused a bit of a panic. Stephen G. Bloom, a writer for the *Dallas Morning News*, was one of a number of reporters to interview Gaines on the occasion of *Mad*'s thirtieth anniversary in 1982. He asked Gaines what he thought *Mad* would be like in generations to come. "I doubt if we'll be around that much longer," Gaines replied, flippantly, adding that for the annual *Mad* trip "last year, we all went to Miami Beach. This year, if we're lucky, we'll go to Brooklyn."

Although Gaines never said anything about *Mad* going out of business, Bloom took the story and ran with it. "Publisher Fears Magazine's on Its Last Leg" screamed the headlines. As befitted the death of an American institution, the story was quickly picked up by Associated Press and appeared in newspapers across the country. *Mad* was flooded with calls, which were fielded by an irate Al Feldstein, who issued statement after statement to the contrary, reminding them that at a current circulation of one million copies an issue, *Mad* was still one of the largest magazines in the country.

Although some have chafed under Gaines's paternalism, his spirit has been responsible for assembling a remarkably talented, diverse, and loyal group of writers, artists, and staff members, many at the top of their fields. Sergio Aragonés described the situation quite succinctly: "*Mad* is kind of like the old father-kids relationship. Bill Gaines is the father image, and he handles the company the way he thinks companies should be handled. And you have an alternative because none of us have contracts. If you don't want to work there, you leave." He adds, "And just like I could never go against my father even if he's wrong, I could never go against Bill Gaines, even if he's wrong, because he's *more* than a friend. Not only a friend, he's more than a friend. To me, things like that are more important than a job or paycheck or a contract. If it was Marvel [Comics Company] it would be different!"

In fact, Aragonés is one of the most ardent opponents to the work-for-hire system that Gaines employs. "This is something Sergio and I have been fighting about for years," Gaines admits, "but we fight with love, because we love each other, and we know that the other one has this opinion that we despise."

Gaines began developing his managerial style when he first took over EC comics, by being sure to run the artist's, then the writer's, credit, and by running one-page artists' biographies in the comics. Gaines encouraged his editors to develop what interested them, rather than jump on the latest popular fad, another major difference between him and other comic publishers. Feldstein says, "We were writing for teenagers and young adults; we were writing for the guys that were reading it in the Army. We were writing for ourselves at our age level...." Years later, this philosophy was responsible for giving readers the feeling that in reading *Mad* they were insiders, friends and cohorts of the Usual Gang of Idiots. For instance, the famous potted plant known as Arthur that appeared in *Mad* for several years was Putnam's office avocado tree, which he "raised from a little nut." The guys around the office were fond of Putnam's pet and began including it in their drawings, to readers' immense delight. Arthur became so famous that the *Saturday Evening Post* once called the plant "a national hero."

Camaraderie was also encouraged in part by Gaines's annual Christmas parties, which he began giving in the comic book days. In the early years he gave out cameras, EC cuff links, and other gifts to his guests; later the gifts became bonuses.

One day in 1960, Gaines called a general meeting of staff, writers, and artists, in all about twenty men. Although some were friends (Meglin, Torres, Woodbridge, and

Several of the group embark on *Mad*'s first European trip, to France. From top to bottom: Bob Clarke, Frank Jacobs, John Putnam, Jack Davis, and Dave Berg. — Irving Schild

For many of artists in the group, the trips are busman's holidays and they carry sketchbooks and watercolor blocks to capture the local scene. Here is Bob Clarke in Venice. — Irving Schild

Stan Hart, George Woodbridge, Al Jaffee, and Nick Meglin take in the shade in Tahiti. — Irving Schild

Have food, will travel. A splinter group made friends with a local driver in Greece, who took them home and fed them grapes from the backyard. Aragonés, Coker, and Irving Schild squat, their hosts stand behind. — Irving Schild

Frank Frazetta had hung out in art school together in a group known as "The Fleagles"), most of the others had never met each other. Assembling them in his office, he distributed copies of guide books to Haiti, and told them that they would soon be going on an all-expenses-paid tropical holiday.

Gaines had spent months planning *Mad*'s first group trip down to the most minute detail. Although a resounding success, the trip was sometimes rocky, as one would expect in a "family" of strangers. At first, there was a natural distrust between the writers and artists, since artists are considered one step above writers in the comic world hierarchy, and writers are considered (by artists) to be disconcertingly quick-witted. "The artists had no use for any of the writers—even to talk to one of them was almost a violation of your honor as an artist," George Woodbridge remembers. "I always thought I was very liberal and open-minded because I befriended Frank Jacobs."

Gaines's elaborate planning became the butt of many jokes during the trip. Don Martin has remarked that "he was sort of like a Sunday school teacher or a first grade teacher. We almost had to stand in line with no talking allowed." But his attention to detail was responsible for one of the most memorable events of the trip. Before leaving New York, Gaines had checked up on *Mad*'s Haitian subscribers. He found that there was only one, and he was about to let his subscription lapse. On arriving on the island, Gaines piled the group into rented jeeps and headed for the man's house. The group greeted the stunned reader at his door, Gaines bestowed on him a gift subscription, and the Madmen drove off into the sunset.

Over the following years, Gaines has led the group on trips that have grown increasingly exotic and lengthy. In 1966 they made their first European trip, to France, which was followed by tours in Italy, Greece, Kenya, Japan, Hong Kong, Thailand, Morocco, and Spain. The Madmen themselves were becoming an increasingly international group, with the addition of Sergio Aragonés of Mexico, Harry North of England, Paul Peter Porges of Austria, Antonio Prohías of Cuba, and Irving Schild of Belgium. Almost everywhere they visited, there was someone in the group who either knew their way around or spoke the language, and helped make friends and get the group through the numerous small difficulties of travel. Foreign editors of *Mad* sometimes joined in when the group was visiting nearby.

In 1971, when *Mad* was reaching the peak of its circulation, Gaines went all out, and the Madmen took a seventeen-day trip with stops in London, Copenhagen, Leningrad, Moscow, and Amsterdam. In Moscow, the group visited the offices of the Soviet humor magazine *Crocodil*, where they were surprised to find that the editors knew as much about what was going on in American politics as they themselves knew.

Eventually, Gaines began to loosen up his iron organizational grip, and the trips became more spontaneous. Women began joining the group in 1980 when wives and girlfriends were welcomed for the second half, and when *Mad* added its first female staffers and free lances in 1985, the trips became fully integrated.

Over the years the group grew to know each other well, and this intimacy made the events of the 1980 trip to Germany all the

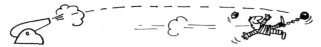

more painful. John Putnam became sick with a severe cold that, because of his childhood tuberculosis, quickly developed into pneumonia. When it was time for the group to return to New York, Putnam had grown too sick to be moved, and George Woodbridge volunteered to stay with him until he recovered. The illness wore on for six weeks as his condition deteriorated. Several attempts were made to fly Putnam back to New York; once a jet was specially chartered, but it became obvious that he was not to recover. On November 29, Putnam died. Several days later Woodbridge flew back alone, ending an era at *Mad*.

In their group travels, the Madmen have developed rituals and interests that set them apart from other groups of working people. One of these is their traditional greeting of their boss. It all began when someone (probably Frank Jacobs) began singing, "Fuck You, Bill" to the tune of "Over There." Others, realizing that the song was a perfect expression of their affection toward maniac Gaines, joined in a rousing chorus. The expression stuck, and to this day is considered the proper, though startling, greeting when approaching Gaines on any special occasion. Another motif of the trips is food and wine, encouraged by Gaines's legendary appetite, thirst, and appreciation of all things gastronomic. Whatever the occasion or location, Gaines makes sure to plan a banquet of the sometimes exotic local specialties, sparing no expense.

Every year, several months after a trip, the group assembles once again for a party to reminisce, share snapshots, and present Gaines with a scrapbook created by the artists and writers. Occasionally, the group will

perform songs they have written. The scrapbooks and the acts are typically as irreverent as the Madmen themselves, but nothing beats Lenny Brenner's contribution to the scrapbook marking the trip to Tahiti in 1974. Under a photograph of Gaines in a lawn chair he placed a note that reads as follows:

Dear Bill;

Seeing you with that book . . . in that shirt . . . those pants . . . those shoes . . . and with that bug spray . . . Well, I thought, what better memento of that wonderful trip to Tahiti . . . or was it Mexico? . . . Spain? . . . Russia? . . . or was it Haiti??

Who can tell!? you were reading the same book, wearing the same crummy clothes and spraying the same sickening bug spray on all the trips!

AND WHO CARES, ANYWAY?

FUCK YOU!

Len Brenner

And so they go.

In 1987, after a fifteen-year romance, Bill Gaines and Anne Griffiths wed, and the wedding provided a setting for a *Mad* reunion.

NOTES

"The only self-censorship we ever had . . ." Benson, "The Transcripts," 22.

"no company that owns Mad magazine . . ." Smith, "Harcourt Has That 'What Me Worry' Look," 22.

"net margin profit . . ." Slutsker, "The Secret," 230, 232.

"Bill always had a very strong intellectual understanding . . ." Benson, "Harvey Kurtzman and Bill Gaines," 86.

"Mad is kind of like the old father—kids . . ." Thompson, "Sergio Aragonés," 73.

"We were writing for teenagers . . ." Benson, "The Transcripts," 23.

"he was sort of like a Sunday school teacher . . ." Haimes, "Don Martin."

"In order to survive . . ." Walsh, "For This Cartoonist, It's a Mad, Mad, Mad World," 20.

PEOPLE

SATIRE

SHEER MAD-NESS

"The brute fact of today is that our youth is no longer in rebellion, but in a condition of downright active and hostile mutiny. Within the memory of every living adult, a profound and terrifying change has overtaken adolescence." The psychiatrist Robert M. Linder raised this warning not in the violence-prone 1980s, nor during the civil unrest of the 1960s, but in his 1954 study of youth in America, *Rebel without a Cause. Mad* appeared at a great transition in American history. The forces and effects were both broader and deeper than just those from the new mobility and increasing affluence. Midcentury men found their deep-seated "American" values of thrift,

10

hard work, piety, and individuality challenged at every turn. The lone rebel, once a universally admired American hero, in the age of the Organization Man began to be seen more as a selfish misfit, or worse — a nonconformist.

While advances in technology were supposed to be making life easier and more en-

  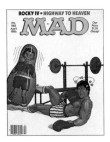

joyable, things in general also became more complicated. A plethora of choices needed to be made for each new purchase, and home and offices were invaded by endless numbers of gizmos and gadgets requiring new skills and maintenance.

Increasingly, the tendency in the face of this technological inundation was to prevail upon experts for help. There was no shortage of specialists to give advice and information: for children there was Dr. Spock (and Dr.

THE MADMEN: *Sergio Aragonés,*
Don Edwing, Don Martin, Paul Peter Porges

Sergio Aragonés's always wordless drawings have embellished *Mad*'s margins since 1962, shortly after the Spanish-born artist moved to the United States from Mexico. He had been cartooning since childhood, amusing his friends with his rapid-fire drawings. He continued during his study of architecture in college, where he also studied mime with Alexandro Jodorowsky, indulging his interest in nonverbal communication. Befitting his reputation as the "World's Fastest Cartoonist," over the years that Aragonés has been a regular contributor to *Mad* he has also illustrated several books and animated films, co-created the humorous magazine *Plop!*, one of the first comics to attempt to assimilate underground comics into the mainstream, and developed the comic book *Groo the Wanderer*, the first creator-owned comic distributed to the general newsstand market. Over the

Wertham), for sex there were the Kinseys, for mental health, psychiatrists — the numbers of which increased sixfold between 1940 and 1964. And there were all those doctors and celebrities who pitched products in print advertisements and on television. Rather than make decisions by the difficult and lonely method of introspection, confused Americans were encouraged by these experts to turn their lives over to those who supposedly knew better, and would, of course, keep their best interests firmly at the top of their minds.

But something was very obviously going awry. For one thing, there was the atomic bomb, its use defended by the U.S. government, but toward which many Americans, in their heart of hearts, felt only repulsion and a sickening lack of control. The terrible effects of radiation were becoming known, as were the consequences of U.S. testing of the weapons in locations around the world.

Lying became a prevalent, insidious, and potent force as Senator Joseph McCarthy waved his lists of nonexistent Communists in the government, while real Communists with professional positions secretly burned their libraries, and movie stars, including Ronald Reagan, turned fink on their left-leaning peers. Madison Avenue hired psychologists to develop new and elaborate ruses to sell products, and executive men learned to fake their way through required, and crucial, corporate personality tests. As visionary Marshall McLuhan put it, "We no longer have a rational basis for defining virtue or vice. And the slogan 'Crime Does Not Pay' is the expression of moral bankruptcy in more senses than one. It implies that if crime could pay, then the dividing line between virtue and vice would disappear." Or as the Man in the Gray

In The Acme Ritz Central Arms Waldorf Plaza Hotel

When Don Martin began contributing to *Mad*, he quickly became known for his grotesque, hinge-footed characters and his unusual sound effects. — Martin/Martin, "In the Acme Ritz Central Arms Waldorf Plaza Hotel," *Mad*, #86

years, Aragonés has won numerous National Cartoonist Society awards in several categories.

Don "Duck" Edwing was introduced to the staff of *Mad* through Harvey Kurtzman, to whom he had been selling "five-dollar cartoons" for *Help!* Edwing began with "Scenes We'd Like to See" as well as other topical short pieces and ideas for Don Martin's cartoons. Through *Mad* he has been able to indulge his taste for the macabre. Edwing now specializes in work that reveals his fascinations, in cartoons about jungles, headshrinking and cannibalism, dungeons, and disease.

If Don Martin had been a medieval artist, he would certainly be known today as "Master of the Shplork." Martin's lantern-jawed, bulb-nosed, flap-footed, thick 'n' thin characters are unmistakable, as are his outrageous and articulate sound effects. As a young man, Martin studied art at the Pennsylvania Academy of Fine Arts in Philadelphia with the idea of becoming a painter, but already he was finding that his main inspirations were the monstrous and grotesque paintings of sixteenth-century artist Hieronymus Bosch and Warner Brothers cartoons. For many years Martin was known as "*Mad*'s Maddest Artist," and although in 1987 he moved on to other work, at *Mad* the title, like a revered football number, seems to have been retired.

Writer and artist Paul Peter Porges's life is the stuff of which 1950s adventure movies are made. His native Vienna was taken over by Nazi Germany when Porges was twelve years old; Porges was adopted along with one hundred thirty other endangered Jewish children by the Baron Edouard de Rothschild and lived in a castle near Paris. When France fell, the children were left to their own devices. Porges wandered southern Europe, looking for a way to reach a safe haven. During these years he worked in a vineyard with other refugee children, escaped, and was caught with false papers and put in a concentration camp in France—the last stop before a camp in Germany. He escaped again, on a garbage truck, and, aided by remnants of the Jewish community, Quakers, and the Swiss Red Cross, finally made it to safety in Switzerland.

After finishing high school, Porges studied art at L'Ecole des Beaux Artes in Geneva. He emigrated to New York City and by 1954 was contributing cartoons to the *Saturday Evening Post* (where he became a contract cartoonist), and later *Playboy* and the *New Yorker*. Porges's humor often has a particularly silly twist. To what does Porges attribute such an absurdist bent? "In order to survive you have to have a cynical outlook on life. You can't take it seriously. It *is* absurd.... It comes out of the minorities, the guy who survives, who remains stable. And the guy the *unfunny* guys are trying to kill."

Flannel Suit exclaimed, "I don't know what honesty is anymore."

And last, but not least, there were the children. By the late 1950s, many of these offspring were growing older, and, perhaps because of their sheer numbers, a new population group was defined: teenagers. But these kids, doted on and indulged like no generation before, were not turning out to be the bundles of joy their parents expected. By 1958, Dwight Macdonald reported in *The New Yorker* that the first association that most adults had with the word "teenager" was "juvenile delinquent."

1986

As the decade wore on the situation grew only more intense. Conformity and affluence were supposed to bring ease and contentment, but Madison Avenue kept upping the stakes; there was no resting place in the climb to success. The *Playboy* era supposedly ushered in sexual freedom, but that freedom was only available to the well-to-do single white man. As Eric Sevareid observed, "The biggest big business in America is not steel, automobiles or television. It is the manufacture, refinement and distribution of anxiety...." The success of this industry was reflected in the sales of Miltown tranquilizers, which soared from $2.2 million when the drug was introduced in 1955, to $150 million by 1957.

Amidst these intense pressures to conform, other voices began to be heard, voices that

ORDINARY CONFORMISTS

. . . play insipid show scores, dismal pop tunes conducted by Jackie Gleason, sickening dance music by Guy Lombardo, rock n' roll hits by Ricky and Elvis, and occasional works of Gershwin and Tchaikovsky on complicated hi-fi sets.

ORDINARY NON-CONFORMISTS

. . . play obscure folk songs sung by obscure folk, dull chamber music played in dull chambers, Wagnerian operas in their entirety, Gregorian chants, and readings of minor Welsh poets on super-complicated stereo hi-fi sets.

MAD NON-CONFORMISTS

. . . play bird calls, tap dancing and exercise lessons, transcriptions of Senate Committee hearings, Gallagher & Shean, The Singing Lady, and theme music from famous monster movies on easy-to-operate hand-wound victrolas.

ORDINARY CONFORMISTS

. . . wear narrow-shouldered charcoal-grey Ivy League suits, button-down shirts with tight collars, silly caps, cramped Italian style shoes. Females wear Empire dresses and shoes with spike heels that constantly break off.

ORDINARY NON-CONFORMISTS

. . . wear sloppy-looking sweatshirts, grimy blue jeans, arch-crippling sandals, and scratchy beards. Among the females of this group, leotards are usually substituted for blue jeans, and the scratchy beards are optional.

MAD NON-CONFORMISTS

. . . wear smart-looking MAD straight jackets, glamorous opera capes, roomy knickers, comfortable Keds, and lightweight pith helmets which offer good protection in bad weather and provide storage space for day's lichee nuts.

ORDINARY CONFORMISTS

. . . go in for uninspired Technicolor musicals, stories with happy endings, migraine-provoking Cinemascope, and 6½-hour double features that destroy the eyes, ears, nose, throat and spine.

ORDINARY NON-CONFORMISTS

. . . patronize stuffy out-of-the-way movie houses that show "experimental" films, arty-type films, documentaries, and obscure foreign language pictures with the sub-titles in pidgin Swahili.

MAD NON-CONFORMISTS

. . . enjoy hand-cranked penny arcade machines which contain film classics like the Dempsey-Firpo fight, Sally Rand's Fan Dance, old Ben Turpin comedies, and Tom Mix pre-adult westerns.

As American society developed a counterculture in the late 1950s, *Mad* positioned themselves at the fringes of the fringes while pointing out that many nonconformists were conformists of a different stripe. Sy Reit's 1959 vision of the *Mad* nonconformist was absurdly wacky at the time, but in light of nouvelle cuisine, clothing designers like Jean Paul Gaultier, movie directors like Pee Wee Herman and David Lynch, and hip-hop and rap music, it can now be seen as surprisingly prescient of the postmodern eclecticism of the 1980s. — Reit/ Woodbridge, "How to be a Mad Non-Conformist," *Mad*, #47

DON MARTIN DEPT. PART I

ONE NIGHT IN A LIVING ROOM

EEE AAAGH!!

What's the matter, Dear . . . cat got your tongue??

27

Yet another trip to the Martin Zone in this slice-of-life quickie. — Martin/Martin, "One Night in a Living Room," *Mad, #159*

Although Harvey Kurtzman provided strong direction for the art in *Mad* during his tenure as editor, his own drawings seldom appeared in the comic book or magazines. His series of one-page "Hey Look" comics were what impressed Gaines and Feldstein at his first interview at EC comics, and later several of them appeared in *Mad* comics. — Kurtzman/Kurtzman, "Hey Look," *Mad, #7*

"I don't think it's going too far to say that for my generation, the generation that protested the Vietnam War, growing up with Harvey's **Mad** *and Harvey's war comics shaped the situation to allow our generation to protest that war. . . . It was comics*

were both a threat and a safety valve. The books *The Lonely Crowd, The Organization Man, Man in the Gray Flannel Suit*, and *The Hidden Persuaders* were all critical of the direction society was taking: all were surprising successes. The movies *The Wild One* and *Rebel without a Cause* celebrated teenage rebellion for its own sake, and hoods became heroes. Some even saw in the rise of Joseph McCarthy a rebellion against the status quo; Richard H. Rovere described it as "the perverse appeal of the bum, the mucker, the Dead End Kid . . . to a nation uneasy in its growing order and stability and not altogether happy about the vast leveling process in which everyone appeared to be sliding, from one direction or another,

into middle-class commonplaceness and respectability." What was called "sick humor" enjoyed a vogue, and iconoclastic humorists Stan Freberg, Mort Sahl, Ernie Kovacs, and Lenny Bruce found audiences.

EC comics was one of these dissonant voices. When Gaines was thrust into the head position at EC at his father's death, he and his mother were already well-fixed financially, and he was not at all sure, or even concerned, that he, as the family failure, would be able to successfully run the company. Years later, DC's then-editor, Sheldon Mayer, recalled, "I got the feeling that Bill went into the business as a joke, to see if he could screw up things, change them for his private amusement, and still manage to make money doing it. . . ." It was having nothing to lose that enabled Gaines to follow his own, and others', caprices and instincts without much regard for EC's reputation in the comic book industry or in American culture at large.

EC comics expressed an individual point of view, anathema in the 1950s. Gaines and Feldstein were writing their horror and science fiction purely for their own enjoyment, and Gaines has stated that "EC stories differed from a lot of stories in comics because 'virtue' did not have to triumph. . . ."

What is obvious in hindsight is that EC stories of bigotry, racism, murder, monsters, and mayhem reflected and gave substance to fears and anxieties of living in an unfamiliar post-industrial world of unlimited war, uncertain morality, and the isolated nuclear family.

These, of course, were not the kind of thoughts that the new and precariously situated middle class, with their mortgaged

about media that made you question how you get your information, and that's a necessary co

houses, G.I. Bill educations, and vivid memories of bad times, wanted to entertain; and it was members of middle class, rather than the elite rich, intellectuals, or poor, who led the attack against comic books. The idea of comics themselves—picture books—seemed a rejection of literacy, and this new middle class had struggled for the right and ability to read, if only *Reader's Digest*. As pundit Leslie

...nt toward taking any kind of political action.” ART SPIEGELMAN

Fiedler explained it, "The high-minded petty bourgeois cannot understand or forgive the rejection of his own dream, which he considers as nothing less than the final dream of humanity."

Many of EC's young readers followed the controversy revolving around comic books more closely than their parents ever realized. The disappearance of the comic books some-

times had an impact as strong as that of the comic books themselves. Through news reports and the EC Fan-Addict Club bulletin, the most far-flung fans learned that their favorite comics were under attack. Gary Arlington remembers trying, as a boy, to buy a copy of Wertham's book, and realizing that "the people who ran this place didn't know what to think. Here was 'little Gary' wanting to special order this book, this *Seduction of the Innocent*." Arlington later went on to run a San Francisco comic shop and EC lending library that was a favorite hangout of many artists who created the first underground comics. Spain

© HARVEY KURTZMAN 1986

Rodriguez, one of those very cartoonists, also vividly remembers the impact of the code. "I was shocked when EC's were effectively banned. It was a severe blow to my youthful idealism. I never thought something like this could happen in America." Skip Williamson, another professional cartoonist, has stated that "in an era of phlegmatic homogeneity they brought color and primal awe to a kid sneaking peeks at his uncle's comics. And to an entire generation, they exposed (through their crucifixion) one of the Great American Lies. The one about freedom of the press."

For the men running EC, the issue was not

DOCTORED DICE

NORMAL DICE

DOCTORED DICE

Again, the gambler's ingenuity is applied, and again our sharp eyes detect his subtle work. Note how "legitimate" dice at left have perfectly square corners, while those

"doctored" dice at right have tiny tiny beveled corners—enough to control roll. Shrewd MAD fans can easily see how gambler can throw winning "seven" almost every time.

Readers could always count on *Mad* to explain the mysteries of life. —Jaffee/Wood, "Mad Investigates the Sordid Business of Gambling," *Mad*, #71

as black-and-white. "The 'experts' gave all kinds of supportive testimony how terrible we were, and what we were doing to the youth of America," Feldstein recalled of the subcommittee hearings. "We became intimidated, and I'm sure that we all did some soul-searching." Although Kurtzman seems always to have been sure that he was on the moral up-and-up, Gaines and Feldstein attempted to clean up their act, producing first the New Directions comics and then the Picto-Fiction line, aimed at more adult readers. But something was missing; Feldstein and Gaines had lost their confidence and enthusiasm for serious comic books. They weren't even writing most of the stories,

and it was almost a relief when both lines failed.

Aside from a few scrapes, *Mad* comics were never the focus of public ire the way EC's horror and crime comics were. *Mad* was probably overlooked because it was seen as a "funny book," although it was often just as subversive of social mores and taste as the horror comics, if not more so. Overtly, cartoon violence was a recurring comic motif in *Mad*, its victims as likely to be women as men. Male and particularly female characters were often physically overendowed, especially as drawn by Elder and Wood; such sexiness was later specifically outlawed by the code.

But less easy to point the finger at was *Mad*'s attitude, an atmosphere that pervaded the comic, and later, the magazine. The images had a labored intensity about them, and close examination of the many details revealed that things were not what they had seemed on first glance. Strange, ongoing subplots developed in the backgrounds, adding another level to the comic. Characters made references to events from previous issues of *Mad*, or made inside jokes, or appeared in cameo roles in other *Mad* stories. Kurtzman began playing with alternative ways to make images, incorporating photographs and found images, having covers that didn't look like comic book covers, and using foreign languages. Not all of Kurtzman's experiments were easy to appreciate, and readers who took the time to read, reread, and decipher *Mad* felt like insiders in a new, and unconventional, adventure. Cartoonist Rick Griffin vividly remembers the first time he saw *Mad*. "There was something unusual about the format of this book. The strange use of 'doctored' photographs mixed with weird art

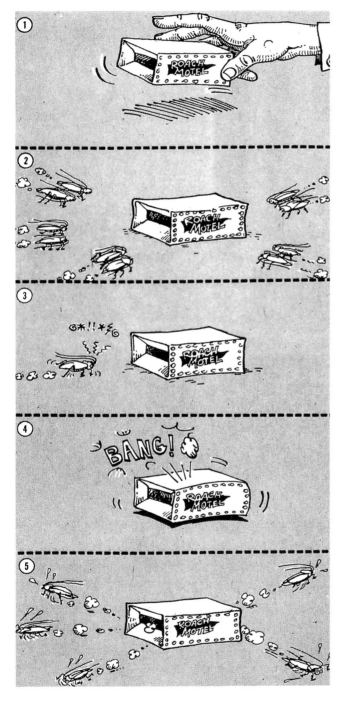

struck me as rebellious and anti-establishment. It gave me a fantastic disorienting effect."

With the encouragement of Gaines and Feldstein, Kurtzman's toying with the conventions of comic art and writing expanded to a general challenge of the culture at large. When Feldstein took over *Mad*, the humor in the magazine became less personal, but by grounding the magazine more firmly in subjects from the mass media, and using the work of a number of writers, he made the humor more varied and accessible to a broader range of people. By the late 1950s *Mad* was enthusiastically unconventional, universally skeptical and honest; it didn't talk down to its readers. *Mad* refused to take anything, including itself, seriously. Unlike General Electric, progress was not *Mad*'s most important product—when something new was silly or unnecessary, *Mad* pointed it out.

Mad championed the cause of the outsider. Soon after its institution in 1954, the Comics

A bit of silliness from *Mad*'s artist of marginal interest, Sergio Aragonés—Aragonés/ Aragonés, *Mad as a Hatter*

While normal folks fantasize about sunnier or more exciting aspects of life, a *Mad* artist's inclination often tilts in a different direction.—Aragonés/Aragonés, "A Mad Look at Bugs," *Mad*, #259

Code Authority had virtually eliminated representations of members of ethnic groups in comics; their restriction against "ridicule or attack on any religious or racial group" had, as historian Pamela B. Nelson has pointed out, "intimidated many cartoonists into avoiding ethnic images altogether." But Joe Orlando sees a more insidious meaning behind the code. "It reflected the society. Look at the advertising, the magazines like

Saturday Evening Post, the kind of people they represented were certainly not a melting pot, they all looked like WASPS, and they were hairless, and they didn't sweat, and the women all wore white gloves." Feldstein and Gaines had been severely burnt enough by the code to avoid the kind of pointed racial and religious morality tales that had been the suspense comics' redeeming feature, but in *Mad* they reveled in contrariness, exalted in pointing out skeletons in closets and dirt swept under the rugs. The strategy of disguising the same social issues as satire worked, and soon *Mad* found a place in living rooms across the United States; by 1960 its circulation reached a landmark one million, and it was read by 58 percent of all college students and 43 percent of all high school students, perhaps the only "cult" magazine to be read by a majority. *Mad* had succeeded in finding a middle ground in a society polarized between squeaky-clean suburban lifestyles like those portrayed on *Donna Reed* and *Father Knows Best*, and the perceived menaces of Communism, ethnicity, and rock-and-roll. When it found that middle ground, it proceeded to throw pies at both sides, its readers, and even itself.

Indeed, self-denigration has been central to the spirit of *Mad*. While obviously proud of its team of artists and writers, announcing awards and honors bestowed on them on the letters page, *Mad*'s masthead refers to them as

"the usual gang of idiots." Bill Gaines is a "fink," and often the butt of jokes about his cheapness and weight. On the letters page editors and readers refer to each other as "clods" while trading compliments, criticism, and insults. Mail-order pictures of Alfred E. Neuman are suggested for lining bird cages or wrapping fish. As historian Todd Gitlin explains it, "With the help of *Mad* and its ilk, a subgeneration crystallized on the curious premise that, *en masse*, it was made up of singularly discerning, superior spirits—who were, at the same time, just plain knuckleheads." If *Mad* encouraged the questioning of authority, it meant *all* authority, including its own.

By the late 1950s, the mass media were beginning to take notice of this upstart magazine that dared to poke fun at the American Dream. In fact, although *Mad* had a number of imitators in comic book form at the time, it was the only mainstream satire magazine available to most Americans. The cold war was still on, and Charles Winick of Columbia University noted in a 1962 study of *Mad* that "the areas of national life in which ridicule is acceptable have diminished steadily. The preoccupation with un-Americanism, and, thus, with Americanism, can only be seen in perspective if we consider how we might feel if we heard of 'Englishism' and 'un-Englishism' and 'Frenchism' and 'un-Frenchism.'"

Nevertheless, the 1960s were bringing ripples of change in the pervasively defensive climate of the previous decade. McCarthy was buried, and the blacklists were beginning to be openly challenged. Families who thought that the move to suburbia or the new mouthwash or late-model car would bring everlasting peace and security were discovering the error of their beliefs. Teenagers were gaining more influence as they aged and began spending money, and they were spending it on *Mad*. As an editor at *Coronet* magazine pointed out, "*Mad*'s habit of deflating everything may indicate that the organization man, conformist wave is not engulfing the younger generation." Adults who read copies of *Mad* that their kids brought home often found its satire to be quite entertaining, and became readers themselves. Judging from letters and comments, new readers often found themselves blinking in surprise that there was anyone else "out there" who shared their consternation with the current state of affairs.

What helped give *Mad*'s editors and contributors their special perspective was that they were mostly first- or second-generation immigrants—outsiders looking in at a sometimes alien social system with the courage to say so. Will Elder used his Brooklyn childhood as inspiration for the *Archie* parody, "Starchie." "We were very poor," Elder says. "We'd go out on dates and a friend would drive us in his car, he with his girlfriend, I with mine. Afterward, he would drop me off first at a house that looked very lovely. And I would walk three blocks down to my apartment, which looked like a hovel, a lean-to. I was very much ashamed. So why not inject that?"

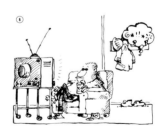

One of the reasons that *Mad*'s readers have felt like part of a family is that their artists and writers often include inside jokes about the humorist's trade. —Aragonés/Aragonés, *Mad as a Hatter*

Turnabout is fair play—a favorite theme in *Mad*. —Aragonés/Aragonés, "A Mad Look at Birds," *Mad*, #140

***Mad* boldly goes where no man has gone before, this time to a *Star Wars* restroom somewhere long ago and far away.** —Aragonés/Aragonés, "A Mad Look at 'Star Wars,'" *Mad*, #197

More sheer absurdity from Basil Wolverton. —Wolverton/Wolverton, "Mad Hats," *Mad*, #36

The Cookie Tin Capote

Cookie tin would be perfect for gal wishing to preserve that "just graduated" look.

The Colander Cloche

Ventilated colander would be just the thing for that hot-headed type dame.

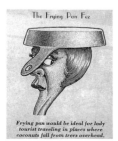

The Frying Pan Fez

Frying pan would be ideal for lady tourist traveling in places where coconuts fall from trees overhead.

Jewish and Italian Americans have predominated on *Mad*'s editorial staff, and artists and writers have included a large number of Jews, Hispanics, and Europeans—a surprising number of them survivors of the persecutions of Nazi Germany and other oppressive regimes. Satire magazines have more of a following and history in Europe and Latin America, perhaps giving these humorists a head start on their fellow American citizens.

Unfortunately, *Mad*'s tolerance and encouragement of outsiders sometimes did not extend to the female or homosexual members of their audience. Homophobic jokes, of the stereotypical limp-wristed and lisping variety, appeared until Feldstein received a visit and a talking-to by representatives of a gay and lesbian rights group. Jokes made at the expense of women were similarly clichéd, and unfortunately, a feminist has never made a formal call, although *Mad*'s editorial staff has grown more sensitive about issues of sexism in recent years.

Mad has provided a detailed, funny counterattack against the hucksterism of Madison Avenue, the chicanery of politicians, the pretensions of those in authority, and the hy-

pocrisy of everyday life. But, for kids, there is another level in reading *Mad*: *Mad*'s unblinking satires allow them to examine unfamiliar social practices and standards, while maintaining the protection of humor and disdain. For many years, *Mad* was the only semi-sanctioned place where kids could read about

sex, divorce, alcoholism, drugs, corruption, other religions and lifestyles, then considered over the heads of, and therefore off-limits to, healthy children. Even foreign readers picked up helpful tips about life in America from *Mad*, a Danish reader revealing that during his first visit to New York City, he was able to identify a cockroach in his hotel room from a picture he had seen in *Mad*.

By including cruder jokes about things like nose-picking and body odor, *Mad* has let its readers know that it has accepted the reality of the human condition, a reality that "polite company" would never even ac-

knowledge. Al Goldstein, publisher and editor of *Screw* magazine, puts the issue rather colorfully: "The *Mad* mystique resides in its expression of the unfulfilled wish, and this is inseparable from the world view of the adolescent male. His is a gender-oriented reality: boys are our true vulgarians and barbarians, and despite the fact that their parents want to 'pretty them up'—as if they were painting a pile of shit—there is a roughness about the male condition that cannot be gentrified." One may question Goldstein's assumption that such a state is sex-specific; it is a condition of childhood in general that kids are awkward and unacceptable to the adult world in their natural unsocialized state, probably as klutzy as Alfred E. Neuman. Robert Warshow, in an article about his son's devotion to EC comics, frames the issue a lit-

tle more gently. "Children do need some 'sinful' world of their own to which they can retreat from the demands of the adult world; as we sweep away one juvenile dung heap, they will move on to another. The point is to see that the dung heap does not swallow them up, and to hope it may be one that will bring forth blossoms."

Although *Mad*'s circulation has, at times, reached almost three million copies, with an estimated pass-along readership of six times that number, it has accepted, and even guards, its stance as an outcast. It has received some help from enthusiastic detrac-

tors, including the Catholic Church. Artist Joe Orlando remembers moving to a new home in Queens and receiving a courtesy call from the local Catholic pastor, who offered to bless his new home, room by room. Soon they arrived at his upstairs studio, where the priest commented on Orlando's large collection of reference books, asking if he was careful to make sure that none were to be found on the *Librorum Prohibitorum*, or Catholic Index of

Before going on to become a Stanford professor in computer science and author of the world's standard set of programming reference books, Don Knuth overhauled the weights and measures system in this, his first published work. Knuth proposed that the system become the standard of the future, but it seems to have had about as much success in the United States as the metric system.—Don Knuth/Wood, "The Potrzebie System of Weights and Measures," *Mad*, #33

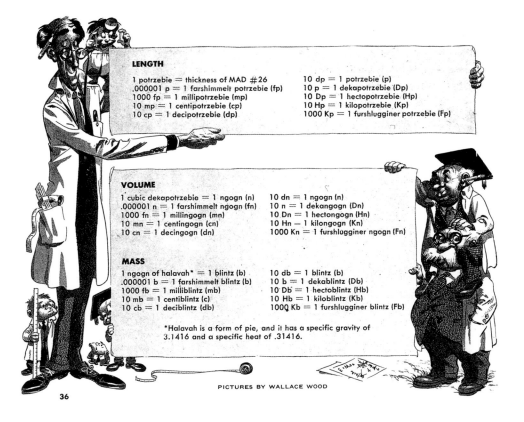

THE POTRZEBIE SYSTEM
OF WEIGHTS AND MEASURES

THE POTRZEBIE SYSTEM

This new system of measuring, which is destined to become the measuring system of the future, has decided improvements over the other systems now in use. It is based upon measurements taken 6-9-12 at the Physics Lab. of Milwaukee Lutheran High School, in Milwaukee, Wis., when the thickness of MAD Magazine #26 was determined to be 2.26334851- 7438173216473 mm. This length is the basis for the entire system, and is called one potrzebie of length.

The Potrzebie has also been standardized at 3515.- 3502 wave lengths of the red line in the spectrum of cadmium. A partial table of the Potrzebie System, the measuring system of the future, is given below.

LENGTH

1 potrzebie = thickness of MAD #26	10 dp = 1 potrzebie (p)
.000001 p = 1 farshimmelt potrzebie (fp)	10 p = 1 dekapotrzebie (Dp)
1000 fp = 1 millipotrzebie (mp)	10 Dp = 1 hectopotrzebie (Hp)
10 mp = 1 centipotrzebie (cp)	10 Hp = 1 kilopotrzebie (Kp)
10 cp = 1 decipotrzebie (dp)	1000 Kp = 1 furshlugginer potrzebie (Fp)

VOLUME

1 cubic dekapotrzebie = 1 ngogn (n)	10 dn = 1 ngogn (n)
.000001 n = 1 farshimmelt ngogn (fn)	10 n = 1 dekangogn (Dn)
1000 fn = 1 millingogn (mn)	10 Dn = 1 hectongogn (Hn)
10 mn = 1 centingogn (cn)	10 Hn — 1 kilongogn (Kn)
10 cn = 1 decingogn (dn)	1000 Kn = 1 furshlugginer ngogn (Fn)

MASS

1 ngogn of halavah* = 1 blintz (b)	10 db = 1 blintz (b)
.000001 b = 1 farshimmelt blintz (b)	10 b = 1 dekablintz (Db)
1000 fb = 1 milliblintz (mb)	10 Db = 1 hectoblintz (Hb)
10 mb = 1 centiblintz (c)	10 Hb = 1 kiloblintz (Kb)
10 cb = 1 deciblintz (db)	1000 Kb = 1 furshlugginer blintz (Fb)

*Halavah is a form of pie, and it has a specific gravity of 3.1416 and a specific heat of .31416.

PICTURES BY WALLACE WOOD

36

Prohibited Books. Orlando assured him that he doubted that any were. "Then he said, 'Ah!

Potrzebie, Hoohah!, Blab! and Zap

To say that EC comic books and *Mad* magazine have an especially devoted following would be an understatement. Although they have been reviled by parents and educators, they have also inspired two alternative literary genres: the comic book fanzine and underground comics.

When EC comics became popular, there were no magazines or publications that reviewed comic books. In *Seduction of the Innocent*, Frederic Wertham charged that, because of this, comic books couldn't be considered a true literary form—fans of EC comics considered this a challenge. Although large distances sometimes separated them, the hard-core EC readers already knew of each other through EC's letters columns. Bhob Stewart in east Texas had been first off the line in 1954 with *The EC Fan Bulletin*. It was modeled after science-fiction fanzines of the 1930s and contained news and ruminations written by Stewart about the whole line of EC comics. The messy hectograph the teenager used limited the press run to about sixty copies and because of this the otherwise well-received *Bulletin* folded after two issues.

Soon Stewart found out that another EC reader from Virginia, Ted White, had acquired a postcard mimeograph machine that would do the job better, if not smaller. They teamed up with Larry Stark, a New Jersey fan who had written EC so many lengthy, thoughtful letters that Gaines had bestowed on him a lifetime subscription to the line. Together they produced *Potrzebie*, which contained upgraded writing, criticism, and commentary about comics as well as news of Wertham's crusade.

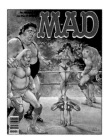

Before long other publications discussing EC's horror, suspense, war, and humorous comics were begun. Notable among them were *Hoohah!*, published by Ron Parker beginning in 1955, the *EC Fan Journal,* and the *EC World Press*. All the publications were available for token subscription fees, or simply in return for letters or articles. They were small-circulation, simply produced periodicals, usually typewritten, mimeographed, and

You're an artist—and who do you work for?' I said, '*Mad* magazine' and he said, '*That's* on the Index!'" Orlando admits, mischievously, that "He left without blessing my studio."

Mad has also had its share of more thoughtful, less dogmatic critics. There are vocal, early fans still around who feel the magazine went downhill when Harvey Kurtzman left. Around the *Mad* offices they are known as the Kurtzman Cult. Even while still under Kurtzman's editorship, *Mad* had begun receiving letters charging pandering and a

lowering of standards. Others have felt that *Mad*'s transition to a magazine took the juice out of it. In 1958, Dwight Macdonald contended that *Mad* "speaks the same language, aesthetically and morally, as the media it satirizes; it is as tasteless as they are, and even more violent." And, in the journal *Dissent*, T. J. Ross charged that "Consistently, and perhaps unwittingly, *Mad* depicts parents as apes and family life as apish, without any upbeat compromise." Cartoonist and playwright Jules Feiffer took this criticism one step further when he asserted that in *Mad* "everything stinks. Everything's a gag, a joke, a put-on. It's all bullshit, so there are no changes to be made and no reason to be involved."

It may not seem so to Feiffer, but the editors of *Mad* do differentiate between what they feel is appropriate and what they do not. "We draw the line at things that might actu-

KING DAVID INSPECTING HIS BAR-MITZVAH GIFTS

Paul Peter Porges gives vivid personality to dry historical figures in his series "Candid *Mad* Snapshots of Historical Celebrities." — Porges/Porges, "Candid Mad Snapshots of Historical Celebrities," *Mad*, #202; "More Candid Mad Snapshots of Historical Celebrities," *Mad*, #203

"In fact, it was the only subversive literature available. I remember actually seeing the original Mad Comics, *when I was about nine, at the shoeshine parlor/ tobacco and magazine shop.*
It was so different from other comics, so rampantly hysterical, it burned my fingers!"

PAUL BUHLE
Genesis

PAVLOV WITH A NON-SALIVATING DOG

ally hurt somebody, no matter how funny they are," stipulates Gaines, a general rule, but one that is strictly enforced. When *Mad* runs an ad parody, it is the advertisement itself that is spoofed, not the product. There has been very little nudity in *Mad*, certainly none of the full-frontal variety, and only lately have a few of the blander four-letter words begun to appear, although such things as sex are often included, obliquely. "We take

hand-stapled, and contained criticism, interviews, and correspondence, created as a labor of love by enthusiasts for other enthusiasts. The earliest EC fanzines were helped along by the E.C. Fan-Addict newsletter. Eventually reaching twenty-five thousand members, the newsletter posted notices for members.

Over thirty years after the last EC comic was published, new fanzines devoted to them continue to spring up. *Squa Tront*, published and edited at first by Jerry Weist, was the most sophisticated, and is still being published. *Squa Tront* (EC Venusian for "Good Lord!") sports a color cover, original art, and unpublished photos and working drawings from EC and other artists. In true amateur fashion (in the best sense of the word), steady contributors have taken turns at editorial and publishing duties: John Benson has been editor of about half the publication's run, and Bill Spicer is about to take the helm. Rich Hauser's *Spa Fon* (Martian for "Good Lord!") also appeared in the 1960s, and the 1980s have spawned Rob Labbe's *Mad Freaks, USA*, Kyle Hayley's *Qua Brot*, and Monte Beauchamp's *Blab!*, which began as an EC-centered publication but has since broadened to other comics and is actually available at well-stocked magazine shops.

Although you won't find them in public library collections, these publications are mother lodes of information, anecdotes, and arcana about the history of comics and their influence. The articles may tend to dwell on the small details that only a devoted fan would love, and the publication schedule may be erratic (since 1967 there have been ten issues of *Squa Tront*), but the contributions are often well researched, original, and insightful.

Underground comic books are a second type of alternative publication that have been directly influenced by the EC comic books and *Mad*. Comic books like R. Crumb's *Zap Comix* began to appear in the late 1960s and, like the EC line and *Mad*, did not bear Comics Code Authority approval—some of the first since the EC line went under in 1955. The publishers/artists/writers got away with it by distributing the comic books through head shops and other countercultural outlets springing up around the United States, such as Gary Arlington's San Francisco Comic Book Company, which also had an EC lending library. Gaines's books were aimed at an older audience, and so are underground comics, although the sex and violence depicted there are sometimes much more explicit than anything ever found in EC comics. Like *Mad*, underground comics are usually published in black and white and don't take advertising.

But more important is the influence of the EC stories and art on the underground artists. Along with George Herriman's *Krazy Kat* and Will Eisner's *Spirit*, the EC comics were an early inspiration to many of the

the position that if the kid is too young to understand our double entendres, they won't hurt him," explains Gaines.

Keeping to these rules, *Mad* has managed to surprise and shock, but occasionally it has truly enraged its readers. Sometimes the

problems are political. Once, an ad parody featuring the "Crime of the Month Club" gave an address as "Mafia, Italy." The Italian government caught wind of it and a member of the State Department paid a call, requesting that *Mad* watch its ethnic references. In the early 1960s *Mad* suggested that readers send off to J. Edgar Hoover for official draft-dodger cards. The FBI was inundated with mail (they wouldn't say how much), and Hoover dispatched two FBI men to convince the editors to refrain from such pranks.

The most infamous incident of *Mad* misjudging its readership occurred in 1974. Nick Meglin came up with the cover idea of a hand giving "the finger" and the words "*Mad*—First in Bad Taste." Feldstein changed the wording to read "Mad—The Number One Ecch Magazine," and mild-mannered Norman Mingo was enlisted to paint the image. The trouble began the moment the issue arrived at newsstands and drugstores, many of which refused to display it. Hundreds of readers sent letters of complaint, charging that the cover was arrogant and offensive. Gaines responded with a personal letter of apology to each one. Ironically, today the issue is one of the most requested back issues of *Mad*, and has become a collector's item.

In the face of criticism, the Madmen have usually taken the tack of pointing out that *Mad* does not proclaim itself to be redeeming in any way, a stance reflected in its admission

of being "trash," and "garbage." About the most that Gaines will admit to is that "editorially, we're trying to teach them 'Don't believe in ads. Don't believe in government.

Watch yourself—*everybody* is trying to screw you!'" In 1967 *Mad* received the boost of an unsolicited champion in the form of theologian Vernard Eller, B.A., B.D., M.A., Th.D., and a professor of religion at La Verne College in California. Eller expounded his views in an article entitled "The *Mad* Morality: An Exposé" for the *Christian Century*. "*Mad* is every bit as preachy as that old codifier Moses," he declared. "Beneath the pile of garbage that is *Mad*, there beats, I suspect, the heart of a rabbi." He pointed out that *Mad* often criticized the same things as Sunday preachers do: alcohol, tobacco, drugs, licentiousness, deceit, and hypocrisy; and that "*Mad* is teaching an old, a real old morality— *but without moralism*." What's the difference?

Progress was never *Mad*'s most important product, and this backward look at auto design became one of the all-time favorite cartoons to have appeared in the magazine.
—Reit/Clarke, "America's Dream Car," *Mad*, #49

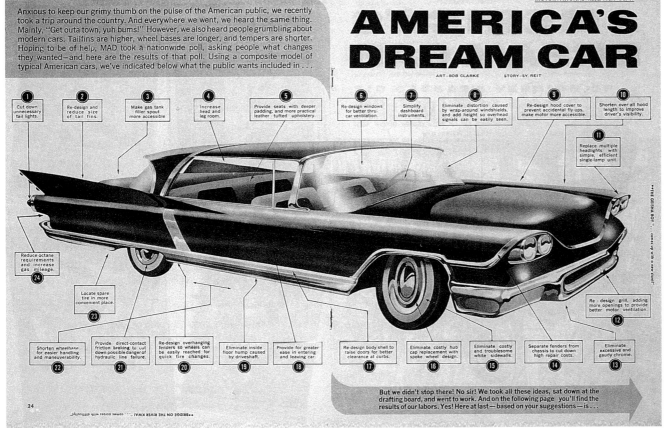

creators of underground comics that comics could be a fully realized art form. Mark James Estren, in his *History of Underground Comics*, called EC comics "the most direct influence on the underground cartoonists" of all and included a reprint of an entire EC horror story in an appendix of his book. Several underground comic books have paid homage to EC as well, such as one titled *Extra!* and another called *Tales Calculated to Drive You Bijou*.

Twenty years of EC fandom culminated in 1972 at the first EC Comics Convention held in Manhattan. Gaines, Feldstein, Kurtzman, Marie Severin, and several of the original EC artists participated in freewheeling panel discussions, to the delight of hundreds of attendees, and to the shock of the ECers, who finally felt vindicated after years of EC's banishment. Many of the most active fans from the early days, like Stewart and Benson, had become full-fledged working members of the comic book world, and many other artists and writers who had cut their teeth on ECs were present as well, in a surprising confluence of fanzine publishers, underground and mainstream comic book creators.

NOTES

"The brute fact of today . . ." Macdonald, *"Profiles,"* 62.

"We no longer have a rational basis . . ." McLuhan, The Mechanical Bride, 29.

"The biggest big business . . ." Barnouw, Tube of Plenty, 355.

"Miltown tranquilizers . . ." Stevens, Storming Heaven, 15.

"the perverse appeal of the bum . . ." Rovere, Senator Joe McCarthy, 48.

"I got the feeling that Bill . . ." Jacobs, William M. Gaines, 52–53.

"EC stories differed from a lot of stories . . ." Decker and Groth, *"William M. Gaines,"* 62–63.

"The highminded petty bourgeois . . ." Fiedler, Cross the Border, 27.

"the people who ran this place . . ."

AMERICA'S DREAM CAR

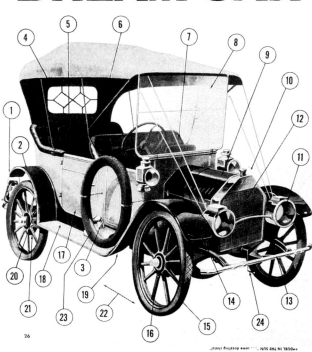

26

"The shift was neat but actually very easy: where the old moralism said 'WRONG,' *Mad* simply reads 'STUPID.'"

"Criticism we can take; praise from his kind could kill us," quipped Gaines and Feld-

stein, in a disclaimer they felt compelled to include in Eller's book-length version of the article. "We reject the insinuation that anything we print is moral, theological, nutritious, or good for you in any way, shape, or form. We live in a corrupt society and intend to keep on making the best of it." Eller's publisher felt equally obliged to include a disclaimer, which began "the officials of Abingdon Press (since 1789), publishers of *The Interpreter's Bible* and the finest works of modern religious scholarship, wish to state that their publication of this book in nowise is to be construed as approval of *Mad* magazine (or even acknowledgment that it exists)."

Whether *Mad* is good for children or bad for them is an argument that may never be resolved, but what *is* verifiable is that *Mad does* have an impact. For three generations, kids have read *Mad* at a time when they are formulating a world view that remains a foundation for the rest of their lives. *Mad* has been designed to be read and reread; lots of readers have kept a stack and scrutinized them over and over. "Those reprint volumes—squeezing down the originals from *Mad* comics . . . became my Book of Life," reveals historian Paul Buhle. "I confirmed all my sus-

picions about the commercial colonization of the mind by studying *Mad*'s satire as I had never studied my school books." John Pound, an underground cartoon artist, remembers that "I...spent hours poring over them, deciphering the STRANGE, dense, sweaty, ugly, funny, *twisted* pix which have since burned themselves deep, deep in my brain. I was fascinated."

"When something touches you at that early age, it really leaves an indelible mark," admits Kurtzman. "It's not important that what I did is of little consequence, but that the stain runs deep." Deep, indeed. Now that some of the earliest readers of *Mad* are entering middle age, the writers and public figures among them are talking about the influence that *Mad* had on them and their peers. It has become obvious that *Mad* is one of the influences to be credited (or blamed) for the political upheaval of the younger generation in the 1960s. Historian Theodore Roszak in his book *The Making of a Counter Culture* cited two "landmarks in affairs of the spirit" that announced the war of the generations: Allen Ginsberg's reading of the poem *Howl* and *Mad*. "The kids who

were twelve when *Mad* first appeared are in their early twenties now [in 1968]—and they have had a decade's experience in treating the stuff of their parents' lives as contemptible laughing stock." Todd Gitlin in his definitive history *The Sixties* devotes a subchapter to *Mad*; in his estimation, *Mad* and its ilk "pried

open a cultural territory which became available for radical transmutation...." And radical activist Tom Hayden was a teenage fan of *Mad*, inspired by it to start his own high school satire magazine, *The Daily Smirker*.

WHEN MAX GAINES CREATED THE COMIC BOOK, he had an idea that comics could be used to educate children. With his *Picture Stories* line of comic books about science, history, and the Bible that lectured kids much like the teachers the ex–school principal once supervised, he achieved little success. Where Max Gaines failed, his son, setting about only to turn the family company upside-down, may have succeeded. *Mad*'s harshest critics have felt that the magazine has had a terminally bad attitude, undermining all authority and points of view and inspiring nothing better than apathy. It may be true that in the face of the institutionalized dishonesty and corruption that *Mad* relentlessly exposes, the urge to surrender is great. The only magic bullet *Mad* offers is its "What—me worry?" boy, but the way of Alfred E. Neuman is a temporary respite, at best. There has always been more going on in *Mad* than mere escapism. It is a cliché to say that in the last fifty years the world has become an immeasurably more complex place, but the gap between the values and ideals that children are taught at home and in school and those that they will encounter in adulthood continues to widen. *Mad* encourages kids to look carefully and question these disparities. *Mad* gives voice to the outrage that these kids, who are not yet "adjusted" to society, feel about the ruses and corruptions epidemic in the world today. And it is an outrage leavened with empowering laughter that many of them will remember and carry with them for the rest of their lives.

Arlington, "Wishing on the Moon," 27.

"I was shocked..." Rodriguez, BLAB!, 44.

"in an era of phlegmatic homogeneity..." Williamson, "Notes from the Underground," 72.

"There was something unusual..." Griffin, "Notes from the Underground," 24–25.

"intimidated many cartoonists..." Hardy and Stern, Ethnic Images, 13.

"58% of all college students..." Gehman, "It's Just Plain MAD," 96.

"with the help of Mad and its ilk..." Gitlin, The Sixties, 36.

"the areas of national life in which ridicule..." Winick, "Teenagers, Satire, and Mad," 184.

"Mad's habit of deflating everything..." Gehman, 97.

"the Mad mystique resides..." Goldstein, "Ill Gotten Gaines," 3.

"Children do need some 'sinful' world..." Warshow, The Immediate Experience, 102–103.

"speaks the same language, aesthetically and morally..." Macdonald, 76.

"Consistently and perhaps unwittingly..." Ross, "The Conventions of the Mad," 505.

"everything stinks..." Cohn and Mann, "Mad Infinitum," 134.

"editorially, we're trying to teach them..." Cohn and Mann, 135.

"We reject the insinuation..." Eller, The Mad Morality, i.

"the officials of Abingdon Press..." Eller, ii.

"Those reprint volumes..." Buhle, "The Jewish Radicalism of Mad Comics," 32.

"I spent hours poring over them..." Pound, "Notes from the Underground," 66.

"When something touches you at that early age..." Kurtzman, MAD, vol. 4, notes following issue #23.

"landmarks in affairs of the spirit..." Roszak, The Making of a Counter Culture, 24.

"pried open a cultural territory..." Gitlin, 36.

APPENDIX A

MAD

BOOKS

A perusal of this bibliography of *Mad* books is likely to convince any reader that the Madmen have made every possible (and impossible) pun on *Mad*'s name. For many years, Gaines tried to keep all the books in print (with the exception of the hard covers), but with more and more of the popular paperbacks being published, he finally gave up. Almost all the books now go regularly in and out of print, as well as sometimes having their titles updated (for example, *Greasy Mad Stuff* was *The Greasy Mad* last time around). Several of the early paperbacks, which have gone through numerous reprintings, have sold over a million copies. Let the buyer beware!

Anthologies (in chronological order):

The Mad Reader. New York: Ballantine Books, 1954. Introduction by Roger Price.

Mad Strikes Back. New York: Ballantine Books, 1955. Introduction by Bob and Ray.

A portrait of a *Mad* reader by a master of the grotesque, Basil Wolverton. Although Wolverton's work was only occasionally used in *Mad*, his style is the quintessence of the magazine's spirit.
— Kurtzman/Wolverton, "Mad Reader!" *Mad*, #11

Inside Mad. New York: Ballantine Books, 1955.

Utterly Mad. New York: Ballantine Books, 1956.

Mad for Keeps. New York: Crown Publishers, 1958. Introduction by Ernie Kovacs. Hardcover.

The Brothers Mad. New York: Ballantine Books, 1958.

The Bedside Mad. New York: New American Library, 1959.

Mad Forever. New York: Crown Publishers, 1959. Introduction by Steve Allen. Hardcover.

Son of Mad. New York: New American Library, 1959.

A Golden Trashery of Mad. New York: Crown Publishers, 1960. Introduction by Sid Caesar. Hardcover.

The Organization Mad. New York: New American Library, 1960.

Like Mad. New York: New American Library, 1960.

The Ides of Mad. New York: New American Library, 1961.

Fighting Mad. New York: New American Library, 1961.

Mad Frontier. New York: New American Library, 1962.

Mad In Orbit. New York: New American Library, 1962.

The Voodoo Mad. New York: New American Library, 1963.

Greasy Mad Stuff. New York: New American Library, 1963.

Three Ring Mad. New York: New American Library, 1964.

The Self Made Mad. New York: New American Library, 1964.

The Mad Sampler. New York: New American Library, 1965.

It's A World, World, World, World Mad. New York: New American Library, 1965.

Raving Mad. New York: New American Library, 1966.

Boiling Mad. New York: New American Library, 1966.

The Questionable Mad. New York: New American Library, 1967.

Howling Mad. New York: New American Library, 1967.

Indigestible Mad. New York: New American Library, 1968.

Burning Mad. New York: New American Library, 1968.

The Ridiculously Expensive Mad. New York: World Publishing Co., 1969. Hardcover.

Good 'n' Mad. New York: New American Library, 1969.

Hopping Mad. New York: New American Library, 1969.

The Portable Mad. New York: New American Library, 1970.

Mad Power. New York: New American Library, 1970.

The Dirty Old Mad. New York: Warner Books, 1971.

Polyunsaturated Mad. New York: Warner Books, 1971.

The Recycled Mad. New York: Warner Books, 1972.

Aurora model, 1963

The Non-Violent Mad. New York: Warner Books, 1972.

The Rip-off Mad. New York: Warner Books, 1973.

The Token Mad. New York: Warner Books, 1973.

The Pocket Mad. New York: Warner Books, 1974.

The Invisible Mad. New York: Warner Books, 1974.

Dr. Jekyll and Mr. Mad. New York: Warner Books, 1975.

Steaming Mad. New York: Warner Books, 1975.

Mad at You! New York: Warner Books, 1975.

The Vintage Mad. New York: Warner Books, 1976.

Hooked on Mad. New York: New American Library, 1976.

The Cuckoo Mad. New York: Warner Books, 1976.

The Medicine Mad. New York: Warner Books, 1977.

A Mad Scramble. New York: Warner Books, 1977.

Incurably Mad. New York: Warner Books, 1977.

Swinging Mad. New York: Warner Books, 1977.

Mad Overboard. New York: Warner Books, 1978.

Mad Clowns Around. New York: Warner Books, 1978.

A Mad Treasure Chest. New York: Warner Books, 1978.

Mad Sucks. New York: Warner Books, 1979.

Super-Mad. New York: Warner Books, 1979.

The Abominable Snow Mad. New York: Warner Books, 1979.

Mad About the Buoy Book. New York: Warner Books, 1980.

Mad For Kicks. New York: Warner Books, 1980.

The Uncensored Mad. New York: Warner Books, 1980.

Pumping Mad. New York: Warner Books, 1981.

Mad Horses Around. New York: Warner Books, 1981.

Eggs-Rated Mad. New York: Warner Books, 1981.

A Mad Carnival. New York: Warner Books, 1982.

The Explosive Mad. New York: Warner Books, 1982.

Mad Barfs. New York: Warner Books, 1982.

Eternally Mad. New York: Warner Books, 1983.

Mad About Town. New York: Warner Books, 1983.

Big Mad on Campus. New York: Warner Books, 1983.

The Endangered Mad. New York: Warner Books, 1984.

Stamp Out Mad. New York: Warner Books, 1984.

The Forbidden Mad. New York: Warner Books, 1984.

Monster Mad. New York: Warner Books, 1985.

The Plaid Mad. New York: Warner Books, 1985.

Son of Mad Sucks. New York: Warner Books, 1985.

Qwerty Mad. New York: Warner Books, 1986.

Monu-Mentally Mad. New York: Warner Books, 1986.

Big Hairy Mad. New York: Warner Books, 1986.

The Wet and Wisdom of Mad. New York: Warner Books, 1987.

Mad Duds. New York: Warner Books, 1987.

'Til Mad do us Part. New York: Warner Books, 1987.

Mad Blasts. New York: Warner Books, 1988.

The Mad Cooler. New York: Warner Books, 1988.

The Spare Mad. New York: Warner Books, 1988.

Mad in a Box. New York: Warner Books, 1989.

Mad Jackpot. New York: Warner Books, 1989.

Soaring Mad. New York: Warner Books, 1989.

Weather Mad. New York: Warner Books, 1990.

Original Paperbacks and Solo Collections (by author):

Aragonés, Sergio. *Viva Mad.* New York: New American Library, 1968.

Mad-ly Yours. New York: Warner Books, 1972.

In Mad We Trust. New York: Warner Books, 1974.

Mad as the Devil. New York: Warner Books, 1975.

Mad about Mad. New York: Warner Books, 1977. Foreword by Albert B. Feldstein.

Shooting Mad. New York: Warner Books, 1979.

Mad Marginals. New York: Warner Books, 1980.

Mad as a Hatter. New York: Warner Books, 1981.

Mad's Sergio Aragonés on Parade. New York: Warner Books, 1982. Oversized paperback.

Mad Menagerie. New York: Warner Books, 1983.

More Mad Marginals. New York: Warner Books, 1985.

Mad Pantomimes. New York: Warner Books, 1987.

More Mad Pantomimes. New York: Warner Books, 1988.

Berg, Dave. *Mad's Dave Berg Looks at the USA.* New York: New American Library, 1964. Midword by Albert B. Feldstein.

Mad's Dave Berg Looks at People. New York: New American Library, 1966.

Mad's Dave Berg Looks at Modern Thinking. New York: New American Library, 1969. Foreword by Jerry De Fuccio.

Mad's Dave Berg Looks at our Sick World. New York: New American Library, 1971.

Dave Berg Looks at Living. New York: Warner Books, 1973.

Mad's Dave Berg Looks at Things. New York: Warner Books, 1974.

Dave Berg Looks Around. New York: Warner Books, 1975.

Dave Berg's Mad Trash. New York: Warner Books, 1977. Oversized paperback.

Mad's Dave Berg Takes a Loving Look. New York: Warner Books, 1977.

Mad's Dave Berg Looks, Listens and Laughs. New York: Warner Books, 1979.

Mad's Dave Berg Looks at You. New York: Warner Books, 1982.

Mad's Dave Berg Looks at the Neighborhood. New York: Warner Books, 1984.

Mad's Dave Berg Looks at Our Planet. New York: Warner Books, 1986.

Mad's Dave Berg Looks at Today. New York: Warner Books, 1987.

Brandel, Max. *The Mad Book of Word Power.* New York: Warner Books, 1973.

Coker, Paul. *The Mad Pet Book.* New York: Warner Books, 1983.

DeBartolo, Dick, Phil Hahn, J. Hanrahan, and Don Martin. *The Mad Adventures of Captain Klutz.* New York: New American Library, 1967.

DeBartolo, Dick, and Harry North. *The Mad Book of Sex, Violence and Home Cooking.* New York: Warner Books, 1983.

DeBartolo, Dick. *Here's Mad in Your Eye.* New York: Warner Books, 1984.

DeBartolo, Dick, and Bob Clarke. *Madvertising.* New York: Warner Books, 1979.

DeBartolo, Dick, and Jack Davis. *The Return of a Mad Look at Old Movies.* New York: New American Library, 1970.

DeBartolo, Dick, Jack Davis, and Mort Drucker. *Mad Look at Old Movies.* New York: New American Library, 1966.

DeBartolo, Dick, and Don Edwing. *Mad Murders the Movies.* New York: Warner Books, 1985.

DeBartolo, Dick, and Al Jaffee. *The Mad Guide to Self Improvement.* New York: Warner Books, 1979.

DeBartolo, Dick, and Harry North. *A Mad Guide to Fraud and Deception.* New York: Warner Books, 1981.

DeBartolo, Dick, and Angelo Torres. *A Mad Look at TV.* New York: Warner Books, 1974.

DeBartolo, Dick, and George Woodbridge. *A Mad Guide to Leisure.* New York: Warner Books, 1976.

Drucker, Mort. *Mort Drucker's Mad Show Stoppers.* New York: Warner Books, 1985. Oversized paperback.

Edwing, Don. *Don Edwing's*

Mad T-shirt, 1959

Mad Bizarre Bazaar. New York: Warner Books, 1980.

Mad Book of Almost Superheroes. New York: Warner Books, 1982.

Mad Variations. New York: Warner Books, 1984.

Mad's Sheer Torture. New York: Warner Books, 1988.

Mad Fantasy, Fables and other Foolishness. New York: Warner Books, 1989.

Ficarra, John, and Paul Coker Jr. *The Mad Book of Fears and Phobias.* New York: Warner Books, 1985.

Hart, Stan, and Paul Coker Jr. *The Mad Book of Revenge.* New York: Warner Books, 1976.

The Mad Guide to Careers. New York: Warner Books, 1978.

Mad's Fast Look at Fast Living. New York: Warner Books, 1982.

The Mad Survival Handbook. New York: Warner Books, 1983.

Hart, Stan and Jack Davis. *A Mad Guide to Parents, Teachers and other Enemies.* New York: Warner Books, 1985.

Jacobs, Frank. *Mad's Talking Stamps.* New York: Warner Books, 1974.

Mad Goes to Pieces. New York: Warner Books, 1984. Foreword by Nick Meglin.

Mad Zaps the Human Race. New York: Warner Books, 1984.

Jacobs, Frank, and Bob Clarke. *The Mad Jumble Book.* New York: Warner Books, 1975.

More About Mad Sports. New York: Warner Books, 1977.

Get Stuffed with Mad. New York: Warner Books, 1981.

Mad's Believe It or Nuts. New York: Warner Books, 1986.

Mad Goes Wild. New York: New American Library, 1974.

Jacobs, Frank, and Paul Coker Jr. *Mad For Better Or Verse.* New York: Warner Books, 1975. Foreword by Nick Meglin.

Jacobs, Frank, and Jack Davis. *Mad Jock Book.* New York: Warner Books, 1983.

The *Mad* Zeppelin, 1965

Jacobs, Frank, and Al Jaffee. *Sing Along with Mad.* New York: Warner Books, 1977. Foreword by Nick Meglin.

Jacobs, Frank, and Paul Peter Porges. *Mad Around the World.* New York: Warner Books, 1979. Foreword by Nick Meglin.

Jacobs, Frank, and Jack Rickard. *Mad About Sports.* New York: Warner Books, 1972. Foreword by Nick Meglin.

Jaffee, Al. *The Mad Book of Magic and Other Dirty Tricks.* New York: New American Library, 1970.

Al Jaffee's Mad Monstrosities. New York: Warner Books, 1974.

Mad's Al Jaffee Spews Out Snappy Answers to Stupid Questions. New York: Warner Books, 1975.

Mad's Al Jaffee Spews Out Still More Snappy Answers to Stupid Questions. New York: Warner Books, 1976.

Al Jaffee's Mad Inventions. New York: Warner Books, 1978.

Mad's Al Jaffee Spews Out More Snappy Answers to Stupid Questions. New York: Warner Books, 1979. Foreword by Nick Meglin.

Good Lord! Not Another Book of Snappy Answers to Stupid Questions. New York: Warner Books, 1980.

Mad's Al Jaffee Freaks Out. New York: Warner Books, 1982.

Mad's Vastly Overrated Al Jaffee. New York: Warner Books, 1983. Oversized paperback.

Snappy Answers to Stupid Questions #5. New York: Warner Books, 1984.

Mad Brain Ticklers, Puzzles and Lousy Jokes. New York: Warner Books, 1986.

Mad's Very Best Snappy Answers to Stupid Questions. New York: Warner Books, 1986.

Once Again Al Jaffee Spews Out Snappy Answers to Stupid Questions. New York: Warner Books, 1987.

Al Jaffee Sweats Out Another Book. New York: Warner Books, 1988.

Mad's All New Snappy Answers to Stupid Questions. New York: Warner Books, 1989.

Jaffee, Al, ed. *Clods' Letters to Mad.* New York: Warner Books, 1974. Foreword by Jerry De Fuccio.

Koch, Tom, and Jack Rickard. *The Mad Weirdo Watcher's Guide.* New York: Warner Books, 1982.

Koch, Tom, and Angelo Torres. *History Gone Mad.* New York: Warner Books, 1977.

Martin, Don. *Mad's Maddest Artist Don Martin Steps Out.* New York: New American Library, 1962. Foreword by Albert B. Feldstein.

Mad's Don Martin Cooks up More Tales. New York: New American Library, 1969.

Don Martin Drops Thirteen Stories. New York: Warner Books, 1973.

Mad's Don Martin Carries On. New York: Warner Books, 1973.

The Completely Mad Don Martin. New York: Warner Books, 1974. Oversized paperback.

Mad's Don Martin Steps Further Out. New York: Warner Books, 1975.

Don Martin Forges Ahead. New York: Warner Books, 1977.

Mad's Don Martin Digs Deeper. New York: Warner Books, 1979.

Mad's Don Martin Grinds Ahead. New York: Warner Books, 1981.

The Adventures of Captain Klutz II. New York: Warner Books, 1983.

Mad's Don Martin Sails Ahead. New York: Warner Books, 1986.

Martin, Don, and Dick De-Bartolo. *Mad's Don Martin Comes on Strong.* New York: New American Library, 1971.

Martin, Don, and E. Rosenblum. *Mad's Maddest Artist Don Martin Bounces Back.* New York: New American Library, 1963.

Meglin, Nick. *Mad Stew.* New York: Warner Books, 1978.

Meglin, Nick, and George Woodbridge. *The Sound of Mad.* New York: Warner Books, 1980.

A Mad Look at the 50's. New York: Warner Books, 1985.

A Mad Look at the 60's. New York: Warner Books, 1989.

Porges, Paul Peter. *The Mad How Not to Do It Book.* New York: Warner Books, 1981. Foreword by John Putnam.

A Mad Book of Cheap Shots. New York: Warner Books, 1984.

Mad Lobsters and Other Abominable Housebroken Creatures. New York: Warner Books, 1986.

Prohías, Antonio. *Mad's Spy vs. Spy Follow up File.* New York: New American Library, 1968.

Koch, Tom, and Bob Clarke. *The Mad Worry Book.* New York: Warner Books, 1980.

The Mad Self Improvement Yearbook. New York: Warner Books, 1985.

The Third Mad Dossier of Spy vs. Spy. New York: Warner Books, 1972.

The All New Mad Secret File on Spy vs. Spy. New York: Warner Books, 1973.

The 4th Mad Declassified Papers on Spy vs. Spy. New York: Warner Books, 1974.

The 5th Mad Report on Spy vs. Spy. New York: Warner Books, 1978.

Mad's Spy Vs. Spy. New York: Warner Books, 1978.

The 6th Mad Report on Spy vs. Spy. New York: Warner Books, 1982.

Mad's Big Book of Spy vs. Spy Capers and other Surprises. New York: Warner Books, 1982. Oversized paperback.

Siegel, Larry, and Angelo Torres. *The Mad Make Out Book.* New York: Warner Books, 1979.

Mad Clobbers the Classics. New York: Warner Books, 1981.

Mad's How to Be a Successful Dog. New York: Warner Books, 1984.

Siegel, Larry, and George Woodbridge. *Mad's Cradle to Grave Primer.* New York: Warner Books, 1973.

Silverstone, Lou, and Jack Rickard. *Politically Mad.* New York: Warner Books, 1976.

Silverstone, Lou, and Bob Jones. *The Mad Tell It Like It Is Book.* New York: Warner Books, 1983.

Silverstone, Lou, and Harry North. *The Mad Book of Horror Stories, Yecchy Creatures and Other Neat Stuff.* New York: Warner Books, 1986.

Silverstone, Lou, and Jack Rickard. *A Mad Look at the Future.* New York: Warner Books, 1978.

The Mad Book of Mysteries. New York: Warner Books, 1980.

SPECIALS AND FREEBIES

Ever since *Mad* began publishing magazine-size compilations of articles from previous issues, gimmicks and freebies have been part of the attraction. Some of these have been particularly memorable: gummed and serrated *Mad* stickers (because they are still to be seen permanently affixed to bedroom doors across the United States), dramatic miniposters, and, of course, the *Mad* zeppelin model.

1956
Worst from Mad 1, September, *Mad* record labels and travel stickers.

1957
Worst from Mad 2, October, "Meet the staff of *Mad*" 33⅓ rpm record.

1958
More Trash from Mad 1, "Eight Pages in BLINDING COLOR."
Worst from Mad 3, September, "Startling full-color 20″ by 30″ Alfred E. Neuman for President Campaign Poster."

1959
More Trash from Mad 2, *Mad* Labels.
Worst From Mad 4, September, eight-page full-color "Sunday Comics Section We'd Like to See."

1960
More Trash from Mad 3, "Six Full Color Reversible *Mad* Textbook Covers PLUS four Extras in Black and White."
Worst From Mad 5, "*Mad* 'Twists' Rock-n-Roll" 33⅓ rpm record.

1961
More Trash from Mad 4, "Sing Along with *Mad*" parody songbook.

1962
More Trash from Mad 5, *Mad* window stickers.

1963
Mad Follies 1, Color fold-out paste-on *Mad* paperback book covers.
More Trash from Mad 6, *Mad*'s version of "TV Guise."
Worst From Mad 6, "Fink Along with *Mad*" 33⅓ rpm record.

1964
Mad Follies 2, The 1965 *Mad* calendar.
More Trash from Mad 7, *Mad* commemorative and Alfred E. Neuman for President stickers.
Worst from Mad 7, fold-out *Mad* protest signs.

1965
Mad Follies 3, color fold-out *Mad* "Mischief Stickers."
More Trash from Mad 8, "Full Color Pop Art Op Art Life-size Picture of Alfred E. Neuman."
Worst from Mad 8, Color pop-out "Build Your Own Hanging Model of the *Mad* Zeppelin."

1966
Mad Follies 4, "Make Your Own *Mad* Mobile."
More Trash from Mad 9, more *Mad* mischief stickers.
Worst from Mad 9, "Alfred E. Neuman Vocalizes" 33⅓ rpm record.

1967
Mad Follies 5, die-cut punch-out *Mad* stencils.
More Trash from Mad 10, more *Mad* mischief stickers.
Worst from Mad 10, "Your Own Ridiculous, Way-out *Mad* Bumper Sticker."

1968
Mad Follies 6, "Would you believe... More *Mad* Mischief Stickers."
More Trash From Mad 11, "Including two, yes two, Free Bonuses, a Full-Color 14″ by 20¼″ Alfred E. Neuman for President Campaign Poster PLUS a Full Color Self Adhesive Alfred E. Neuman for President Bumper Sticker."
Worst from Mad 11, sixteen *Mad* car-window stickers.

1969
Mad Follies 7, "*Mad* Nasty Cards with Full Color Picture and Insulting Poem."
More Trash from Mad 12, thirty-six *Mad* pocket medals.
Worst from Mad 12, twelve "Get *Mad*" picture postcards.

1970
Special 1, Fall, "The *Mad* Voodoo Doll."

The *Mad* "Straight Jacket," 1959

1971
Special 2, Spring, "16 Framed and Ready to Hang *Mad* Wall Nuts."
Special 3, color fold-out *Mad* protest stickers.
Special 4, sixteen color *Mad* miniposters.
Special 5, fold-out *Mad* flag poster.

1972
Special 6, *Mad* mischief stickers.
Special 7, sixteen *Mad* miniposters: "eight wild, shocking message posters and eight presidential candidate posters."
Special 8, 16-page full-color bonus: "The TV Guise Fall Preview."
Special 9, The Nostalgic *Mad* #1.

1973
Special 10, color fold-out: Don Martin nonsense stickers.
Super Special 11, "Gall in the Family Fare" 33⅓ vinyl record PLUS 16 extra pages.

1974
Super Special 12, The Nostalgic *Mad* #2.
Super Special 13, *Mad* "Sickie Stickies" PLUS 14 pages of never before published material.
Super Special 14, "Don Martin Vital Message Posters PLUS 8 Don Martin Art Depreciation Paintings."
Super Special 15, The Nostalgic *Mad* #3.

1975

Super Special 16, "*Mad*-hesives PLUS 16 pages of never before published material."

Super Special 17, "Don Martin Vital Message Posters PLUS 8 Don Martin Literary Heroes Portraits PLUS 16 pages of never before published material."

Super Special 18, The Nostalgic *Mad* #4.

1976

Super Special 19, "200 Year Old *Mad*de, Bicentennial Year *Mad* Collectors' Item."

Super Special 20, Don Martin Give 'em Hell election year stickers.

Special 21, The Nostalgic *Mad* #5.

1977

Special 22, "16 Diplomas, Certificates and Other Awards ready for framing."

Special 23, Don Martin sound effect stickers.

Special 24, The Nostalgic *Mad* #6.

Super Special 25, Don Martin 20″ by 30″ rock music posters.

1978

Super Special 26, "Makin' Out" 33⅓ rpm vinyl record.

Super Special 27, "*Mad* Shock Stickers PLUS 16 pages never before published material."

1979

Super Special 28, Fall, "The Nostalgic *Mad* #7 PLUS 16 pages never before published material."

Super Special 29, Winter, "*Mad* Collectable Connectables."

1980

Mad Disco, thirty-minute two-sided extended LP of "*Mad* Disco Music."

Barrie Chase and Fred Astaire, 1958

Super Special 30, Spring, 100 pages.

Super Special 31, Summer, "The *Mad* Mystery Record."

Super Special 32, Fall, The Nostalgic *Mad* #8.

Super Special 33, Winter, forty-one full-color Alfred E. Neuman for President stamps and stickers.

1981

Super Special 34, Spring, "*Mad* Look at TV."

Super Special 35, Summer, 14 *Mad* "Car and Home Window Stickers."

Super Special 36, Fall, "A 96 page Look at the Comics over the Years."

Super Special 37, Winter, Sergio Aragonés' 20″ by 30″ "*Mad* Map of the USA."

1982

Super Special 38, Spring, "A 96 page Look at Sports Over the Years."

Super Special 39, Summer, "The *Mad* Laugh Record."

Super Special 40, Fall, "*Mad*vertising: A 92 page Look at *Mad*ison Avenue over the Years."

Super Special 41, Winter, "A 100 page Look at Summer."

1983

Super Special 42, Spring, "100 page Look at Cops, Politicians, Teachers and other Corrupt Professions."

Super Special 43, Summer, "A 100 page Look at Horror, Sci-Fi and Other Weird Things."

Super Special 44, Fall, "A 100 page Look at Sex, Love and other Things Your Parents Are Against."

Super Special 45, Winter, "*Mad* Book of Silly Nonsense."

1984

Mad '84, "A *Mad* Extra: 84 pages of all new never before published wild and insane *Mad* Trash."

Super Special 46, Spring, "Movies II: a 100 page Look at Hollywood."

Super Special 47, Summer, "Violence! A 100 page Look at the Great American Pastime."

Super Special 48, Fall, "Another 100 page Look at TV."

Super Special 48, Winter, "The Worst From *Mad*: Eight Shocking all new full color *Mad* Wall Signs."

1985

Super Special 50, Spring, "The *Mad* Book of Sillier Nonsense: 100 pages of Idiocy from Past Issues."

Super Special 51, Summer, "More Trash From *Mad*: Eight Shocking, Ridiculous Full Color *Mad* Mini Posters."

Super Special 52, Fall, "*Mad* Super Stars #1: Martin, Prohías, Drucker, Berg."

Super Special 53, Winter, "The Worst From *Mad*."

1986

Super Special 54, Spring, "Classic Flops."

Super Special 55, Summer, "More Trash From *Mad*."

Super Special 56, Fall, "Eight Full Color Posters."

Super Special 57, Winter, "The Knockout *Mad*."

1987

Super Special 58, Spring, "*Mad* Book of Silliest Nonsense."

Super Special 59, Summer, "*Mad* Bombs: 10 Page portfolio of Spy vs. Spy."

Super Special 60, Fall, "The Totally Crooked *Mad*."

Super Special 61, Winter, "Four Star Super Special."

1988

Super Special 62, Spring, "*Mad* Mania: 16 page portfolio of Sergio Aragonés Classics."

Super Special 63, Summer, "The Hot Air *Mad*."

Super Special 64, Fall, "*Mad* Grosses Out."

Super Special 65, Winter, "*Mad* Bombs Again: 10 page top secret file on Spy vs. Spy, PLUS 5 rare episodes of Spy vs. Spy."

1989

Super Special 66, Spring, "The *Mad* Event: 32 page exhibition spotlighting the Battle of the Ages: Parents vs. Kids."

Super Special 67, Summer, "Sizzling School Sucks Super Special."

Super Special 68, Fall, "*Mad* Shorts: 96 pages of Flimsy Material."

Super Special 69, Winter, "*Mad* Mania."

1990

Super Special 70, Spring, "*Mad* Sports 2."

Super Special 71, Summer, "*Mad* in Your Face: Dorky Door Hang-Ups."

Super Special 72, Fall, "Our Creature Presentation."

Super Special 73, Winter, "*Mad* Bombs in a Big Way."

1991

Rock Super Special 74, Spring, "96 pages of Moldy Oldys."

Super Special 75, Summer, "Computer Virus Edition: Bug-Infested Alfred E. Neuman Program."

Super Special 76, Fall, "*Mad* Collector's Series 1: 17 Mischief Stickers."

FOREIGN

MAD

As early as 1959, *Mad* was exporting its brand of insanity to other countries. First came the British-language edition—yes, that's right, the magazine *was* translated: apartments became flats, dollars became pounds, and bathrooms W.C.s. The British edition was very well received; fans loved the wordplay and spontaneously joined in just as readers in the United States had on *Mad*'s debut. Other countries soon made arrangements with *Mad* to begin their own editions. Foreign editors face a number of challenges in producing their versions of *Mad*, holding television and movie parodies until the programs are released locally and weeding out articles that may have no reference to their readership, as well as dealing with the problems of translating *Mad*'s often idiomatic English into their own tongue. Many foreign editions also add original art and writing of a high caliber; notable in this regard are the British, Danish, Dutch, and German editions. Some of this material goes far beyond the bounds of what the U.S. editors would include: the Dutch edition once included a prophylactic as a special bonus (they stapled it in).

British edition: 1959, Ron Letchford, editor.

Swedish edition: 1960, Kell Stähl, editor; Semic Publishing.

Dutch edition: 1964, Rob Bakker, editor; Nellie Werkman, publisher.

Danish edition: 1979, Erling Stenby, editor; Semic Publishing.

Australian edition: 1980, Susan Horwitz, editor; Stanley Horwitz, publisher.

Finnish edition: 1981, Marjaana Tulosmaa, editor; Semic Publishing.

Norwegian edition: 1981, Hege Høiby, editor; Semic Publishing.

Brazilian edition: 1982, Otacílio Dássunção Barros, editor; Alfredo C. Machado, publisher.

South African edition: 1985, Waldean, publisher.

Chinese edition: 1990, Ason Chen, editor; Johnny Duann, publisher.

Italian edition: 1991, Games SRL.

German edition: Herbert Feuerstein, editor; Klaus Recht, publisher.

Discontinued foreign editions: Argentinian, Puerto Rican, Spanish, French, and Mexican.

Dutch *Mad*

MAD

BIBLIOGRAPHY

"Alfred E. Neuman Joining Superman." *New York Times*, June 10, 1964, 3.

"Are Comics Horrible?" *Newsweek*, May 3, 1954, 60.

Arlington, Gary. "Wishing on the Moon." *BLAB!* 2 (Summer 1987), 27.

Baker, Eric, and Tyler Blik. *Trademarks of the 20s and 30s.* San Francisco: Chronicle Books, 1985.

Barnouw, Eric. *Tube of Plenty: The Evolution of American Television* (1975). Reprint: New York: Oxford University Press, 1982.

Barrier, Michael, and Martin Williams. *A Smithsonian Book of Comic-Book Comics.* New York: Smithsonian Institution Press and Harry N. Abrams, 1981.

Benson, John. "A Conversation with Harvey Kurtzman and Bill Elder," *Squa Tront #9*, New York: John Benson, 1983.

———. "A Conversation with Harvey Kurtzman and Bill Gaines." *Squa Tront #9.* New York: John Benson, 1983.

———. "The Transcripts: 1972 EC Convention, the Horror Panel." *Squa Tront #8*, New York: John Benson, 1978.

Benson, John, ed. *MAD.* 4 vols. West Plains, MO: Russ Cochran, 1986–1987.

Benton, Mike. *The Comic Book in America.* Dallas, TX: Taylor Publishing Company, 1989.

Bloom, Stephen G. "Mad Turns Thirty." *Dallas Morning News*, April 4, 1982, F1.

Boatner, E. B. "Good Lord! choke...gasp...It's E.C.!" *The Comic Book Price Guide #9*, Robert M. Overstreet, ed. Cleveland, TN: Overstreet Publications, 1979.

Boni, John, Sean Kelly, and Henry Beard. "Mad Parody." *National Lampoon*, October 1971, 43+.

Bray, Glenn. *The Illustrated Harvey Kurtzman Index, 1939–1975.* Sylmar, CA: Glenn Bray, 1976.

Buhle, Paul. "Beware of Imitations! The Jewish Radicalism of Mad Comics." *Genesis* 2 (Summer 1987): 32–35.

Casty, Alan H., C. R. Greenwood, and Edward R. Hagemann. "Item: Some Parodies of News Media." *Writers in Action.* Englewood Cliffs, NJ: Prentice-Hall, 1959.

Cohn, Fred, and Charles C. Mann. "Mad Infinitum." *Manhattan inc.* August 1986, 133–136.

"Comic-Book Hearing to Start Tomorrow." *New York Times,* April 20, 1954, 32.

Congressional Digest 33 (December 1954), 293.

Cook, Bruce. "Yecch! Alfred E. Neuman Is No Idiot." *National Observer.* October 27, 1969, 1.

"Crazy Like a Fox." *Newsweek,* August 31, 1959, 57.

Crouch, Bill. "Alfred E. Neuman's Portrait Painter." *Cartoonist Profiles,* June 1975, 16–21.

Decker, Dwight R., and Gary Groth. "An Interview with William M. Gaines." *The Comics Journal* 81, (May 1983): 53–84.

Decker, Dwight R., and Kim Thompson. "Newswatch: Wally Wood Dead at 54." *The Comics Journal* 69, (December 1981): 8–12.

De Fuccio, Jerry. "Norman Mingo and Alfred." *The Comic Book Price Guide.* 12th ed. New York: Crown Publishers, 1982.

Duncan, David D., with Mort Drucker. *Familiar Faces, The Art of Mort Drucker.* Redford MI: Stabur Press, 1988.

Elkind, David. *The Hurried Child.* Reading, MA: Addison-Wesley, 1981.

Eller, Vernard. "The 'MAD' Morality: An Exposé." *The Christian Century.* December 27, 1967, 1647–1649.

———. *The Mad Morality.* Nashville: Abingdon Press, 1970.

Estren, Mark James. *A History of Underground Comics* (1974). Reprint: Berkeley: Straight Arrow Books, 1987.

Fiedler, Leslie. *Cross the Border—Close the Gap.* New York: Stein & Day, 1972.

Fiore, Robert, and Gary Groth, eds. *The New Comics.* New York: Berkley Books, 1988.

Flagler, J. M. "The MAD Miracle." *Look,* March 19, 1968, 46.

Bust of Alfred E. Neuman, c. 1958

Friedman, Richard P. "Frankly, My Dear . . ." *Circulation Management,* September–October 1988, 50.

Gaines, M. C. "Good Triumphs over Evil! More about the Comics." *Print,* vol III, no. 3 (1943).

———. "Narrative Illustration: The Story of the Comics." *Print,* August 1942.

Gehman, Richard. "It's Just Plain MAD." *Coronet,* May 1960, 96–103.

Gifford, Denis. *The International Book of Comics.* New York: Crescent Books, 1984.

Gitlin, Todd. *The Sixties: Years of Hope, Days of Rage.* New York: Bantam Books, 1988.

Goldberg, Jeff. "A Conversation with William M. Gaines." *Oui,* February 1979, 70–76, 125.

Goldstein, Al. "Ill Gotten Gaines." *Screw,* August 1, 1988, 4–15.

Goodman, Roger B., ed. *Americans Today.* New York: Charles Scribner's Sons, 1969.

Goulart, Ron. *The Great Comic Book Artists.* New York: St. Martin's Press, 1986.

———. *The Great Comic Book Artists, Vol. 2.* New York: St. Martin's Press, 1986.

Griffin, Rick. "Notes from the Underground." *BLAB!* 1 (Summer 1986): 24–25.

Groth, Gary. "William M. Gaines." *The Comics Journal* 100 (July 1985): 103+.

Haimes, Norma. "Don Martin." *Cartoonist Profiles,* nos. 52, 53 (December 1981).

Halliwell, Leslie. *Halliwell's Film Guide.* 6th ed. New York: Charles Scribner's Sons, 1987.

Hardy, Charles, and Gail F. Stern, eds. *Ethnic Images in the Comics.* Philadelphia: The Balch Institute for Ethnic Studies, 1986.

Harrigan, Claire Kathleen. "Don Edwing Mad's Bizartist." *Cartoonist Profiles,* no. 61 (March 1984).

Harrison, Hank. *The Art of Jack Davis!* Redford, MI: Stabur Press, 1988.

Hauser, Rich. "Bill Gaines Talks with the Fanimals." *Spa Fon* 5, (September 1969): 70–79.

Henderson, Robbin Legere, et al., eds. *Prisoners of Image: Ethnic and Gender Stereotypes.* New York: Alternative Museum, 1989.

Hertzberg, Hendrik. "Part of the Solution, Part of the Problem." *New York Times Book Review,* June 21, 1987, 1.

Hine, Thomas. *Populuxe.* New York: Alfred A. Knopf, 1987.

Hiss, Tony, and Jeff Lewis. "The 'Mad' Generation." *New York Times* Magazine, July 31, 1977, 14–20.

Hoberman, J. "Vulgar Modernism." *Artforum,* February 1982, 71–76.

Hogben, Lancelot. *From Cave Painting to Comic Strip.* New York: Chanticleer Press, 1949.

Horn, Maurice, ed. *The World Encyclopedia of Comics.* New York: Chelsea House, 1976.

Horn, Maurice, ed. *The World Encyclopedia of Cartoons.* New York: Gale Research Co. 1980.

Hunt, Darryl L. "Who Reads *Mad?*" *Catholic Family Magazine,* July 1965, 32.

Hurd, Jud. "MAD Magazine's Allan Jaffee." *Cartoonist Profiles.*

Inge, M. Thomas. *Comics as Culture.* Jackson, MS: University Press of Mississippi, 1990.

Jacobs, Frank. *The Mad World of William M. Gaines.* New York: Bantam Books, 1973.

Jacobs, Frank. "The Madcap Travels of MAD Magazine." *New York Times,* February 25, 1973. VII, 22.

Jung, C.G. *The Archetypes and the Collective Unconscious.* 2nd ed. Princeton, NJ: Princeton University Press, 1977.

Katz, Bill and Berry G. Richards. *Magazines for Libraries.* New York: R. R. Bowker, 1978.

Kauffmann, Stanley. "Theater: Mad Magazine Transferred to the Stage." *New York Times,* January 10, 1966.

Kihss, Peter. "No Harm in Horror, Comics Issuer Says." *New York Times,* April 22, 1954, 1.

Kihss, Peter. "Senator Charges 'Deceit' on Comics." *New York Times,* April 23, 1954, 29.

Krebs, Albin. "Louella Schwartz Is Like a Melody to Mad." *New York Herald-Tribune,* March 25, 1964.

Kunitz, Stanley J., ed. *Twentieth Century Authors.* New York: H. W. Wilson, 1955.

Kurtzman, Harvey. *Kurtzman Komix.* Princeton, WI: Kitchen Sink Enterprises, 1976.

Kurtzman, Harvey, and Will Elder. *Goodman Beaver.* Princeton, WI: Kitchen Sink Press, 1984.

Kurtzman, Harvey, with Howard Zimmerman. *My Life as a Cartoonist.* New York: Minstrel Books, 1988.

LeGoff, Michael. "Working MAD." *How,* July–August 1988, 92–101.

Leiberman, Irving. "How Harmful Are Your Child's Comic Books?" *Liberty,* March 1955, 18–19.

McCarten, John. "The Theatre." *The New Yorker*, January 22, 1966, 74–75.

Macdonald, Dwight. "Profiles: A Caste, A Culture, A Market—II." *The New Yorker*, November 29, 1958, 76.

McLuhan, Marshall. *The Mechanical Bride*. New York: Vanguard Press, 1951.

———. *Understanding Media*. New York: New American Library, 1964.

McNeil, Alex. *Total Television* (1980). Reprint: New York: Penguin Books, 1984.

"MAD Comes to Yale." *Yale Alumni Magazine*. May 1973, 18–21.

"Madcappery." *Newsweek*, January 24, 1966, 82.

"Maddiction." *Time*, July 7, 1958, 63.

"Magazine's Right to Parody Lyrics Backed on Appeal." *New York Times*, October 13, 1964, 1.

Mann, Martin. "This Month in Science." *Popular Science*, February 1961, 23.

Marston, William Moulton. "Why 100,000,000 Americans Read Comics." *American Scholar*, September 1943, 35–44.

Martin, Richard, and Harold Koda. *Jocks and Nerds: Men's Style in the Twentieth Century*. New York: Rizzoli International, 1989.

Meglin, Nick. *The Art of Humorous Illustration* (1973). Reprint: New York: Watson-Guptill Publications, 1981.

Montane, Diana. "The Minister of Sinister." *New Times, Miami's News and Arts Weekly*. May 17–23, 1989, 13+.

Morton, Charles W. "The Case for Mad." *The Atlantic*, September 1963, 100.

Murphy, T. E. "Progress in Cleaning Up the Comics." *Reader's Digest*, February 1956, 105–108.

Norris, Vincent P. "Mad Economics: An Analysis of an Adless Magazine." *Journal of Communication*, Winter 1984, 44–61.

"Not-so-vital Statistics on Admiral Crowe." *New York Times*, June 12, 1986, 12.

"Now Comics Have Gone Mad." *Pageant*, June 1954, 88–93.

Packard, Vance. *The Hidden Persuaders*. New York: David McKay, 1957.

Pinkwater, Daniel. "On First Looking into Kurtzman's Mad." *Fish Whistle*. Reading, MA: Addison-Wesley, 1989.

Pound, John. "Notes from the Underground." *BLAB!* 2 (Summer 1987): 66.

Pringle, Henry F. "The Anatomy of Ballyhoo: A New Type of Magazine—Smutty or Smart?" *Outlook*, January 6, 1932.

"Property Rights: The Best Things in Life Are Free." *Time*, April 3, 1964, 68–71.

Ranzal, Edward. "Parody of Songs Upheld by Court." *New York Times*, March 24, 1964, III, 1.

Reeves, Richard. "Mad Magazine—Witness for the People." *New York*, October 1, 1973, 40–45.

Robinson, Dane, ed. *Twenty Five Years of British Mad*. London: Suron International Publications, 1984.

Ross, T.J. "The Conventions of the Mad." *Dissent*, no. 8 (1961), 502–506.

Roszak, Theodore. *The Making of a Counter Culture: Reflections on the Technocratic Society and Its Youthful Opposition*. New York: Doubleday and Company, 1968.

Rovere, Richard H. *Senator Joe McCarthy*. New York: Harper Calophon Books, 1973.

Sanders, Betty. "Mad Magazine in the Remedial English Class." *English Journal*, February 1970, 266–267, 272.

"Sassy Newcomer." *Time*, September 24, 1956, 71.

Sayres, Sohnya, et al., eds. *The 60s Without Apology*. Minneapolis: University of Minnesota Press, 1985.

E.C. Fan-Addict Club membership certificate, 1953

Schechter, Harold. *The New Gods: Psyche and Symbol in Popular Art*. Bowling Green, OH: Bowling Green University Popular Press, 1980.

Schott, Jinny. "*Mad*-ness Has Its Method." *The Ohio State Lantern*, February 6, 1970, 8.

Sherr, Lynn. "Some Mad Predictions." *More*, April 1972, 8–9.

Simonean, Joseph R. "Mad Magazine's Alfred E. Neuman: A 400 Year Old Ancestor?" *Boston*, August 15, 1979.

Skow, Jack. "Mad: Wild Oracle of the Teenage Underground." *Saturday Evening Post*, December 21–28, 1963, 62–65.

Slutsker, Gary. "The Secret Is in the Repackaging." *Forbes*, June 15, 1987, 230–231.

Smith, Randy. "Harcourt Has That 'What Me Worry' Look." *New York Daily News*, February 7, 1981, 22.

Standard, Jim. "City 'Mad' Trial Pits Bitter Foes." *Oklahoma City Times*, September 24, 1962, 1–2.

Stevens, Jay. *Storming Heaven: LSD and the American Dream*. New York: Harper and Row, 1987. Reprint: New York: Perennial Library, 1988.

Stewart, Bhob. "Memories of Wally Wood: There Are Good Guys and Bad Guys." *The Comics Journal* 70, (January 1982): 50–67.

"Stuff v. EC Publications, Inc., et al." *U.S. Patent Quarterly*, Fed. Ct. of Appeals for the 2d Cir.: 1965, 560.

Thompson, Kim. "Interview: Sergio Aragonés." *The Comics Journal* 128, (April 1989): 67–98.

Thompson, Kim, and Gary Groth. "An Interview with the Man Who Brought Truth to the Comics, Harvey Kurtzman." *The Comics Journal* 67, (October 1981): 68–107.

"Thousands May Laugh But We Call It a Stupid Insult." *Sunday Pictorial*, April 31, 1959, 1.

"Thunder on the Far Right." *Newsweek*, December 4, 1961, 18–22.

U.S. Congress. Senate. "Subcommittee to Investigate Juvenile Delinquency of the Committee on the Judiciary." 83rd Cong., 2nd sess. 1954.

Walsh, Patrick. "For this cartoonist, it's a Mad, Mad, Mad world." *Reading Eagle*, January 9, 1983, 20.

Warshow, Robert. *The Immediate Experience* (1946). Reprint: New York: Doubleday and Company, 1962.

Wasserman, Jeffrey H. "Conversations with the Brother-in-Law of Underground Comix." *Inside Comics*, vol. 1, no. 2 (Summer 1974): 16–25.

Webb, Michael. *Hollywood: Legend and Reality*. Boston: Little, Brown, 1986.

Wertham, Fredric. *Seduction of the Innocent*. New York: Rinehart and Company, 1953.

———. *The World of Fanzines*. Carbondale: Southern Illinois University Press, 1973.

Whitman, Arthur. "The Mad Mad World of Alfred E. Neuman." *New Haven Register*, November 1, 1964.

Whyte, William H. *The Organization Man*. New York: Simon and Schuster, 1956.

Wilkes, Jack. "Charley Gaines—Comics Pioneer." *Independent News*, March 1944, 7.

Williamson, Skip. "Notes from the Underground." *BLAB* 1 (Summer 1986): 44.

Wilson, Robert Anton. "Don't Go Away, *Mad*." *Fact*, November–December 1965, 32–39.

Winick, Charles. "Teenagers, Satire, and Mad." *Merrill-Palmer Quarterly of Behavior and Development*, July 1962, 183–203.

Winn, Marie. "What Became of Childhood Innocence?" *New York Times Magazine*, January 25, 1981, 14–17.

INDEX

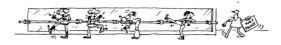

"Drawn Out Dramas" by Sergio Aragonés